Home Is Where Your Politics Are

Home Is Where Your
Politics Are

Home Is Where Your Politics Are

Queer Activism in the U.S. South and South Africa

JESSICA A. SCOTT

RUTGERS UNIVERSITY PRESS
NEW BRUNSWICK, CAMDEN, AND NEWARK, NEW JERSEY
LONDON AND OXFORD

Rutgers University Press is a department of Rutgers, The State University of New Jersey, one of the leading public research universities in the nation. By publishing worldwide, it furthers the University's mission of dedication to excellence in teaching, scholarship, research, and clinical care.

Library of Congress Cataloging-in-Publication Data

Names: Scott, Jessica A., author.
Title: Home is where your politics are : queer activism in the U.S. South and South Africa / Jessica A. Scott.
Description: New Brunswick : Rutgers University, [2024] | Includes bibliographical references and index.
Identifiers: LCCN 2023044021 | ISBN 9781978836082 (hardback) | ISBN 9781978836075 (paperback) | ISBN 9781978836099 (epub) | ISBN 9781978836105 (pdf)
Subjects: LCSH: LGBT activism—Southern States. | LGBT activism—South Africa. | Sexual minorities—Political activity—Southern States. | Sexual minorities—Political activity—South Africa. | BISAC: SOCIAL SCIENCE / LGBTQ+ Studies / Gay Studies | SOCIAL SCIENCE / Gender Studies
Classification: LCC HQ73.73.U6 S368 2024 | DDC 320.90086/60975—dc23/eng/20240124
LC record available at https://lccn.loc.gov/2023044021

A British Cataloging-in-Publication record for this book is available from the British Library.

Copyright © 2024 by Jessica A. Scott

All rights reserved

No part of this book may be reproduced or utilized in any form or by any means, electronic or mechanical, or by any information storage and retrieval system, without written permission from the publisher. Please contact Rutgers University Press, 106 Somerset Street, New Brunswick, NJ 08901. The only exception to this prohibition is "fair use" as defined by U.S. copyright law.

References to internet websites (URLs) were accurate at the time of writing. Neither the author nor Rutgers University Press is responsible for URLs that may have expired or changed since the manuscript was prepared.

⊖ The paper used in this publication meets the requirements of the American National Standard for Information Sciences—Permanence of Paper for Printed Library Materials, ANSI Z39.48-1992.

rutgersuniversitypress.org

For Funeka Soldaat and Jane Bennett

Contents

1 Introduction 1

2 Positionality and Method 20

3 Sites of Struggle 33

4 Welcome to Modernity 61

5 Metronormativity as Alienation 82

6 Queer Organizing in Out-of-the-Way Places 105

7 When Whiteness Gets in the Way 129

Appendix 151
Acknowledgments 159
Notes 163
Bibliography 183
Index 195

Home Is Where Your Politics Are

Home Is Where Your
Politics Are

CHAPTER 1

Introduction

Unreliable Assumptions

In 1996, then-president Bill Clinton signed the Defense of Marriage Act (DOMA) into law.[1] DOMA not only prohibited the recognition of same-sex marriages by the U.S. government, it also guaranteed that individual states did not have to recognize same-sex marriages performed in other states (or countries).[2] By 2008, only two states in the South did not have a constitutional amendment banning same-sex marriage.[3] Those states were North Carolina and West Virginia. By 2012, North Carolina had emerged from a battle over the meaning of marriage and family, and the state had adopted Amendment 1, a constitutional amendment banning same-sex marriage.[4] When same-sex marriage became legally available through the *Obergfell* decision in 2015, West Virginia remained the only state in the South without a ban on same-sex marriage.[5]

Since 2012, there have been many other contestations over LGBT rights in North Carolina, across the South, and in the rest of the United States.[6] However, as I was traveling the South in 2015 from my home state of West Virginia, conducting interviews for this book, the struggle over Amendment 1 was still fresh in people's minds. When I attended the "Bold Not Broken" Louisiana Queer Conference at the University of Louisiana in Baton Rouge in 2015, a keynote speaker and veteran activist in queer politics in North Carolina, recounted the story of the campaign against Amendment 1. The activist also did something else: "We had a marriage amendment happen in North Cackalacky, I'm not going to deny—it happened in 2012, way later than everybody else's in the South except West Virginia . . . because they never had to vote on one. Woo, West Virginia. Progressive. Progressive as hell. I like that joke."[7] "West Virginia . . . progressive as hell" does not work as a "joke" without access to a map of states with reputations that precede them. In a consideration of the spatial politics of sexuality, those reputations are already established as being correlated with political conservatism or progressivism, based on a set of relational dynamics that operate regionally, nationally, and internationally. In the keynote address I excerpted above, "the South" is a place where "everybody else" already had a "marriage amendment" outlawing same-sex marriage. The activist's suggestion is that West Virginia would have had a marriage amendment too if they/we had "had to vote on one" because the idea of West Virginia as progressive is a joke.

In the imaginary of the spatial politics represented by this excerpt from a keynote I attended at a conference in Louisiana, the reality that West Virginia never did have a constitutional amendment outlawing same-sex marriage is not acknowledged as something that could be the result of the state's one statewide LGBT advocacy organization successfully preventing a constitutional amendment from ever being placed on the ballot. The reality that West Virginia has never had a constitutional amendment banning same-sex marriage is not something that could have been a result of West Virginia being one of the only states in the South with a Democratic majority in its state legislature until a Republican supermajority took over the state in 2015.[8] The reality that West Virginia has never had a constitutional amendment banning same-sex marriage is not something that could have been an embrace of the state motto: Mountaineers are always free. The reality that West Virginia never had a constitutional amendment banning same-sex marriage is not something that needs to be explained because, according to the speaker, West Virginia as a progressive state is a joke.

Whether the idea of West Virginia being progressive is a joke or not—I know many West Virginians who themselves would argue that the joke works—is not my concern here. My interest in this story is the shared sense of spatial politics *outside of the state* of West Virginia that allows such a joke to land. As I write, in 2024, West Virginia is more embattled than ever by the far-right political agenda of a Republican supermajority that has swallowed the state government. Abortion has been criminalized. Bill after hideous bill threatens to criminalize parents who wish to provide gender affirming care for their transgender children, criminalize drag performers, and legalize discrimination. However, that was not the context of the state in 2015 when the keynote speaker made West Virginia the punchline of a joke about regressive politics and attitudes.

In 2016, same-sex marriage in South Africa had been legally available for ten years.[9] One of the events to commemorate the adoption of the Civil Union Act—the piece of legislation that legalized same-sex marriage in South Africa—occurred at the Pink Loerie Festival, an annual Pride festival in Knysna.[10] Knysna is a small town along South Africa's scenic "garden route" on the southeastern edge of the country. The Pink Loerie Festival celebrated its sixteenth year in existence and the tenth year of same-sex marriages in South Africa with a mass same-sex wedding. During the mass wedding—an event where some of the couples were renewing their vows rather than actually getting married—the mayor of Knysna expressed enthusiasm about what the occasion meant for Knysna and South Africa. The mayor began those remarks by observing that this was not only the first mass same-sex wedding in South Africa, but it was also the first mass same-sex wedding on all of the African continent. Since same-sex sexuality is criminalized on much of the African continent and same-sex marriage is only available as a legal possibility in South Africa, this is unremarkable as an observation. Yet, such a statement takes on exaggerated significance as it is employed to create a celebratory atmosphere around "the successes we have achieved in overcoming the struggles to create a truly equal society and a nation free from discrimination."[11] For this public official in Knysna, the mass same-sex wedding put Knysna "on the map":

> I need to thank... the organizers of the... festival for always putting Knysna on the map. As you may recall, we were the proud host of Mr. Gay World. That happened last year, and this year, we're having this great and auspicious occasion once again. I don't know what's in store for next year, but let's see what's going to happen.... [This event] is a great milestone for LGBT rights and indicative of the successes we have achieved in overcoming the struggles to create a truly equal society and a nation free from discrimination. Allow me, however, to lament the sad truth that these rights are still not afforded in many African nations. I find it a sad state of affairs that there are still those in power who think they can dictate who are allowed to be loved or not.

For the mayor of Knysna, events like the Pink Loerie Festival, the first mass same-sex marriage in Africa, and Mr. Gay World "put[] Knysna on the map. The mayor was sure that another "great and auspicious occasion" would be part of the festival in 2017 that would again put Knysna on the map. The mass same-sex marriage, "a great milestone for LGBT rights," marks South Africa, through the speaker's lens, as "a truly equal society and a nation free from discrimination." Despite the ideal shape that policy in relation to LGBT rights takes in South Africa, not a single person I spoke to during my time there would suggest that South Africa was "a truly equal society and a nation free from discrimination."

Both of these examples—one from the U.S. South and one from South Africa—reference a map of LGBT rights that is something speakers understand as shared with their audiences. In order to understand the map that Knysna could be put on, and in order to tell a joke about space and politics that translates, the audience has to have some prior knowledge of a spatial dynamic to sexual politics.

There are other ways this map works. To statewide LGBT equality organizations in the U.S. South, the production of maps that measure progress at the state level produce empty spaces where no positive policy developments happen because changes in statewide policy were never going to go their way in state legislatures dominated by Republican lawmakers, regardless of how much work the organizations did changing policy from district to district or municipality to municipality. To friends of one organizer who moved from Michigan to North Carolina, the South was a harrowing place; they urged the organizer to stay safe and not get killed. In one rural North Carolina county, the city of Asheville was referred to as "the gathering of the gays." To a colleague of mine who saw a poster hanging in my office in 2014 that said "Out in Africa," commemorating the Out in Africa film festival that began in South Africa in 1994 and continued annually for over a decade, Africa was "a scary place to be out"—a remark this colleague made so casually, without ever having been to the African continent, that it was announced as a taken-for-granted truth. This was a discursive truth to my colleague, regardless of the reality that South Africa has one of the most progressive constitutions in the world when measured by LGBT rights. As my colleague stood in my office, it was not lost on me that in South Africa at that very moment, there were legal rights available to lgbtiq people that I did not believe would be available to Americans in my lifetime. It turns out that I was wrong about the latter, but that is part of my argument in this book. As unpredictable as legislative changes and even interpersonal exchanges are in any context while battles over gender and sexual norms play out around us, I contend that the boundaries on the map of "good" and "bad" places to exist as lgbtiq people are drawn by metronormative logics that demarcate not only where queer people are likely to live, but *how* they are likely to live in locations that are either on or off of the map of LGBT rights.[12]

I argue in this book that until we come to terms with the spatial dynamics of queer existence, we will see the continued alienation of queer people from our homes because of contests about space that take place both in and outside of our contexts—political contests that play a direct role in shaping our existence within the places we call home. The "pink line" theory advanced by South African journalist Mark Gevisser, whereby "same-sex marriage and gender transition are celebrated in some parts of the world" and "laws are being strengthened to criminalize homosexuality and gender non-conformity in others" is a clear indication of the persistence of discourses of spatial politics that perform the work of metronormativity in relation to sexual politics.[13]

Gevisser's pink line theory obscures the complexity of the politics and lives of lgbtiq people in the world. Under the hegemonic discourse of "same-sex marriage and gender transition" being "celebrated in some parts of the world" and "laws . . . being strengthened to criminalize" same-sex sexuality and gender non-conformity in other parts of the world, exists wild variation.[14] This book does not argue that legal landscapes do not vary from country to country or municipality to municipality. However, the book does argue that the laws in existence—policies that can be reflected on maps designed by advocacy organizations interested in depicting color-coded guides to communicate how safe or dangerous it is to be queer in any given area—are unreliable as indicators of safety or danger. This unreliability is due not only to the variation permeating any given geography, but also to the varied ways in which queer- and trans-identified inhabitants of every global space navigate their own contexts, often with few resources and under significant pressure from overlapping stories about the discursively inhospitable places in which they live.

Thinking in Place

Place-labeling discursive mechanisms allow the spatial politics of sexuality to position some locations as incompatible with queer life. The U.S. South and the African continent as a whole both have a history of being characterized as inhospitable to queer life. South Africa is a place that has a policy landscape positioning it among the most progressive nations in the world when it comes to LGBT rights, and yet it is also one of few sites to have generated a specific "genre" of sexual assault: corrective rape. Harrowing descriptions of corrective rape eclipse international media coverage of the country's constitutional protections of lgbtiq people.

South African scholar, thinker, teacher, and activist Zethu Matebeni writes about South Africa as a country of paradoxes when it comes to sexual politics: "On the one hand, the country has the most progressive Constitution with a widely-praised Equal Rights Clause. On the other hand, many South Africans live under severe measures of inequality, and for some attaining equal rights ends on paper. The everyday lives of those South Africans threatened by violence, rape, and murder make a mockery of the constitution."[15] To queer and transgender Africans elsewhere on the continent, South Africa is a place full of possibility because of the promise of its constitution. South African scholar of transgender and refugee politics B Camminga writes about the version of South Africa that draws queer- and trans-identified refugees from other African countries across the South African border as an "imagined South Africa."[16] Devastatingly, what the transgender refugees Camminga speaks to find on their arrival in South Africa is disappointment layered on disappointment. According to Camminga, "Transgender-identified people who enter the country do so because they believe something exists here that does not exist for them in their country of origin."[17] The spatial politics of sexuality result in contradictory characterizations of South Africa as a place where human rights are protected or where anti-queer and anti-trans violence abounds, depending on the lens through which the country is being viewed. Internal discourses vary from those that circulate outside South Africa within the African continent and those that circulate about South Africa in the rest of the globe outside of the African continent.

Kenyan feminist researcher and teacher Mumbi Machera reflects on views about sexualities in multiple contexts by considering conversations with students, after introducing the question of same-sex sexuality to them in a classroom in Kenya.[18] After they exclaim that same-sex sexuality is "not African . . . a purely Western development," Machera asks what they would say if their siblings expressed that they experienced same-sex desire or love. The students, affronted, exclaimed that such a thing is impossible, but then hypothesize, "I would advise them to go to America."[19]

Machera was writing in 2004. Fifteen years later, in 2019, Camminga reports the circulation of very similar narratives again in East Africa, but the site of exile has moved closer to home. Camminga interviewed transgender refugees in South Africa who had left East Africa, after being told that they would be killed, if they didn't "go overseas or go to South Africa."[20] In the case of both the United States and South Africa, there is a narrative about the possibility of queer life that circulates globally, while at the same time, refugees who apply for asylum on the basis of sexual orientation or gender identity are likely to find racism, xenophobia, and violence upon their arrival. In both countries, violence against queer people persists despite the reputations of these countries in other African nations that these are the destinations to which queer and trans Africans should flee.

The U.S. South is a region often shrouded in narratives about its incomprehensible strangeness. Rural sexualities scholar Mary Gray speaks to the strangeness of the region when writing about choosing Kentucky as a site for ethnographic research focused on the lives of young queer people.[21] In the introduction to *Out in the Country: Youth, Media, and Queer Visibility in Rural America*, Gray includes a section called "Methods: Locating the Rural." Gray explains the focus on "the rural" for the study: "I wanted to locate my research in an archetypal rural space that loomed large in the cultural imaginary of the United States." Though Gray is from California where there are also rural areas, Gray tells the reader that California rural is not the same as Kentucky rural, which is partly due to "PBS documentaries about President Johnson's War on Poverty fram[ing] the few images I had of this region."[22] Before Gray even left California, a story about what it meant to be queer in Kentucky had informed Gray's research. Gray's account of the decision to locate the study in Kentucky demonstrates how saturated media coverage of the U.S. South and other areas characterized as predominantly rural is with messages about strange people, incomprehensible beliefs, and dangers that may or may not be elaborated.

South Africa and the United States are both places where queer and trans individuals on the African continent might be told to go if the story of same-sex sexuality and/or gender nonconformity being "unAfrican" is mobilized against them. From the perspective of policy maps, the United States and South Africa do not bear the stigma of a peculiar hostility to queer existence and are instead often celebrated as the sites most conducive to queer thriving. Both of these countries, however, have complicated internal politics when it comes to queer habitability.

This book argues that there are hegemonic discourses shaping both the way that space is perceived and the way material resources are distributed and/or available to marginalized queer populations struggling for their/our own dignity and safety. Despite important disruptions to the hegemony of these discourses on the ground and in academic publications, discourse continues to position some spaces as "out-of-the-way places" in relation to the ideal policy landscape for LGBT rights.[23] To be out of the way does not mean to be a rural dweller. It does not mean "to be African." To be out of the way, in the sense I am using it, means to occupy a geography that is peripheralized by the hegemonic discourse of where it is "good" or "bad" or "safe" or "dangerous" to exist queerly.

The reality of safety, mobility, and risk of violence for queer people is that neither gayborhoods, nondiscrimination legislation, nor same-sex marriage laws can guarantee the first or protect against the last. Historians Marcus Hunter and Zandria Robinson write similarly about the cartographies that are shaped by Black life in their impressively intersectional history *Chocolate Cities: The Black Map of American Life*. What Hunter and Robinson assert about the violence of racism resonates with the reality of violence against queer people: "Histories and incidents of racialized violence abound at every location on Black maps, then and now."[24] Violence that reaches out from centuries of criminalization and pathologization overlaps at the intersections of race, gender, ability, and sexuality. These intersections are the most fertile places for understanding and unsettling the dominance of metronormative logics and narratives because they go beyond the identity politics that invariably privilege the least marginalized within a group.

In the anthology *Boldly Queer*, Irene Fubara-Manuel provides the reader with one interviewee's interpretation of the International, Lesbian, Gay, Bisexual, Transgender and Intersex Association's map that is coded from red to green.[25] Red countries are countries where same-sex sexuality is criminalized to the extent that death is a potential punishment. Green countries are countries where same-sex marriage is a legal possibility. (The map has become much more complex in recent years, including more variety in both its color scheme and legislative possibilities.) Fubara-Manuel's interviewee is more interested in what *cannot* be seen by the map's color scheme. Their *specific* experience as a queer African immigrant does not align with the assumptions that are more easily categorized through reliance on the law as an indicator of "climate" for queer people. The map, as a measure of their safety, is unreliable. Similarly, the law, as a rubric for the safety and possibility of queer life, is unreliable.[26]

Kenyan author and journalist Binyavanga Wainaina also speaks to assumptions about safety, mobility, and belonging in the edited volume *Boldly Queer*.[27] Wainaina sometimes identified as a "public homosexual" because of the way Wainaina documented coming out so publicly in letters to Wainaina's late parents. The letters have been published in the *Guardian* and by *Granta*; they have also been chronicled in a TEDx Talk and documented in interviews elsewhere.[28] When colleagues in Nigeria and Uganda invited Wainaina for speaking engagements and readings at their universities, Wainaina was concerned, but the colleagues insisted. When Wainaina attended the events, the venues were full, and audiences were excited to receive Wainaina. Wainaina realized that there was work that had gone into making the spaces safe and welcoming, and that it was the people who had extended the invitation and who cherished Wainaina's presence who had done that work. Wainaina's experience of a warm welcome as a public homosexual in countries where same-sex sexuality is criminalized is evidence that it is possible to "struggle" such a "welcome" into existence everywhere in the world, even in places maligned by the metronorm as inhospitable to queer life. The ethnographic accounts of queer organizers working at the margins in this book speak to what that struggle entails.

Colonizing Narratives, Colonized Discourse

While I emphasize the importance of the local in this project, the local does not exist in a vacuum, nor does it live outside of the forces of globalization that act for good or ill on environments, economies, governments, and possibilities for human survival and mobility. During the time I was first in South Africa (2009–2010) enrolled as a student at the University of Cape Town, two Malawians were arrested after they threw an engagement party. They were charged under colonial-era "sodomy laws" and sentenced to fourteen years of hard labor.[29] The campaign that followed resulted in the release of the two individuals, both of whom had been held in a gender-segregated men's prison. That campaign was initiated in Malawi by Malawian lgbtiq activists and organizations and then amplified at the global level to the point that global aid monies to Malawi from the United States and Europe hung in the balance.

However, during the course of this campaign, African activists lost ownership of the narrative, which circulated internationally as a violation of gay rights. Because colonial-era law does not distinguish between punishment for same-sex sexuality and gender nonconformity, the story was originally reported in the Malawi newspaper the *Nation* under the headline "Gays Engage" and distributed through international media as an incident involving violations of the rights of a "gay couple."[30] Though Tiwonge Chimbalanga, one of the individuals who was arrested and charged for celebrating the engagement to Stephen Monjeza, has never identified as a man, "international media and international advocacy groups went into a frenzy of activity reporting on the violation of 'gay rights' in Africa."[31] The effects of shallow understandings of context by those who have the power to shape entire narratives about a place and the people living there unfolded around this example through "the obliteration of non-conforming gender identities, trans lives and beings in the insistence on referring to Tiwonge as gay even though she stated that she identified as a woman."[32] Another consequence of this discourse affected "the LGBTI movement in Malawi, whose voices couldn't rise above the cacophony of interests speaking for, about, and against them but whose communities were driven deeper underground in fear."[33]

International gay advocates might point to the release of Chimbalanga and Monjeza as a "win," suggesting that it was more important that the two were released from prison than that Chimbalanga's gender identity was honored and recognized (though they would likely not say it that way). Ryan Thoreson, whose ethnography of the International Gay and Lesbian Human Rights Commission (IGLHRC)—an organization that has since changed its name to OutRight International—tells a story that captures the relationships between an international rights organization and the countries in which they work. Thoreson's observations of the workings of IGLHRC indicate that a sense of urgency often takes precedence over lived complexity for rights organizations, and that such urgency is further used to justify the decisions made by large organizations with more capacity and larger audiences.[34] International transgender advocates might point to a systemic problem in LGBT(I) rights work that sacrifices the dignity of transgender individuals worldwide for a more immediately accessible narrative of gay rights, but that is not the story Thoreson tells.

What happened in Malawi and what happened in many of the narratives I encountered during my research for this book demonstrates that the complexities of local contexts cannot be understood as purely distinct from, or purely a product of, hegemonic narratives of space, sexuality, and rights. Without acknowledging the capacity of the local to theorize itself and the world, as well as the relationship between the two, *from its vantage point*, hegemonic discourses will continue to have the authority to generalize the local out of its specific existence.[35]

In some ways, the argument I set out to make in 2014, when I began the research project that would become this book, has become even more relevant to the world I find myself writing in in 2024. Gevisser's formulation of a simple dichotomy of countries that celebrate same-sex marriage and gender transition and countries that criminalize those things is more tenuous now than it was when I heard Gevisser present it in a lecture theatre at the University of Cape Town. Political figures like Barack Obama and Hillary Clinton are no longer traveling the globe to lecture formerly colonized nations about their position on LGBT(I) rights as human rights abuses. South Africa continues to be mocked by other African nations for its constitutional embrace of LGBT(I) rights. Lesbians in South Africa are still wondering: if plans for land expropriation come to fruition, will they be included in the redistribution of land?[36] The United States is fracturing internally over the question of drag performances, censorship of queer reading material for adolescents, and gender-affirmative care for minors. The contestation of these things that had always been there, but had also been masked under a story about the United States as one of the gayest places in the world—remember Machera from above?—is taking center stage in American politics. The narrative of historical progress in the United States was so strong when I began this research that the questions I raise in this book about contestations over place, sexuality, race, and rights seemed, at that time, much harder to see. In 2024, after a decade has passed since beginning this research, so much dramatic change has occurred that this story will be much easier to follow now. We've seen Donald J. Trump as president of the United States; we've lived through the recriminalization of transgender people; and the story of history as progress that I grew up with in the United States is crumbling. Generations behind me do not buy into that story in the way my generation was asked to buy into it. When we wanted to speak dissent during the presidency of George W. Bush, we were often told that we should respect the office of the president. Now, however, there is widespread public permission to treat the entire presidency of Trump as a joke. The story of American exceptionalism has perhaps reached its expiration date. The good news is that this makes my argument in this book easier to follow. I think the bad news is clear.

On Rights, Strategies, and Norms:
Marriage, Visibility, and Urgency

In this book, I am less concerned with the type of strategies activists employ and more concerned with how they navigate the limitations placed on them by discourses about their homes as sites of LGBT(I) activism. I wanted to know what the discursive terrain on which activists work looks like and how they navigate that terrain. When I first began this research, I had a sense that the primary limitation facing organizations in both the U.S. South and South Africa would be in relation to funding. That was true to some extent. It wasn't that organizations could not receive funding. An organization like Free Gender in Khayelitsha at the edge of Cape Town is very attractive to, and regularly approached by, funders. However, the burdensome process of extensive reporting and the requirement of international organizations that such reporting be done in English (or other colonial languages) has led Free Gender to refuse meetings with most funders. From the perspective of Funeka Soldaat, founder of the organization, accepting funding means that you begin doing the work of funders. Funeka has indicated to me multiple times that Free Gender does not have time to do the work of funders because they have work of their own that they need to do.

The subordination to national organizations (for the U.S. South) and international organizations (for South Africa) seemed to me to be something that would be a limitation in both locations. This was also true in some sense. When attending Pride events in the U.S. South, the national LGBT advocacy organization with the ubiquitous equality sign sticker—the Human Rights Campaign (HRC)—would be set up with tables and tents that took up four or five times the space of the state equality group or other local organizations also present. The HRC collected names and donations in the same way that local and state organizations collected names to expand their presence in the state and the region. The HRC, however, has a nationally recognized logo. Not only did it come into the Pride events with more resources, it also had a bigger infrastructure for extracting more resources and taking them back to Washington, DC. By the time I was traveling the U.S. South in 2015, organizers, activists, and staff at different LGBT(I) advocacy organizations located in southern states were also noting that instead of sending resources to southern organizations, the HRC was establishing its own offices in states across the South. From the perspective of several of the people I interviewed, this was another form of extraction because by establishing these offices, the HRC was poaching the capacity of local organizations instead of contributing to that capacity. Local and state-based organizations were trying to translate issues affecting lgbtiq people into their own contexts. On top of worrying about their own limited resources and capacity, they now had to worry about national organizations descending into their contexts and taking over.

For South African organizations, the difficulty with funding was that they thought they were ineligible for some funding because they weren't based in Uganda or Zimbabwe. To some international funders, South Africa looked too good on paper to receive funding when there were more urgent needs in other African countries due to their highly visible homophobic legislation. The irony in the ramped-up concern—the *urgency*—with which Uganda and other countries were discussed was that these were countries with anti-sodomy laws dating back to European colonization. Nothing was changing legislatively in those countries at the time I was having these conversations with activists in South Africa. Yes—same-sex sexuality was being recriminalized, and that attempt at recriminalization was being used to amplify homophobic rhetoric, but the legislative terrain was not going to radically shift as a result of the recriminalization of same-sex sexuality in Uganda or other countries with similar legislation under consideration.

Among the events I attended and the interviews I conducted, there are a range of perspectives and approaches to the work of LGBT(I) advocacy that organizations and individual activists take. Thoreson noted that individual activists may also have political perspectives that do not neatly align with the work that they are doing.[37] When Thoreson spent time working at the IGLHRC for research, Thoreson found that staff had individual views that were critical of some of the norms in human rights work, even as they worked for an organization that officially embraced those norms.[38]

Much of the work advanced by organizers and activists I interview here is rights-based work. My interest in that work is how organizers and activists strategize within the dynamics that spatial politics establish. I am less interested in judging whether organizations take the right or wrong approach, or whether their politics are "good" or "bad" queer politics, and more interested in how metronormativity shapes the work that organizations and activists are able to do in their own contexts. "Metronormative," in my framing, refers to the hegemony of city-based cultural productions of queer life. However, "metronormative" in this book also refers to the kinds of American exceptionalism that have come to characterize and travel with what Arab thinker and writer Joseph Massad refers to as the "Gay International."[39] The language of LGBT rights is a U.S.-based language. Narratives about LGBT presence in the United States are metronormative—from messaging used in advocacy campaigns to the assumption that queerness flourishes unimpeded in cities.[40] When LGBTI rights language and cultural productions dominate global formations of what queerness is, and even the rubric by which queerness is measured, that language travels as a metronormative language. I see the metropole as the center of colonial norm-making. "Metropolitan," in my theorization, is not limited to being city-based; the term expands to encapsulate a global regime of knowledge and political practice used by some countries (primarily the United States and European nations) to submit other countries (most commonly formerly colonized nations) to their political will.

South Africa is discursively subordinated in relation to this U.S.-based global discourse of rights. I would argue that this discursive subordination is partly because South Africa is located on the African continent (characterized, as queer African scholars Sokari Ekine and Hakima Abbas note, as particularly homophobic), and partly because contemporary South African political leadership is more ambivalent about LGBT rights than the authors of the 1994 Constitution, who were committed to the codification of those rights.[41] William Spurlin, who has written about queer life in the American Midwest and South Africa, characterizes this ambivalence by describing threads of nationalism that position same-sex sexuality as "un-African."[42] Though South Africa has one of the best constitutions for LGBT rights in the world, it is not common (in the United States or globally) to see South Africa held up as a model for queer life. In fact, while it was common knowledge in South Africa that the U.S. Bible Belt was a scary and difficult place to be gay, South Africa never once came up in discussions in the U.S. South as a policy model for LGBT rights.

Metronormative narratives, then, are not only about loving cities or city life. Nor are those narratives simply about fear of the uninhabited countryside. Ryan Lee Cartwright, in a study of the intersection of space, ability, sexuality, race, and gender in rural America, notes that political ideologies are rarely free of an association with location. Rhetoric generated by the Christian right in the 1980s, as a part of so-called Christian values, was "often spatialized and called 'small town values,' locating a prescriptive conservative sexual politics . . . in rural white landscapes."[43] This discursive move not only associates conservative homophobic values with small towns and rural areas, it also whitens those spaces, which, as I explore more extensively in chapter 7 of this book, are not as white as this rhetoric would suggest. Given these layers of complexity in the interplay between norms, politics, race, class, gender, sexuality, ability, and what it means to live in a place that has been locked into association with a particular kind of politics, I'm most interested not in exploring which kinds of queer politics are worth enshrining but in asking this question: What does it mean to operate within a space that has itself become emblematic of a kind of politics that is meant to curtail your work and your very being?

Writing about the corporatization of nonprofit work in LGBT rights, Alexandra Chasin has demonstrated what happens when "the LGBT movement goes to market," so it is true that there are larger political implications to the choices that activists and organizations make in pursuing their goals.[44] My primary argument, though, is that metronormativity—which subordinates regional and rural norms and politics to metropolitan logics—constrains the choices it is possible to make in the first place. That said, there are some principles that metronormative LGBT rights organizations embrace that are questioned by the data I've collected here. Here I want to highlight three influences of metronormativity, in places that are at the edge of its reach: marriage, visibility, and urgency.

Discussions about marriage permeated the environment of the U.S. South in 2015. It was a marriage moment. How organizations did their work rarely unfolded without some reference to marriage. Even the multi-issue southern justice movement Southerners on New Ground (SONG) incorporated a reference to marriage in one of their campaign videos. The request in their video was that SONG members and other queer southerners would "marry the movement"—a formulation, which to SONG went well beyond the legalization of same-sex marriage and included other issues that shape life chances for queer and trans people in the South.[45] With strong roots in North Carolina, it was difficult for SONG not to engage the marriage question during the battle over Amendment 1. Though marriage is not usually an issue the organization would have mobilized around, context demanded that they respond. When BreakOUT!, an organization that describes itself on Facebook as "fighting the criminalization of LGBTQ youth in New Orleans, LA," declined to serve as a marshal at New Orleans Pride, they cited their "priority to [their] vision of liberation where [they] walk down the street without fear."[46] In some of their materials, they ask how they could "walk down the aisle" when they couldn't "walk down the street" without experiencing police harassment or violence.

Other organizations that were committed to the traditional suite of LGBT advocacy goals often had to decide how to approach marriage in their work. Would they embrace a full-fledged marriage equality campaign? Or would they acknowledge that marriage was not a possibility in their context until it was federally available and work on other things? West Virginia's only state-wide LGBT rights advocacy organization, Fairness WV, poured enormous energy and resources every year into stopping a constitutional ban on same-sex marriage. Georgia Equality, though, saw more pressing issues around health care and HIV education that needed to be addressed and focused their energy in those directions. Even Free Gender, a Black lesbian organization in Khayelitsha, just outside of Cape Town, mobilized around marriage but without marriage being the end goal, since same-sex marriage had already been legally available in South Africa for a decade. I will elaborate on this campaign in chapter 4. My argument is that campaigns like "Troubling the Civil Union Act," led by Free Gender, might use the metronormative marriage discourse, but they use it to accomplish something specific in their communities, not because marriage is their primary concern or even the thing they think is going to make a difference in their lives.

Visibility is another strategy that LGBT rights organizations have accepted as an unmitigated good. And yet, rural American sexualities scholar Carly Thomsen has demonstrated how by LGBT advocacy organizations' very own logic, Matthew Shepard's death is attributable to Shepard's visibility. Thomsen does not believe that Shepard was murdered because of visibility, but if one applies the logic used by mainstream national advocacy organizations that gay, lesbian, and transgender people should be "out and proud" (as Thomsen notes) to the assertion that Shepard was killed because others knew Shepard was gay, it would be difficult to argue that being out and proud ensures one's safety or acceptance. In fact, Thomsen has built a meticulous argument that visibility as a measure of liberation (of individuals) or acceptance (of queer populations) is not only unreliable but also harmful.[47] I would add to Thomsen's argument that measuring an organization's strategies by a rubric of visibility sets up a dynamic where it is difficult to understand the relationships that people and organizations have to their communities, to their contexts. Thomsen demonstrates this through exploration of what Thomsen characterizes as a misunderstood context—the rural American Midwest—but I argue that Black lesbians in townships in South Africa are *already* visible in their communities and that their concern is not visibility, but safety.

Ashley Currier, an American scholar who has written about lesbian organizing in Namibia and South Africa, seems to suggest that Black lesbians are somehow ineffective in their contexts when they "work from a default position of invisibility and insularity to target local audiences and recruit Black lesbians."[48] However, most accounts of hate crimes against Black lesbians in South Africa suggest that it is because of their very visibility (and vulnerability), which is seen as an affront by some heterosexual men in their own contexts, that Black lesbians are murdered. Ironically, Currier contributes to that invisibility by not acknowledging that the title of the book *Out in Africa* is the same as the name of a film festival that began in South Africa in 1994 and existed for more than two decades.

Thomsen, meanwhile, points out that LGBT rights organizations in the United States called on lgbtiq Americans to come out and be visible at work during a time when no employment protections existed for lgbtiq individuals federally or in the marginalized geographic spaces that concern rural queer studies scholars. This call to be visible at work did not coincide with a time when LGBT rights organizations were prioritizing workplace protections. Instead, the call to be visible (and vulnerable!) at work came at a time when national LGBT rights organizations were most heavily invested in arguing for same-sex marriage protections. Part of the metronormative visibility logic extends to how organizations are legible themselves. Ekine and Abbas note that some queer political work is located in other types of organizations in Kenya.[49] This was something that participants in the U.S. South spoke to as well. For an organization to be legible as "visible," though, through the lens of the Gay International, their work must be focused on LGBT(I) rights specifically. This type of legibility affects whether an organization is eligible for funding to work on LGBT(I) rights issues.

Another characteristic of transnational LGBT(I) advocacy work identified by at least one South African activist is a tendency toward urgency. I heard many organizers discuss this tendency on the part of organizations from outside of their region who came in to help, ran a campaign, and left. This sense of urgency on the part of those who do not themselves live in a place being characterized as hostile to queer and trans existence aligns with Massad's characterization of the Gay International as projecting a "missionary" posture. Not only will outside organizations with bigger budgets and presumably more expertise come in to "save" organizations under duress, there is no acknowledgment on the part of someone with an urgent (or missionary) approach that duress *endures*[50] and has its source in complex histories that cannot be undone through a single campaign or negative press coverage or even an approach to a place that makes its leaders latch on to defensive nationalisms.[51]

Outside of Massad's compelling exploration of the Gay International, what is often *not* critiqued in literature querying the limits of rights as an approach to liberation is the way that hegemonic discourses of rights position some places differently from others in a way that makes it harder for those of us in places maligned as hostile to queer existence to do the work of pursuing our own liberation. The project of this book, then, is to work beyond the confines of national boundaries in order to think about place as something that is significant in the lives of queer people in our attempts to build liberatory politics at home.

My choice of the U.S. South and South Africa as areas of exploration is based partly on my own positionality and partly on a political commitment to pushing back against the United States as the global center of queer politics. These are the two regions of the globe with which I am most familiar. I have lived in West Virginia for most of my life and—rightly or wrongly—the state is considered a part of the southern/southeastern United States where most regional or national LGBT advocacy organizations are concerned. There are two regional LGBT advocacy organizations in the U.S. South. The aforementioned SONG does not provide a list of states that comprise the South in their vision, but the Campaign for Southern Equality lists West Virginia as a state in the region they serve. The other reality that links West Virginia to the South is that our policy landscape is more likely to resemble that of other southern states and less likely to resemble that of northeastern states.

My relationship to South Africa extends back to 2009 when I traveled there to complete an academic program called Gender and Transformation at the University of Cape Town. I lived in Cape Town between January 2009 and July 2010. Since then, I have maintained friendships and traveled regularly back to South Africa (usually to Cape Town), completing a master's degree and a PhD in Gender Studies at the University of Cape Town. As part of that PhD work, I lived in Cape Town for another extended period of time between January and July 2016. I address positionality, along with other methodological considerations, in much greater detail in chapter 2.

The U.S. South and South Africa are not the only locations through which it is possible to explore the spatial politics of sexuality. These locations *are*, however, locations I am committed to, locations I know better than other places, and, because of their similar histories of colonization and formalized policies of racial separation, they are locations that have a lot to say to one another.

Outlining the Book

Based on what I characterize as a rubric or measure for LGBT(I) rights, spatial politics designates some spaces as on or off of a map that is shaped by the achievement of legal accomplishments such as same-sex marriage, nondiscrimination protections, and other policy formations. The material I analyze here suggests that these spatial politics shape what it is possible to do in places written off the map because they become characterized as always already inhospitable to queer life.

In chapter 2, I provide a framework for my methodological approach to the wild and wide-ranging journey of immersing myself in the programs and presentations, actions, and events hosted by organizers focused on questions of queer and trans rights and liberation in South Africa and the U.S. South. Because I am a white person with an American passport who has worked in many spaces where I have both a great deal of privilege and many limitations (the biggest of which is speaking absolutely zero African languages), I spend some time locating myself and explaining my approach to an ethic of research to which I mean to remain faithful in the writing of this book. Part of that ethic is clearly recounting where I went and how I ended up with the language from interviews and presentations that form the substance of this book.

In chapter 3, I trace the historical outline of the politics of land and labor that resulted in wide-scale disenfranchisement of various global populations from their original homes. This approach to the spatial politics of land contextualizes the emergence of the global dynamics of capitalism and neoliberalism through which contemporary language of rights have taken shape. In order to do this, the chapter considers the history of the land lived and struggled on by people who are framed as subjects of rights in both contexts. This is the terrain on which lgbtiq activists in the contexts represented in this book do their work. There is ample theoretical engagement with the question of how out-of-the-way places are marginalized through discourses that position them as inhospitable to queer life, but a major question of spatial politics is how some populations have been removed from the land that was their home and other populations have acquired access and "ownership" of that same land.[52] It is imperative to consider colonial histories of displacement in the context of larger stories about home because while current residents of the areas I examine in this text have deep and meaningful attachments to the places we/they consider home, the physical space to which that home is attached was almost never our/their original home. Instead, histories of colonization, displacement, forced removals, and dispossession have resulted in our/their occupation of the land we/they consider home in both the United States and South Africa.

I begin a book that argues for the centrality of context in the pursuit of queer liberation with a discussion of land because land *is the context* on and over which struggles for rights unfold. The suggestion that queer people move to a major metropolitan area or another country in order to live more freely and more comfortably tells us/them that our investment in rights should matter more than our/their investment in context. This chapter begins the book's story of the damage of metronormativity to queer well-being through discussions of land *not* because the rural is the opposite of the metropolitan and to be marginalized means to be dismissed as "backward" through the metronormative lens (although the latter is true from the perspective of this book). Instead, this chapter begins the book's story of the damage of metronormativity to queer well-being through discussions of land because the alienation of queer populations from the land has been encouraged by metronormative versions of rights *and* because metronormative narratives of queer rights often drive a wedge between what is framed as being in the interest of queer people and what is framed as being in the interest of those who feel some claim to land.

Two contemporary moments from each context highlight what it means to reconnect to land for communities that have been historically alienated from that land by colonialism or capitalism. Both of these examples—a panic over the recruitment of lesbian farmers by the U.S. Department of Agriculture and the question of how lesbians register (or don't) in the process of land redistribution in South Africa—demonstrate the way these contexts continue to be spaces characterized by anxieties over land, legacies of colonial occupation, and contestations over who deserves the protection of citizenship. Alienation takes many forms in a consideration of out-of-the-way queer contexts, but alienation from the land was first.

Stories about place, sexuality, and rights travel through expectations expressed in public discourse in a way that shapes the terrain on which work that values queer lives can unfold. Though policy goals have been framed as ideal achievements for spaces in which it is possible to live queerly, there is a gap between ensuring queer safety and mobility and campaigns to achieve the goals of policy. When law and policy are positioned and pursued as the ideal accomplishments of LGBT(I) rights advocacy, the cessation of violence against queer bodies is not guaranteed. In fact, it often persists, providing a clear view of the inadequacy of policy and law based on a rights model to transform the daily conditions in which queer people live.

With that reality in mind, chapter 4 considers rights a form of metronormativity emerging alongside the expansion of the colonial and capitalist norms detailed in chapter 3. Chapter 4 considers the evolution of a relationship between temporal and spatial meanings of queerness. It incorporates literature from scholars who have considered the spatial and temporal politics of queerness as the product of a metronormative discourse with a very specific (not universal, as rights discourse contends) origins and enormous implications for those situated geographically and symbolically outside of the metropole.[53] The literature in this chapter is put into conversation with discourse from activists who work in out-of-the-way places and contend with both local norms and the demands that metronormativity exerts through its ownership of the meaning of queerness. Literature questioning the usefulness of a hegemonic discourse of universal rights suggests that advocacy mobilizing such discourses risks pursuing a more symbolic form of equality than approaches mindful of people's material needs. To neglect the material conditions of queer people in our/their homes in out-of-the-way places means to ignore the exploitative and extractive economies that have shaped those places. Lived equality or liberation for queer subjects of rights would instead mean addressing the context holistically, including addressing the specificity of queer people's needs in out-of-the-way places.

Chapter 5 examines rifts between different groups of queer people in two urban areas: Cape Town and Atlanta, Georgia. Though the discussion of out-of-the-way places in this book begins with land, I contend that metronormative narratives do not alienate rural queer people from their homes exclusively. In fact, metronormativity's historic domination by assumptions shaped by whiteness and the accumulation of capital outlined in chapter 4 indicates that there are inhabitants of many urban areas that are also alienated from their homes by metronormative frameworks of rights. Hal, a participant quoted extensively in chapter 5, details how the twin histories of capitalism and white supremacy shape current realities for queer, trans, and gender nonconforming residents of Atlanta. While the dominance of whiteness and cisnormativity in LGBT rights work is well documented,[54] many participants spoke to the persistent forms those erasures continue to take. Understanding how racism, racial marginalization, and white supremacy function in metropolitan centers and LGBT rights discourse is critical to understanding the way that even urban-dwelling populations can be marginalized by metronormative discourses of rights. Therefore, I examine these erasures as a product of the dominant shape taken by the metronormative framework of LGBT rights.

Cape Town Pride, too, has been a site of contestation between organizations located in the city center and those representing Black lesbians and other marginalized groups at the city's periphery for years.[55] Khumbulani Pride and Alternative and Inclusive Pride are two organizations that have confronted the exclusions reproduced by Cape Town Pride in different ways. Khumbulani Pride refuses the party atmosphere of Cape Town Pride generated by white gay men situated in Cape Town's gayborhood, Green Point. Alternative and Inclusive Pride staged disruptions of Cape Town Pride for several consecutive years, protesting the insensitive names for Pride festivals chosen by the white gay men on the Cape Town Pride organizing committee.[56]

Atlanta, Georgia, on the other hand, is described by some organizers as a "Mecca" for (especially) Black gay men in the South, but a mecca that does not live up to the promises it holds out to folks who want to remain in the South but live in a city where they can live fulfilling queer lives. Organizers based in Atlanta discuss their experience of Atlanta and their perceptions of life for residents of what one nonprofit director described as "two Atlantas."

Chapter 6 explores what it means to live and organize queerly in homes that are out-of-the-way places. These organizers work in places that are not the kind of major metropolitan areas that Cape Town and Atlanta are. Living and working toward queer liberation in out-of-the-way places is much more deeply textured than a narrative of hospitable and inhospitable or any other binary-driven spatial politics will allow.[57] The depth of the challenges faced by those working with an interest in sustaining queer life in out-of-the-way places is not eclipsed by their love of and commitment to spaces that have often been left behind or fetishized by national and transnational LGBT(I) rights organizations.

Chapter 7 returns the text to my original interest in this topic. If the argument of this book is that home is where we are likely to develop our most profound relationship to politics, I close the book with an extended reflection on what that looks like, from the vantage point that is my geographical home. In this final chapter, I ask how whiteness gets in the way of organizing when it comes to LGBT(I) rights. Because many of the counties surrounding where I live are 90–95 percent white according to census data, I find the question of whiteness—what it is, what it does, how it goes unremarked—a fertile one to explore in relation to literature that has something to say about how whiteness and queerness interact and intersect with one another.

Our relationships with one another are messy wherever we live. The fault lines around who constitutes "community" are under continual negotiation. Though hegemonic discourses of "good" and "bad" places to be queer attempt to structure the world so that some places are on the map of queer habitability and some places are off, out-of-the-way places do not cohere to this dichotomized cartography. Their realities are much more complex. If the story of what places *are* in relation to LGBTIQ existences and possibilities is always told from the metropole, the dynamic process of carving out space for existence and the multiple possibilities for building communities will not register in the narrative of what is legibly queer.

This book argues that queer people struggle not only within our/their own contexts but in relation to a metronormative narrative that has the capacity to alienate us/them from our/their contexts. To be outside of the metropole does not mean to be rural. To be outside of the metropole means to be at a temporal and spatial distance from a narrative establishing the norms that govern modernity. Metronormativity is harmful not only because it is an inaccurate, oversimplified, and ahistorical approach to understanding global queer politics. Metronormativity is harmful because it alienates queer bodies from the land that would otherwise be home to us/them, just as homo-/trans-antagonism does.

CHAPTER 2

Positionality and Method

CRITICAL GESTURES

Following the example of Donna Haraway, Amina Mama, Anna Tsing, and others, this book is an attempt to construct knowledge about specific geographical and discursive locations through an examination of two spaces that are exemplificative of the process of discursive marginalization within hegemonic discourses of LGBT(I) rights.[1] This chapter tells the story of how I worked with a body of cross-disciplinary critical literature to create a theoretical and methodological framework for the examination of the two spaces under consideration here. Haraway's observation that "the need [for] the power of modern critical theories of how meanings and bodies get made . . . in order to live in meanings and bodies that have a chance for a future" demonstrates the necessity of analyzing the processes at work in discursive marginalization of queer experiences, lives, and bodies outside of the metropole (and marginalized spaces within it).[2] The first step toward realizing a more just future for varied queer bodies and lives in multiple locations is to be able to see and resist such discursive marginalization in an effort to disrupt its effects.

The ethics of transnational research have rightly been queried and scrutinized.[3] Haraway, who is a feminist biologist and someone invested in the survival of interconnected ecosystems, suggests that when in doing transnational research one is "at best a guest who might reciprocate appropriately, and at worst another in a long line of colonizers, always taking land and giving advice."[4] It is also Haraway, however, who theorizes the value of developing connections across multiple differently situated locations to not only produce "situated knowledges" but also work toward a world that can resist and survive the dehumanizing legacies of colonialisms and the onslaughts and aftermaths of exploitative and destructive economic systems.[5] Building those connections requires cultivating curiosity and resilience through seeing linkages between spaces where linkages seem unlikely. To build these connections in a way that fosters resilience rather than contributing to the precarity of the local within globalized economies (by producing narratives that situate out-of-the-way places even further out of the way) requires a deep attention to multiple contexts.

A transnational project of the kind I'm describing demands a critical approach, conscious of the histories of the places in which it unfolds and aware of the relationship between the researcher and the places that are linked through such transnational work. Jim Thomas, who elaborates what makes critical ethnography critical and distinguishes it from other approaches, makes the claim that the critical approach "deepens and sharpens ethical commitments by forcing us to develop and act upon value commitments in the context of political agendas. Critical ethnographers describe, analyze, and open to scrutiny otherwise hidden agendas, power centers, and assumptions that inhibit, repress, and constrain."[6] I want to present in this book one model for how "deepen[ed]" and "sharpen[ed]" ethical and political commitments can look in considering two disparate contexts together. This is particularly important in light of something that Carly Thomsen notes in an examination of place in the lives and representation of lesbians in the American Midwest: "A stated focus on rural place may do nothing to shift perceptions about place or inspire a more nuanced approach to understanding differences that manifest along spatial lines."[7] Simply because a place is identified as a subject of study does not mean that place is being understood or worked with on its own terms. In my approach to understanding how metronormativity shapes queer presences in two places, I prioritize an effort to understand those places on their own terms rather than through the lens of metronormativity.

Thomas advocates for "wildness" in research because to domesticate knowledge means to submit it to normative regimes that deny knowledge production its transformative potential. The wildness, or the response "to a call to reject inhibitions imposed by assumed meanings and to cultivate in their place the fiercely passionate and undomesticated side of our scholarly nature that challenges preconceived ideas," of this study is most easily identifiable in its design.[8] The linking of two distant contexts as similarly situated in complex global dynamics involves invoking multi-sited methods, but pushes beyond multi-sitedness as consideration of multiple locations within a geographically bounded site such as a state or a country.[9] This aligns more closely with Tsing's 2015 study that traces the changing meanings of the matsutake mushroom as it shifts from commodity to gift, its existence both material and symbolic, in its circulation around the globe.[10] Tsing is also the person whose phrase "out-of-the-way places" is central to my theorization of space in this text.

Amina Mama also writes about a kind of epistemological wildness, using the term "undisciplined" to refer to anti-imperial thinkers who refuse to be governed by disciplinary boundaries: "Consciousness, culture, ideology, politics, and economics are all discussed by the same writer, often in the same text."[11] Mama's exploration of the undisciplined nature of much of the anti-imperial intellectual work that has been produced on the African continent by African scholars themselves takes place within the context of broader questions Mama raises about the ethics of research, especially in relation to the African continent. In Mama's 2006 lecture to the African Studies Association in San Francisco titled "Is It Ethical to Study Africa?" Mama does not give a definitive answer to this question, neither for the American scholars gathered at the meeting nor for the African scholars whose work preoccupies much of Mama's paper. However, Mama suggests that it is the ethical commitment to African people themselves, to their liberation and their well-being, that has driven an anti-imperial refusal to adhere to disciplinary boundaries. This refusal, for Mama, distinguishes African thought about global power relations from neoliberal logics common in other intellectual traditions.[12]

I believe the question of whether or not it is ethical for me to write about the African continent is not one for me to answer. This nonanswer is one of the things that I believe distinguishes my work from other white American/European scholars who are not linked through their own lives/positionality to an African context but write about those contexts anyway. As the queer feminist scholar of difficult questions Sara Ahmed says, "Ethics requires keeping the question of ethics alive."[13] In response to Mama's question, however, I want to articulate my own approach to engaging ethically with research. Frustration with American exceptionalism was what led me to South Africa in the first place. When I first enrolled in an educational program in South Africa (an act itself indicative of my own privilege), my desire was to learn from a vantage point outside of American exceptionalism. I contend that there is much to be learned from perspectives with American logics at the periphery.

I suggest that this intentional and self-aware approach to knowledge production that queries taken-for-granted logics distinguishes my work from other transnational approaches taken by white Americans. Two texts that are often credited for their transnational approach to queer Africa take normative American political frames and apply them to African contexts.[14] Ashley Currier does this through an exploration of visibility in South African and Namibian lesbian organizing.[15] Ryan Thoreson, meanwhile, does this through an examination of a globally reaching U.S.-based LGBT rights organization that Thoreson ultimately concludes justifies its existence because it does the best it can.[16] These studies do seem to me to be representative of work that claims to be transnational but that ultimately recolonizes the contexts that form their interest through a reading based on frameworks generated in the Global North. These transnational studies demonstrate the necessity of applying a decolonizing lens to marginalized geographies.

My work aligns with Mama's call to engage with the African continent ethically because I recognize my own limitations as a white American and I seek solidarity with scholars who are less interested in using the African continent (and other marginalized-through-colonization geographies) as a case study to prove my theory and more interested in understanding that the contexts I present here have something to contribute to a collective, global understanding of the world. Local politics exist in a complex relationship between local norms and global structures of power. This is the starting place for my inquiry, and it is something that I observed moving through marginalized geographies—American ones and ones in South Africa, Uganda, and Kenya, especially. Because I identify the metropole as the center of colonial thought and political power, all out-of-the-way places have some perspective to contribute to a decolonial approach to spatial politics. My political commitment in this work is to the liberation of the people I write about and all marginalized people across the globe. I contend that my research design embodies the complexity of that commitment. The two locations I am considering here are two of many possible places that have knowledge to contribute to an understanding of the contemporary spatial politics that shape queer existence across the globe. My consideration of these places is an entry point, not an end point. This exploration is an invitation to others to take up this project in other diverse spaces informed by the global politics that interact with local stories.

Methods: Driving South/Showing Up

> Strategies of quite literally following connections, associations, and putative relationships are thus at the very heart of designing multi-sited ethnographic research.[17]

The scenes I describe here come from recorded meetings and/or interviews that I collected between August 2014 and July 2015 in the U.S. South, as same-sex marriage was becoming a national reality in the United States and before the election of Donald Trump to the presidency. During that time, I attended and recorded thirty-four events hosted by LGBT advocacy organizations across the U.S. South. Additionally, I conducted and recorded eighteen semi-structured, in-depth interviews with queer and trans organizers across the same region. Between January and June 2016, I attended and recorded twenty-four events hosted by LGBTI advocacy organizations in South Africa. The year 2016 was significant because it marked ten years since the legalization of same-sex marriage through the Civil Union Act of 2006 in South Africa. The events I attended took place in the Western Cape and Eastern Cape provinces. Additionally, I conducted and recorded thirteen semistructured, in-depth interviews with queer and trans organizers in the Western Cape, Eastern Cape, and Guateng provinces. The interviews were conducted with founders, directors, staff, organizers, and activists involved in LGBT(I) rights and organizing work positioned in grassroots, regional and national organizations.

Participants are identified by pseudonyms. This was not strictly necessary, but because I planned to ask questions about funding, funders, and relationships with larger organizations, I began the research planning to refer to participants by pseudonyms. I did not want to jeopardize relationships between small and large organizations, local and national organizations, or organizations and the funders they rely upon for support. In hindsight, this was naïve, both in the expectation that organizers might share sensitive information with me and in the anticipation of the potential provocation of my words about disparities between organizations in the LGBT(I) rights world. I likely overestimated the potential influence of my words in the organizing/activist/nonprofit context *and* the sensitivity of what organizers might be willing to share in the context of an interview because most of the organizers I interviewed indicated that they did not have a preference whether I used pseudonyms or not. However, the few participants who indicated a strong preference to be referred to anonymously in the research were part of smaller, grassroots organizations with less funding. Based on this vulnerability of grassroots organizers to the whims of powerful funders and larger organizations, I decided to refer to all participants by pseudonyms.

Where organizations are referred to by name in the text, it is because I had permission to refer to them by name, I was attending a public event, I was relying on public documents to write about an event, or I was part of the organization. To see where and how the participants are situated, consult the appendix, which includes all the events I attended and all the interviews I conducted between 2014 and 2016. I will, however, rely on participants' own language about their race, gender, and sexuality in relation to their work to add the texture of intersecting identities to the pseudonyms used throughout the text. For the most part, the work that participants did was an extension of their own identity. LGBT(I) rights organizations that did not specify a particular focus tended to be almost exclusively run by white, cisgender gay men or white, cisgender lesbian women. Organizations that did articulate a particular focus, such as organizations focusing on the experience of Black gay men, transgender women, or Black lesbian women, were, in these examples, run by people whose identities aligned with the focus of their organization.

One notable exception to this pattern is my friend Liesl Theron, who founded the first transgender advocacy organization on the African continent as a white, cisgender woman. However, at the time I was conducting interviews, Liesl had stepped away from that role and was doing other kinds of work. All of Liesl's successors have been transgender people of color. I did not encounter any organizations that claimed to advocate for lgbtiq people with transgender individuals in a director role. I also did not encounter any organizations in the U.S. South with a Black director when the focus of the organization was not explicitly the intersection of race and LGBT issues. That was not true in South Africa, where I interviewed many Black organizers who were founders of their organizations. Sometimes they founded those organizations because of a sense that another organization was not responsive to the needs of Black lgbti people—there was plenty of racial tension in relation to LGBTI spaces—but the leadership of organizations was not nearly as exclusively white in South Africa in the way that it tended to be in the U.S. South.

Following connections took me enormous distances and to many unexpected locations. During the course of collecting material, I attended conferences, workshops, queer and trans camps, strategy sessions, fundraisers, pride marches, public talks, and presentations in various settings. In the U.S. South, I drove a total of 14,716 miles over weekends and school recesses to attend events and cultivate contacts. I was asked to serve on the board of directors of a nascent organization that subsequently dissolved in the space of the year. As part of my involvement in "the field," I've written reports, edited pamphlets, drafted statements, written letters to the editor, washed dishes, and walked fifty-four miles in a commemorative march for racial justice. During the course of this travel in the field, I attended events and/or interviewed individuals doing activist and/or advocacy work in seven states: West Virginia, Virginia, North Carolina, South Carolina, Georgia, Alabama, and Louisiana. Some states, such as Virginia, I only visited once. Others, like South Carolina, North Carolina, and Georgia, I visited repeatedly.

I began showing up in the U.S. South in August 2014. As noted above, I attended events and conducted interviews in that region from August 2014 to July 2015. The period during which I conducted my fieldwork in the United States was almost twice as long as the period of time I spent in South Africa because I was working full time during the entirety of my fieldwork in the U.S. South, while my fieldwork in South Africa took place during a concentrated seven-month period for which I took a semester-long leave of absence from my current teaching position. I was aware of the state equality organizations before beginning this research because of the board position I held at my own state equality organization, Fairness WV. I was aware of several South African LGBTI organizations from living in Cape Town, from conducting master's research in South Africa, and from my friendships with some South African activists. To learn about events that would be taking place in the U.S. South in relation to LGBT issues, I subscribed to the e-mail lists and followed the Facebook pages of all the organizations I could find based in the region.

At one point, I heard a story on West Virginia public radio about a newly formed organization in my own state. I knew one of the people involved through our mutual involvement with Fairness WV, so I contacted that person and asked if I could spend some time with the organization for my research. This was the nascent organization mentioned above, which didn't survive beyond the year that I was doing my research, but for a few months I was on the board of the organization and drove two-and-a-half hours (one direction) once a month for their meetings. Through this experience I became acquainted with a dynamic young person who worked in the state to make the world better for lgbtiq people, with a special focus on lgbtiq youth.

Some events I planned to attend I was already aware of because they were annual events, and I had attended them with students on a regular basis. These were events like the Appalachian Queer Film Festival and Fairness WV's annual conference and gala, held in October and November, respectively. In July 2014, I began sending e-mails and making phone calls to individuals I thought would be able to connect me to LGBT organizing and advocacy work in the U.S. South. I began with two contacts that allowed me to set up a weeklong visit to North Carolina. There were many canceled interviews and meetings during the course of the year I was conducting fieldwork in the U.S. South, but when participants had some personal knowledge of me in advance of an interview or when I had been introduced to participants by a colleague they trusted, the interview was usually rescheduled. During many weekends between August 2014 and August 2015, I was driving to events in another state. I would find out about these events through the e-mail lists I joined or on Facebook pages that I followed. As I learned of events, I attended them. I drove great distances (flying only once—to Baton Rouge) to attend conferences, keynotes, Pride events, queer camps, advocacy trainings, film screenings, community gatherings, and every type of event I could find.

Showing up at these events often resulted in meeting the individuals involved in planning or organizing the events. Meeting organizers in person often allowed me to schedule an interview with those individuals. These interviews were either done later over Skype, by phone, or in person during another trip. Balancing the twelve-to-twenty hours of driving I did most weekends with a full-time teaching job was very difficult in terms of logistics and in terms of cultivating the kinds of relationships that I would have liked to have been able to form with individuals and organizations during my fieldwork in the U.S. South.

At the same time that I was touring the U.S. South, a campaign to introduce a nondiscrimination ordinance that added "sexual orientation" and "gender identity" as protected categories to the city's employment policy began in my own town. A first-year student of mine learned during a conference I hosted on campus that it was legal to discriminate against lgbtq individuals in our state. Finding this situation unacceptable, the student leveraged contacts with several members of the Elkins City Council to propose a change in policy that would address this issue. This change did not occur as quickly or as easily as the student thought that it might due to some very vocal opposition by a few members of the council, one of whom in particular tried to sabotage the effort at every stage. What began as a quietly proposed change in policy became a months-long campaign to get the city's residents and business owners to support a nondiscrimination resolution. In March 2015, the city council adopted the resolution, after an extensive campaign to raise public awareness and support around the issue. I reflect in greater depth on this particular campaign in chapter 7.

Watching this campaign unfold in my own hometown while I was traveling so many miles to events in other states was a surreal experience in many ways, but it also provided me with some key insights in my own research because of the rural setting where we live. Rural spaces were some of the most difficult spaces to access, and I had not anticipated my own hometown becoming the site of an extended campaign around LGBT inclusion/nondiscrimination.

In November 2014, when I was unable to secure permission to attend a meeting hosted by Southerners on New Ground called Out South, I worried that I was not connecting to a wide enough range of organizations. I sent a message to the Gender Benders (an organization I discovered through an internet search) over Facebook messenger. I did not expect much to amount from this message because of my experience of needing a personal contact within an organization and the general difficulty I had had accessing some directors of organizations or securing permission to attend events such as Out South. However, I received a warm message back inviting me to attend any meetings/events that the organization was having, in addition to some information about upcoming events. The person with whom I was corresponding communicated that the organization had had a very positive experience with a researcher who had been working with them over a period of time, and because of that, they welcomed more opportunities to collaborate with researchers.

I drove seven hours to attend a regular Sunday evening meeting of the Gender Benders in Greenville, South Carolina. I stayed overnight and interviewed one of the organization's co-founders the following day. This interview took place on the property where the person lives. During the interview, another member of the group and the co-founder were busy screen printing shirts for the Campaign for Southern Equality, a regional LGBT advocacy organization with which the Gender Benders work very closely. I was not able to contribute meaningfully to the work that the Gender Benders do by volunteering my time or skills, but I did become a part of the organization, moving from "honorary" Gender Bender, as I attended several of their meetings and events to *being* a Gender Bender, as I participated with a small contingency of Gender Benders in the commemoration of the march from Selma to Montgomery in March 2015 to mark the adoption of the Voting Rights Act fifty years earlier.

We walked fifty-four miles, learning about the legacy of the Civil Rights Movement in our country together. I have attended Camp Gender Bender twice and have learned there just how crucial the space that is created to affirm transgender individuals, their partners, and friends is to the survival and well-being of those who attend. My connection to the Gender Benders helped me to access other organizations with which the Gender Benders work collaboratively and opened other opportunities during the rest of my fieldwork in the United States that might not have been available otherwise.

In January 2016, I arrived in South Africa to begin the portion of my research that was to take place there. I spent January through July in South Africa, based in Cape Town. One of my closest friends, the founder and former director of a prominent and well-funded advocacy organization, was also in the process of conducting research. We decided to approach organizations together. My friend already knew all of the organizers we met with, but needed permission to conduct a study. If directors or other staff were amenable, I could interview them about their work while we were there. There were ways that traveling together allowed me to access organizations and individuals I don't believe I would have been able to access otherwise.

The time I spent as a volunteer with another organization—the Black lesbian advocacy organization Free Gender—shaped the way I saw and interpreted the context not only of Cape Town but of relationships between LGBTI rights and advocacy organizations as those relationships unfolded around me. My work with Free Gender was not primarily for research. Rather, it was to embed myself in a marginalized South African context in a way that allowed me to be useful and to offer some small contribution of my own resources toward the work of the liberation of queer people in out-of-the-way places, the political commitment I outlined above. I was not interested in mining the membership of the group for their stories.

Still, serving as a volunteer with Free Gender opened up meetings and events that I would have been unable to access on my own as a researcher. While serving as a volunteer driver for the founder of the organization, I attended many meetings that dealt with law and policy issues in addition to planning meetings for local and regional events. It was not always possible to make a clear distinction between my presence in the organization as a volunteer and my presence in the organization as a researcher, except that the organization and its members were not themselves the subject of my research. Gaining the trust of the founder of this organization, Funeka Soldaat, was something I had to earn. The first time I met Funeka was after I had attended a planning meeting for the Alternative and Inclusive Pride (AIP) network. I learned that there would be another planning meeting to finalize the details for the action at Cape Town Pride in Wetlands Park in Khayelitsha where Free Gender often meets. The morning portion of the meeting was still happening when we arrived at the park. When the portion of the meeting that was relevant for planning the actions at Cape Town Pride began, Funeka spoke in English for a few minutes. Funeka explained some of the possibilities for actions at Pride and talked us through what the possible responses to or risks of those actions might be. Funeka then began speaking in isiXhosa (a language I do not speak or write), expressing a desire to "Xhosa-ise this thing as quickly as possible," which I learned is the way Funeka prefers to operate, especially when organizing.

I was eager to be involved in any and all public events that might be happening, and I understood that there were several that would be hosted by Free Gender as part of the AIP events. I talked with Funeka after this meeting to ask if I could attend the event Free Gender was hosting that week—a community discussion about the Civil Union Act. I asked if I could record the event. I offered to take notes to make myself useful. Without a moment's hesitation, Funeka told me that I could take notes on the event for the organization's records. I laugh now at my naïveté, and others, too, have laughed with me and admired Funeka's handling of a hopeful but probably helpless-seeming (white, American, non-isiXhosa-speaking, etc.) researcher eager to participate in events in Khayelitsha. Funeka told me the venue for the event. I finally managed to find the Nonceba Family Counselling Centre with the help of GPS and several pedestrians I asked for directions along the way after driving in circles in Khayelitsha, missing the street each time.

At the end of the event, I had two hours of recorded material—almost entirely in isiXhosa. Because there was a lot of English legal jargon involved and because my master's research had been focused on lesbian experiences of the Civil Union Act, I was able to understand a shocking amount (to me) of what had been discussed, but there was no way I would have been able to turn that recording into notes or minutes, let alone a transcript in either isiXhosa or in English. After the event, Funeka asked if I could come to the house with other members of the organization so that they could put the recording I had made onto Free Gender's computer. That day, Funeka gave me a tour of the organization's offices, a visiting *sangoma* (traditional healer) from the community told me that I would now be called Nosipho and that I should never answer to Jessica again, and Funeka said that it would be nice if I came back to volunteer.

Over the course of the following few weeks, Funeka asked me for the notes from the event at the Nonceba Family Counselling Centre. I had naïvely believed that I would be exempt from providing notes, since I did not have the facility to generate the notes on my own. However, I said that I would try to work with one of the members of Free Gender to create a translation, and I did that. It took us several hours of listening to the recording, the Free Gender member saying in English what had been said in isiXhosa, while I typed the translated talk sentence by sentence. Funeka appeared in the office at odd intervals, occasionally asking what was taking us so long. This is how my relationship with the founder of Free Gender began. Throughout the rest of my time in South Africa during 2016, there wasn't one week when I didn't see Funeka. Most weeks I spent several days driving Funeka to meetings and anywhere else Funeka needed to go. Most of those days we spent time talking about politics—South African politics, international politics, U.S. politics, LGBTIQ politics, redistributive politics—and debriefing about meetings and events we had attended.

Day-to-day volunteer work with Free Gender meant that I was immersed in the politics of LGBTI rights work in South Africa from a very specific vantage point. I became aware of events, campaigns, and activities happening in Cape Town and nationally. My conversations with the founder of this organization helped me to interpret the dynamics surrounding much of the work I encountered. This would be a very different book without the friendship that grew from this relationship with Funeka Soldaat, who insists on being named in this work.

Because participants were situated in vastly different roles at a wide range of organizations, the specific questions I asked were often adapted for each individual participant, though they were derived from a similar set of questions. My questions were designed with an interest in how participants position themselves and their geographic and political locations for a number of audiences, how they perceive others' perceptions of them and the space they (and their organizations) represent, and how they represent their work in order to engage with funders. These thematic areas provided me with the discursive material to situate participants' responses within their respective historical, social, and political contexts. As Thomas notes, critical approaches to research mean "shifting from discrete instances of phenomena to their broader social context" and require situating the local within the global dynamics of power in which the world is enmeshed.[18]

The range of material I collected by "showing up" was vast and varied. I decided to attend public talks and events because I wanted to focus on the ways in which public discourse travels. I also wanted to talk to individuals working in these areas because their understanding of language, power, urgency, and relationships between a range of actors, such as activists, clients, donors, and others they encounter in their work, plays an important interpretive role in understanding what public discourse about LGBT(I) rights is *doing*. The work that organizers and activists, founders, and directors do is shaped by the "discursive formations" that structure hegemonic conceptions of LGBT(I) rights.[19] This means that speaking to activists directly provides some insights into how they navigate the constraints and opportunities structured by hegemonic discourses of LGBT(I) rights that originate in the metropole. Advocates and activists do not do this work without an awareness of the larger political context in which their work is based. They make strategic decisions about advocacy and activism and can live an embrace and a critique of human rights discourses simultaneously.

No matter where I traveled in the U.S. South or South Africa (outside of Buckhannon and Elkins in West Virginia, where I also participated in and observed actions that inform this book), the sense of my own whiteness was heightened for me because I live so much of my life in an area that is dominated by whiteness (95 percent according to U.S. Census data) to the extent that it is often easy to forget my own whiteness at home.[20] In South Africa, whiteness locked me into a specific relationship to the space. As a white American, I was always already caught up in a narrative that preceded my arrival—a narrative about tourists, a narrative about researchers, a narrative about researchers as tourists—that meant I had to earn any trust that I might eventually get. There is no rubric by which gaining an activist's trust can be measured. However, this book would not be possible without the relationships I cultivated with organizers who knew that this was the project with which I was preoccupied. South Africa is a space that is wary of researchers in a way I did not encounter in the United States because the country is saturated with researchers—looking for participants, gathering data, and drawing conclusions.[21] I encountered many other researchers through my research, through my volunteer work and in other spaces I traveled.

These researchers (and me, too) are part of a politics, an economy, and a terrain that have been shaped by what it means to be a site "mined" for data. My whiteness was a constant reminder of that to me (and maybe to others, as well). Whiteness in America provides one with endless permission for individuality, meaning one is rarely judged in advance or seen as representative of a particular group unless one announces one's membership in such a group. Living with an awareness of whiteness at the forefront of one's consciousness, when one's own whiteness usually goes unremarked, is a disconcerting experience. Discomfort around being a researcher, being white, and being in South Africa (when I am there) demands of me a fidelity to the space. To me, this means relationships I formed in South Africa needed to have enough depth to withstand the tensions around historical and contemporary problems with research. A recognition of the fidelity to the space that I had tried to cultivate while in South Africa was confirmed for me during one of the meetings I attended at the conclusion of a coalition-sponsored advocacy activity. While reflecting on things that went well or could be improved, one of the members of the coalition, someone who splits their time between academia and activist work, said to me: "When we read what you have written, we will know that you were here." The suggestion was that rather than simply observing their efforts, I had attempted to contribute to the work that the coalition was doing. This was a recognition I did not take lightly. There seemed to be some appreciation for my contributions, but also, since many of them have my phone number on WhatsApp, they could let me know if I got it wrong.

There is one final observation I would like to make on the process of piecing together multiple bits of discourse to tell a larger story. I think of what emerges from this process as a mosaic or a quilt, both of which are endogenous art forms in the places from which the analysis in this document emerges. Mosaics adorn many public parks and township households in South Africa. When visiting Meadowlands, Soweto, for the first time in 2010, I was in awe of the beautiful patios in which shards of glass and pottery were repurposed into art by the residents who lived there. I was visiting someone in their home in order to interview them and later walked through some of the surrounding streets of Meadowlands. I found that most homes were adorned with such mosaics on patios, walls, and walkways. When I visited Wetlands Park in Khayelitsha for the first time in 2016, I saw the elaborate mosaics adorning the low walls inside the park and the entryways.

In Appalachia, we have our own legacies of pieces of functional goods repurposed as art. Grandmothers, aunts, mothers, and others who quilt piece together bits of fabric that have outgrown their usefulness as clothing to patch together quilts that help keep bodies warm on cold nights. In Alice Walker's (1973) short story, "Everyday Use," there is tension around the metropolitan politics that unsettle the story's rural characters.[22] Walker expertly demonstrates how both or either (mosaic and/or quilt) of these art forms could become commodified—assigned a high commercial value in a place where they are detached from their usefulness. The quilt and other goods are valued in the southern rural home for their functionality in relation to both subsistence and the familial ties they represent. The quilt and other goods are valued in the city, from which a prodigal daughter has returned for a brief visit in Walker's story, for their rustic charm and commercial value.

Through this story of contested family heirlooms, but especially the story of the quilt, Walker shows how out-of-the-way places fall outside the consciousness of metronormative politics. The prodigal daughter has returned with a newly awakened political consciousness, but her own view of her sister and her home through the metronormative gaze does not register in the political consciousness she acquired in the city. The daughter wants to take a quilt that is a family heirloom back to New York City, where it has commercial value. The sister, however, the daughter who has remained at home, uses the quilt, imbuing it with another kind of value. To gain a critical race consciousness (which Walker's representation even treats in this story as a fashionable trapping), the daughter has had to renounce a critical consciousness about what home might mean when home is a place you have to leave behind to become legible in metronormative discourses.

I read this story as a gesture toward the necessity of critical consciousness that is multiple and able to hold contradictions. Walker's portrayal of the prodigal daughter and the daughter's Black Panther boyfriend is both playful and incisive, but the message about the quilt, home, and the status of out-of-the-way places framed through the city's gaze is clear. Because the story is told from the mother's perspective (who politely tries to pronounce the boyfriend's name, but finds both him and her daughter strange in their estrangement from home), Walker turns the city's gaze back on itself. The playfulness with which the mother treats the difficult-to-pronounce name and the other strange things she encounters about her daughter are transformed into a garish materialism by the time the mother intervenes in the prodigal daughter's scavenging.

In the same way that no two mosaics would be alike and no two crazy quilts ever turn out the same, another researcher may have taken the same bits of discourse (of tile, of glass, of fabric) that I've collected and create a different quilt or mosaic, but these pieces fit together to tell a story about queer life outside of the metropole, queer life at the margins. Had I not come from Appalachia, I might have asked different questions of the interviews collected here. Many Americans might come to South Africa and never ask about the relationship between the two spaces because we are taught to see the United States as the place in the world where other people want to be. We are taught that the world is disciplined by our gaze. However, it was in South Africa that I learned to ask the critical questions I pose here. In this way, for me, these spaces are inseparable influences on my "world sense" and my approach to making meaning.[23]

In the way the fragments that make up mosaics and crazy quilts had their own lives before they were organized by the artist's hand into the shape of a mosaic or quilt, the discourse that I collected here had its own life before it became part of this analysis. The picture that I present here is not the one and only story of LGBT(I) rights in out-of-the-way places or anywhere else. Unresolved tensions in these two locations being considered together animate this document, but these tensions are a reminder that all knowledge is partial. Like feminist epistemology, mosaics and crazy quilts do not attempt to hide their partiality.[24] Instead, their beauty is a product of their brokenness and the evidence that they lived another life before their current incarnation. My own analysis of the material I gathered includes both critical reading of participants' reflections as content alongside sustained engagement with analysis which highlights the coherence of particular discourses across a varied collection of material.

CHAPTER 3

Sites of Struggle

To be both a 'philosopher' and 'of the soil' required an uneasy estrangement from each.
—Ryan Lee Cartwright, Peculiar Places

Lesbian Farmers and Questions of Land

On May 7, 2014, the National Center for Lesbian Rights announced a novel collaboration with the U.S. Department of Agriculture (USDA) to reach out to queer farmers.[1] Leslie, the person tasked with running this program, explained that for USDA, "rural America is our territory first and foremost."[2] I had the opportunity to meet with Leslie at a couple of regional conferences in the U.S. South, and then interviewed Leslie on the phone after I attended one of the USDA-organized sessions in Atlanta, Georgia. In an interview with me, Leslie described a transitional period experienced by USDA during President Obama's leadership. This transitional period was related to USDA revising its nondiscrimination policy to be in alignment with the Obama administration's nondiscrimination policies, which were broader than those of Title VII.[3] Sexual orientation and gender identity were not explicitly protected categories at the time that the Obama administration piloted this program. However, the administration preferred to move in a direction toward the protection of those two categories, which meant that their agencies revised nondiscrimination policies to be more in line with the administration's ethic. USDA became the "second agency to explicitly add gender identity and gender expression" as protected categories in their agency's policies.[4]

This might have been a trickier task in USDA than in some other agencies because of the power of metronormativity to frame narratives about lgbtiq people *and* rural space in a way that made outreach to lgbtiq people from USDA seem unnecessary. What I mean by this is that queer farmers don't immediately come to mind when a person thinks about implementing government policy and the mission of USDA. In Ryan Lee Cartwright's words, "Rural has typically been defined in opposition to the urban or the metropolitan, by both census-makers and queer theorists alike."[5] Leslie recounts how these efforts to transform the agency's interactions with lgbtiq folks were "not immediately welcomed" by all staff in the agency "because folks didn't understand that rural America and LGBT communities are one and the same, and they didn't realize that same-sex couples, transgender individuals, transgender couples, they live in every single community that we serve." Leslie was clear that the neglect of rural queer folks is not a USDA-specific problem. Other organizations that exist because of their claim to care about queer folks, for instance, are often located in major cities, which really limits their availability to, programming for, and responsiveness to rural queer folks. As Leslie explained, "Rural LGBT people are not invited to the table, and it's not just us as government, it's national LGBT organizations" as well.

When USDA realized that it "had work to do," the leadership in the agency wanted that work to be more than a press release because, as Leslie recounted, "it was very easy to just send out a press release saying that these new protections existed." Secretary of Agriculture Tom Vilsack and USDA's Assistant Secretary for Civil Rights Joe Leonard wanted to do "better outreach . . . on a different level" than USDA had ever done before.

Leslie was tasked with putting together a series of LGBTQ summits in different states where USDA has a presence and where rural communities would benefit from USDA services. This was an attempt to connect the government services that are available to farmers and other rural residents with lgbtiq people who may be a demographic alienated from USDA services and programs. Financial support from USDA, for instance, might allow rural lgbtiq people to remain connected to their homes from which so much of the metronormative narrative alienates them. Recognizing the potential for this kind of historical and structural alienation of lgbtiq people from their programs and services, Leslie and colleagues "wanted to step out first and show [LGBTIQ people] why they should care about what programs we have to offer." With census data showing that "99.3% of U.S. counties have a same-sex couple," Leslie and colleagues in the agency had the mandate they felt they needed to reach out to self-identified LGBT rights organizations that might have the resources to bridge the gap that Leslie sensed existed between USDA and lgbtiq folks. As Leslie said, "With that kind of stat on your side, you're ok to go out and do this . . . because it makes sense." USDA thus reached out to organizations like the National Center for Lesbian Rights, the Center for Transgender Equality, and the True Colors Fund, which "have a connection to the LGBT space that the government just doesn't always have."

The summits took different forms, relied on local networking for their attendees, and USDA planners never knew exactly what to expect from each event. Each event introduced new challenges for the organizers, but they considered as thoroughly as they could how to make the events accessible to rural queer folks. One event, in West Virginia, prompted USDA to set up remote streaming technology for some of the events when a potential attendee said, "I wanted to be there, but it was just too far, and I don't have transportation to get me there." Saying "those were the very folks we want to connect with . . . we don't want transportation and access to be a barrier," Leslie and the team planning the summits figured out how to stream and record the event by contracting a local gay-owned technology company to stream and record the summit. Even though the team did not know what to expect, the summits were popular and well attended. To demonstrate the appeal of these summits, Leslie recounted this memory: "We just came back from Nebraska where we didn't know if we were going to get seven, seventy, or seven hundred [attendees]. We ended up with close to 250 people from Nebraska, and we weren't even in Omaha; we weren't in Lincoln. We were in Wayne, Nebraska." People who are not familiar with Nebraska might have heard of Omaha or Lincoln, but the suggestion here is that 250 people showed up to a USDA-sponsored event for queer farmers that was hosted in a town people outside of Nebraska had never heard of.

The Great Lesbian Farmer Takeover of Rural America

The series of summits hosted by USDA to expand their outreach to more populations in rural America was amplified into a conspiracy to take over the last frontier of conservatism by various right-wing blogs before drawing the attention of conservative media figure Rush Limbaugh. Limbaugh's "strange and surreal" reaction to the announcement of the summits was critiqued by Dan Nosowitz in a piece for the *Modern Farmer* website.[6] Nosowitz reproduces what Limbaugh said on a talk radio show about the summits: "They are trying to bust up one of the last geographically conservative regions in the country; that's rural America... So here comes the Obama Regime with a bunch of federal money and they're waving it around, and all you gotta do to get it is be a lesbian and want to be a farmer." As Nosowitz writes, "There are many obvious things wrong with this line of thought. One is the strange obsession with gay women; all the blogs and Limbaugh specifically reference 'lesbians,' even though the USDA is extremely clear about this being an event for the entire LGBT community."

Another example of the "strange and surreal" accounts of the USDA summits is the following, authored by Elizabeth Harrington of the *Washington Free Beacon*: "The all-day summit will teach lesbian and transgender hillbillies how to get subsidies from the government like rural housing loans and 'community facility grants.'"[7] Excluding this loaded sentence, Harrington otherwise presented a neutral summary of the aims and events of the summit, using USDA's own language. While there are links to other right-wing news publications and blogs embedded in Harrington's story, they mostly contain similar summary language punctuated by a few suggestions of the ridiculousness of USDA's project. This article is so devoid of the type of editorial commentary Limbaugh invoked, I struggle to conclude whether the writer's primary goal was to inform readers that these summits are happening because they otherwise might not know—given how unlikely they are to follow LGBT-related news—or to suggest that the ideas in the language used by USDA should seem so ridiculous to Harrington's readership that they require no commentary beyond "lesbians and transgender hillbillies" getting "government subsidies."

As pointed out by Nosowitz, there is a contradiction between the rugged individualist image of rural dwellers and the reality of farming in twenty-first-century America. Agriculture in this country is heavily subsidized, meaning that the government already has a significant stake in insuring and subsidizing large-scale farms in rural America.[8] Limbaugh's story about this event relies upon assumptions (not exclusive to Limbaugh's conservative audience) about who farmers are, what they do, how they think (including, presumably, how they vote), what they do or do not do in bed, and how farmers relate to the rest of the country.

USDA attempted to answer the question of who is a farmer differently than Limbaugh did. Acknowledging that queer people live in every community and are likely a part of every profession, USDA attempted to reach out to the lgbtiq-identified farmers they assumed already lived and worked in rural America. To inform this alternative definition of "farmer," USDA was relying on census data to operate from the starting point that queer and trans people already live in rural America, and the fact that USDA has programs already in existence that could benefit queer and trans rural dwellers, if they were not already alienated from government services by decades of discrimination. Limbaugh was mobilizing a discourse antagonistic to queer bodies in rural spaces. This discourse about where queer and trans people do live, should live, are welcome, and are not welcome is deeply embedded in a spatial politics of sexuality that shapes queer and trans people's relationship to the land. Limbaugh's narrative of spatial politics is much more closely aligned to the metronormative narrative of queerness than proponents of metronormativity are likely to ever admit. USDA's programming directed at lgbtiq-identified rural inhabitants was an attempt to disrupt the alienation that queer and trans people have experienced as a result of government-sanctioned discrimination *and* the metronormative narrative of queerness.

The picture of "lesbian farmer overlords" seizing control of rural America satirically painted by Nosowitz traveled much further as a joke than it did as a conservative conspiracy theory.[9] Some commentators had enormous fun writing elaborate satires about the lesbians who would be donning their flannel and moving to rural America in their U-Hauls in order to infiltrate the last conservative landscape remaining in America. In addition to coverage in mainstream media outlets like NBC and *Huffington Post*, queer-centric media sites like *Pink News*, and climate-focused media sites like *Grist*, Limbaugh's outrage inspired a shirt, a sold-out hat (formerly available on raygun.com), and a self-published satirical novel available on Amazon.[10] The novel features lesbians who arrive with "laser-shooting dairy cows" to infiltrate formerly conservative farmland.[11] The idea of queer farmers coming back to the land and calling it home was a bizarre idea to commentators from every political angle. This story only works as a joke if the idea of lesbian farmers is as absurd to liberal commentators as it is threatening to conservative ones. These responses, then, demonstrate the metronormative terms for queer existence and queer activism that shape reality for queer and trans-identified people living in out-of-the-way places. The question of how queer bodies should relate to land as home comes up again in the example that closes this chapter. That example is from South Africa where discussions of land redistribution are much more immediate than they have been in the United States.

Moved by Discourse

Alienating bodies from their homes requires a story. The stories that are told about people and the lands they call home are stories that make spatial politics work. About the out-of-the-way places many of us call home, Catherine Venable Moore says, "I cannot live inside the story" of the narrative of disaster that is repeatedly projected, rehearsed, internalized, and perpetuated.[12] The story of lesbian farmers invading "one of the last geographically conservative regions in the country" circulated by Rush Limbaugh and caricatured by liberal bloggers is not only a story that resonates in rural American contexts; it is also a story that is told by both Limbaugh and the satirical bloggers as if *no one* lives where the lesbian farmers are predicted to make their appearance. That sense of uninhabited land full of electoral votes is perpetuated by both Limbaugh and the satirical bloggers.

Moore is writing specifically about Appalachia, a site of extraction and exploitation since bodies that considered themselves white arrived there. In places inhabited by indigenous populations, then populations of settlers, and then laborers from other parts of the world, those who call the land home now were not among its original inhabitants. Often, the original inhabitants were displaced centuries ago. However, the original inhabitants and subsequent generations of occupants were all reviled by extractivists who wanted what was under the earth but had to get it out from under those who lived *on* the earth first. The histories and the stories of the people who live on this (and other) land are layered like the earth beneath its inhabitants' feet. I present a brief discussion of Appalachia in this section for three reasons. Firstly, I want to demonstrate that even where whiteness is most prevalent, racialization (through narratives that "socially blacken"[13]) continues to be a tool for removal and/or alienation from land and for exploitative labor practices. Secondly, not only is there significant geographical overlap between the U.S. South and Appalachia, there is a shared imaginary of these regions as places of "backwardness," even when the cultural traditions in those places are likely to be seen as originating from different sources. Thirdly, the only state that sits entirely in the Appalachian region—West Virginia—is often seen as "ground zero" for "Trump Country." It is much more likely to share policy trends (consistent with "Red states") with southeastern states than northeastern states, yet is least likely to be meaningfully included in the programmatic work of LGBT organizations focusing on the southern United States as a region. The liminality of West Virginia in this example speaks to the instability of labels that are meant to capture geographic locations, labels that are likely to carry the stigma of value-laden cultural narratives as well. I write about this dynamic much more in chapter 7 but want to introduce it here so that the text is conscientious about the constructedness of spatial politics from the beginning.

While people often think of places like Appalachia as populated by poor white hillbillies or rednecks (the newest iteration of this story comes in the form of "Trump Country" narratives circulated in every major media outlet since just before the 2016 election), stories that are told about people who live on lands in which the state and/or multinational corporations have an interest are stories that are always already racialized. In most cases there is social blackening applied to any population living on land that is desired for the profit of extraction. Matt Wray and Elizabeth Catte have demonstrated the strange turn that such narratives take when populations that might be otherwise called "white" by appearance, ancestry, and/or census categorization become disposable labor or inconvenient presences on land desired by the state. Wray calls these populations "not quite white," and Catte demonstrates how their removal (even when accomplished by force) is said to be done for their own good.[14] Both scholars discuss the ways in which poor white populations—populations understood to have "trashed" whiteness—are the targets of eugenics logic (along with communities of color) at different times and in different places, but most especially in rural America.

I myself have written about how sexual, racial, and spatial politics are intertwining parts of a complex web of relationships establishing who is "worthy" (or, in the language of eugenicists, "fit") to benefit from the rights that are said to be universally attached to the modern citizen.[15] Just as race has never been a static category, but has instead had permeable boundaries constructed more to sustain social and political hierarchies than to reflect any particular biological reality, it is possible for populations considered "unworthy" or "unfit" under one set of norms to "redeem" themselves by assimilating into the universal subject who is worthy of rights.[16] The labor of such assimilation is often in the direction of whiteness.[17] In the case about which I was writing, the character of Tiffany Doggett in Netflix's *Orange Is the New Black*, it was Tiffany's whiteness itself that was redeemed through substantial transformations that disidentified the character from the Appalachian region with which Tiffany (who was nicknamed Pennsatucky in the show) had previously been exclusively associated. Pennsatucky assimilated into a normative (untrashed) whiteness after getting new teeth, new friends, and new perspectives that more properly reflected modern sensibilities. This assimilation allowed Pennsatucky to move from being "not quite white" to being the universal subject of neoliberal rights. Entrance into modernity is premised upon such assimilations.

LGBT(I) rights are not usually written about in relation to the land queer bodies occupy, but spatial relations have long been fraught for queer individuals and populations.[18] The question of how it is possible to live queerly has never been a separate question from *where* it is possible to live queerly. So, in contextualizing the two geographic sites I work with in this book, I will trace histories that have resulted in alienation from the land for different populations who have made their homes on land desired by capital for its expansion.

At the Intersection of Land and Rights

Land and labor have long been connected in the imaginary of those seeking laborers so they might accumulate capital from land *and* in the imaginary of those struggling against the expropriation of their labor and their land. Silvia Federici traces questions of labor and land back in European history when in order to expropriate labor (making labor a condition of earning a living and having a place to live), it was necessary to expropriate land (feudal lords removed peasants from the land they used for subsistence), making work (in the service of feudal lords) a requirement to survive.[19] Contestations over land involving labor and capitalist accumulation unfolded differently in the spaces we now know as the United States and South Africa. The contemporary forms of governance and the shape that human rights take in both of these countries cannot be understood outside of a global history of colonial erasure, displacement, and dispossession of indigenous populations.

Sioux scholar and indigenous historian Vine Deloria Jr. details the history of the sovereign indigenous nations who signed treaties that were ultimately breached and violated by the U.S. government, along with any trust that could possibly have existed between the United States and sovereign indigenous nations who were signatories to such agreements.[20] As Deloria describes them, "Treaties initially marked off the boundaries between the lands of the Indian nations and the United States."[21] Deloria details this history by creating list after list of broken treaties, attempted "terminations" of tribal sovereignty, and constant curtailments of land held collectively by tribal authorities.

One of the strategies for dispossessing indigenous American peoples of their lands is a strategy that Federici identifies as central to capitalist accumulation: the privatization of land ownership, through which the individual to whom land was "allotted" became invested with sole authority to sell that land to another individual or corporate entity.[22] One example of this is the Choctaw people who were moved gradually westward over time through treaty after "renegotiated" treaty. The Choctaw "preferred to hold their lands in common" and specified that arrangement in a treaty with Congress in 1825. However, Deloria recounts that "just before the admission of Oklahoma as a state, the lands of the Choctaw were allotted" by Congress in violation of that treaty agreement.[23]

Private, individual land ownership meant that the federal government and individual prospective white buyers had to contend only with individual landowners rather than the governing bodies of entire tribes when attempting to buy or take land that belonged to indigenous peoples. Deloria describes white Americans in the nineteenth century as eager to possess land that through treaty and occupancy belonged to indigenous peoples. Like other land removals in both South Africa and the United States, the interests of white Americans and the state were accompanied by stories that justified taking land from indigenous peoples. Deloria suggests that the U.S. government viewed ideal inhabitants of land in the American west as white farmers. This is consistent with the trajectory Federici maps of capitalism valuing land used for the production of food for sale and consumption over land relied upon for subsistence.

Federici frames these processes as sharing an origin in European approaches to land expropriation and resource exploitation.[24] The coercion exerted by European colonial norms was not restricted to the privatization of land and the extreme restriction of indigenous mobility. Norms dictating binary understandings of gender and sexuality were part and parcel of that colonial coercion.[25] Legal codes criminalizing a wide range of sexual behaviors between bodies of the same gender and bodies of different racial configurations were used to further police indigenous mobility *and* to police interactions between indigenous and European populations.[26]

Architectures of Apartheid

The racially constructed policies of apartheid, premised on whiteness as superior and indigenous Africans as a source of labor, remain evident in the contemporary architecture of South Africa's municipalities.[27] South African historian Tembeka Ngcukaitobi follows the trajectory of such removals in early twentieth-century Cape Town when "public health" was invoked as a reason to put Africans in "locations" at a distance from Europeans who lived in the city center. As recounted by Ngcukaitobi, the colonial government did not miss an opportunity to exert control over land and African bodies.[28]

Sol Plaatje, who chronicled the establishment of laws that turned "native South Africans" into "pariah(s) in the land of (their) birth" and who was involved in establishing active resistance to these laws, was adamant that the 1913 Natives Land Act set in motion the irrevocable disenfranchisement and marginalization of "native South Africans" who were no longer allowed to purchase land.[29] Bessie Head, too, who contributed the foreword to a later edition of Plaatje's text, describes the Natives Land Act as having "created overnight a floating landless proletariat whose labour could be used and manipulated at will, and ensured that ownership of the land had finally and securely passed into the hands of the ruling white race."[30] The Natives Land Act was followed by a series of additional laws that articulated further restrictions on the mobility and autonomy of South Africans in South Africa: "On it [the Natives Land Act] rest the pass laws, the migratory labour system, influx control and a thousand other evils."[31]

A system of pass laws criminalized freedom of movement for African people. In writing about the various forms labor took in the colonies that made up what is now South Africa, Ngcukaitobi also writes about the relationship between land dispossession, accusations of "criminality," and coerced labor. One form that coerced labor took was through the use of prison labor. One way of incarcerating more people is to criminalize their movement on land where they once lived. (Incidentally, but most certainly not accidentally, at the moment of the abolition of slavery in the United States, the Thirteenth Amendment abolishing slavery contained a clause that allowed for coerced labor as a condition of criminal punishment or incarceration.)[32]

South African scholars Henry Trotter and Christiaan Beyers have separately investigated the impact on group identity of being forcibly removed from home. South Africans who were identified and might now identify as coloured were forced to vacate areas such as District Six in Cape Town "through drastic measures taken to segregate the city" because such areas were so "racially entangled" and characterized by "diverse... living conditions" before they "were homogenized by racial zoning."[33] Beyers describes District Six as "one of the principal sites on which coloured identity is symbolically claimed and contested," partly because even now "a large portion of District Six remains undeveloped and subject to a land claims process under the post-apartheid Land Restitution Programme."[34] While these forced removals were from one part of the city (center) to another (periphery), they, too, were linked to labor exploitation: "The policy was designed to remove Africans from the region and to promote a stronger sense of colouredness by privileging coloureds economically, relative to Africans. And within urban areas, coloureds were to be relocated to racially homogenous townships."[35]

Trotter argues that forced removal from home or the land on which one lives (even in urban spaces like District Six) creates loss that takes a particular form: "Apartheid social engineering determined the spatial limits within which coloured memories circulated, creating a reflexive, mutually reinforcing pattern of narrative traffic. Over the past four decades, the constant circulation of these nostalgic stories has developed a narrative community among coloured removees in the townships. This experience of popular sharing and support in the context of loss gives coloured identity in Cape Town a salience today that would be lacking if it were based solely on political or economic interests."[36] Apartheid, though, as noted by journalist Mark Gevisser and judge Edwin Cameron in their landmark collection of essays on LGBTI South African history *Defiant Desire*, attempted to legislate every aspect of South African life: "Apartheid legislated who we were, what work we could do, where we could live, who we could associate with, what we could read and see and what kind of sex we could have."[37] The intimate details of daily life were legislated through the division of space—*where* you were able live, *where* you were able to work, *where* you were able to go, *where* your entrance would be granted, and *where* your entrance would be denied were all subjects of apartheid policy. Apartheid policy was not only racial policy; it was spatial policy.

This historical spatial separation has structured different experiences for South Africa's queer and trans populations. Sexualities scholar Andrew Tucker, for instance, has organized an account of "queer visibility" in Cape Town around "white," "coloured," and Xhosa queer men. While Tucker's analysis seems to take those categories for granted as *essential* identity categories that are themselves the source of the differences between the communities Tucker studies, the spatial and structural barriers between these differently racialized populations are obvious and entrenched enough that Tucker was able to frame an entire spatial analysis of queer visibility in Cape Town around these three *racial* categorizations, instead of around, for instance, specific neighborhoods or other geographic markers.[38]

"A Rich and Impoverished Land"

As one participant in this study noted, the U.S. South has a history of being "a rich and impoverished land." Similar to the struggle over land in South Africa, indigenous people were removed from the land on which they lived in order to make way for white colonizers in the country that now calls itself the United States of America. Indigenous populations were also forcibly removed to other parts of the country, where they were contained on land that was mostly unsuitable for subsistence.

Deloria calculates that by 1934, an overwhelming "90 million acres" was taken "through land sales, many of them fraudulent," not to mention the reality that indigenous peoples had often "never heard of buying and selling land by means of a paper."[39] Land sales, however, were accompanied by even more coercive means of taking land that was meant to be protected by treaties. Deloria describes incidents in which tribes were given a choice to sell their land or to lose it anyway to projects such as dams for energy production, railroad projects, hunting and fishing preserves, and even what has been called "conservation" by the U.S. government.[40]

Public intellectual, writer, and journalist Ta-Nehisi Coates, too, identifies deprivation of land and home as central to the case for reparations for Black Americans.[41] This deprivation—from slavery, from theft, from segregation, from redlining, and myriad other *legal* discriminatory practices—was central to denying Black Americans access to resources and opportunities that were available to and plentiful for white Americans, especially as economic incentives in the middle of the twentieth century.

In 2001, the Associated Press audited hundreds of thousands of public records revealing land theft from Black Americans on a massive scale.[42] In the 1950s and the 1960s, land ownership by Black individuals and families radically decreased in the U.S. South.[43] As with redlining, the federal government is complicit in the resulting disparities in land ownership by white individuals and families and land ownership by Black individuals and families. Vann Newkirk, a journalist telling the story of land theft from Black farmers in the U.S. South, weaves a complicated tale of racist land dispossession that takes place on a vast scale when the mechanisms that are available to assist farmers to secure and keep their land through lending and financial support are controlled by the same people who want to see Black Americans disenfranchised and stripped of their potential political influence. Newkirk writes that while "most of the black land loss appears on its face to have been through *legal* mechanisms—'the tax sale; the partition sale; the foreclosure'—it mainly stemmed from *illegal* pressures, including discrimination in federal and state programs, swindles by lawyers and speculators, unlawful denials of private loans, and even outright acts of violence and intimidation."[44] Acts of violence, discrimination, and other forms of intimidation that resulted in sales and foreclosures when Black farmers were unlawfully deprived of government assistance enabled land theft from Black farmers :

> Major audits and investigations of the USDA have found that illegal pressures levied through its loan programs created massive transfers of wealth from black to white farmers, especially in the period just after the 1950s. In 1965, the United

States Commission on Civil Rights uncovered blatant and dramatic racial differences in the level of federal investment in farmers. The commission found that in a sample of counties across the South, the FHA [Federal Housing Administration] provided much larger loans for small and medium-size white-owned farms, relative to net worth, than it did for similarly sized black-owned farms—evidence that racial discrimination "has served to accelerate the displacement and impoverishment of the Negro farmer."[45]

Bayard Rustin, Black gay confidante to Martin Luther King Jr., described documents taken from founders of the White Citizens' Council that detailed a plan to "force hundreds of thousands of Black people from Mississippi in order to reduce their potential voting power."[46] Each time that Black Americans attempted to build wealth and community through acquisition of land, those efforts were eviscerated in the name of American "development." There are few better examples of this than the highway system that was built to connect American cities. Highways were commonly routed directly through neighborhoods predominantly populated by Black Americans. Marcus Hunter and Zandria Robinson describe the destruction of North Memphis, "an enclave of Black homeowners and business elites" that declined, like many Black neighborhoods, in the wake of postwar highway construction that bifurcated communities and caused neighborhood disinvestment." This "disinvestment" occurred only after "an interstate bypass . . . originally planned through a wealthy White community was blocked by a Supreme Court decision and rerouted through North Memphis."[47]

However, it wasn't only Black landowners who were disadvantaged through legal and illegal means. Black sharecroppers, who were even more vulnerable to the vindictiveness of white people who resented their increased mobility after the adoption of the Thirteenth Amendment, worked and lived on land owned by white property owners in the South. Sharecroppers were also disadvantaged through federal legislation. The Agricultural Adjustment Act adopted in the 1930s was meant to alleviate poverty across the southern United States. However, financial support was disbursed only to landowners. While federal lawmakers "never intended for government subsidies to result in displacement of landless sharecroppers," this program and other federal subsidies "set forces in motion that would result in the permanent displacement of scores of landless tenants."[48]

One popular way to dismiss claims to reparations in the United States is to suggest that slavery happened so long ago that it would be difficult to know who would now owe or be owed reparations. Such a claim is factually inaccurate: dismissals of reparations claims based on a sense that slavery began and ended long ago miss all of the ways that Black wealth was stolen after the end of slavery.

Slavery was institutionalized in the U.S. South, and it was institutionalized with race at the heart of what it meant to be enslaved. Therefore, while every geographic region of the United States has cities that are segregated as a result of housing policies such as redlining (a pernicious legacy of the legal discrimination against Black Americans in the twentieth century), the most definitive forms of racial separation and racial oppression have their deepest roots in the U.S. South. Historian Cynthia Griggs Fleming, writing about the Alabama Black Belt, describes that oppression this way: "The restrictions on black lives were endless, and the consequences for challenging them were deadly."[49] Legislation aimed at enfranchising Black Americans in the twentieth century was created because, while slavery ended in 1865, the violence of racial terror kept Black Americans from voting and running for office until a hundred years later, when the march from Selma to Montgomery during the Freedom Summer project in 1965 resulted in the passage of the Voting Rights Act. As Fleming notes, the legislation was necessary because "as late as 1960, some 70 percent of southern African Americans were still unable to register to vote," even though they were supposed to be enfranchised.[50]

The divide between the North and the South in the United States is well known as the impetus for the Civil War in the nineteenth-century. That war was over the institution of slavery. The massive wealth generated by the cotton industry built the United States. While cotton was grown and harvested in the South, it was processed and shipped to a global market from the North. Not only did the North not have a total moral investment in ending slavery, northern states, and especially metropolitan centers in those northern states, had a deep financial investment in its continuation: "The nation's financial and manufacturing centers, New York and Massachusetts, spun gold from the slave fields of the South."[51]

In their book *Complicity*, journalists Anne Farrow, Joel Lang, and Jennifer Frank tell the story of the role of the North in maintaining and benefiting from slavery. While the northern states are often credited with a "liberal" and abolitionist reputation, the historical reality is that the foundation of both the northern and southern economy was the cotton industry. The North's domination of the U.S. economy was extended through control of ports and many other facets of the trade in cotton: "Northerners' influence and control infused nearly every phase of the trade. Most ships that carried the cotton from plantation to port to market were built in the North, and they were usually owned by Northerners. Their captains and crews were often New Englanders. Northern companies sold the insurance to protect a farmer's crop and all of his property, including his slaves. And hundreds of Northern textile mills clothed those slaves."[52] The spatial politics surrounding the war suggest that the North was the site of abolitionist politics while the South clung to the institution of slavery, ultimately driving the country to the brink of separation. However, the North had an investment in the institution of slavery so deep that it could not be taken for granted that abolitionism was the political stance of individual northerners or the region collectively.[53] In other words, the historical reality is that the North and South were both complicit in and reliant upon the institution of slavery to generate capital at the expense of the human dignity of the enslaved people upon whose backs the wealth of the United States was generated. These sites—north and south—are framed as distinct political entities with specific political goals in approaching the Civil War and political postures that have distinguished themselves from one another since the

19th century. However, there is a global economy in which both of these geographical sites are imbricated: a global economy that generated enormous capital for white wealthy landowners at the expense of enslaved, colonized, and displaced populations. The entire fortune of the United States was invested in the institution of slavery, and while northern states remained at a geographical distance from the ugliest parts of slavery as a daily practice, both the North and South are implicated in the maintenance, perpetuation, and practice of slavery. Hunter and Robinson, too, argue that while the U.S. South has been characterized as the most hostile for Black life, racism pervades the landscape of the entire United States.[54] As they note, "The notion that there is no 'North' is one that runs through Black political culture" because geographical location is not a reliable indicator of when and where the violence of racism will occur.[55] The reality is that "histories and incidents of racialized violence abound at every location on Black maps, then and now."[56] Violence that reaches out from centuries of criminalization and pathologization overlaps at the intersections of race, gender, ability, and sexuality. What South African scholar Zethu Matebeni notes about South Africa is true of queer and trans histories in the United States as well: "Legacies of apartheid continue to segregate groups who in the past were together classified as outsiders because of their sexual orientation, but privileged or oppressed based on their race."[57]

When thinking about land and racial politics in the U.S. South, it is also necessary to think about how the body fit into the logic of property in the United States. Enslaved people were not land, but they were considered "property," and they were governed by the same laws that governed property ownership.[58] Black feminist thinker Imani Perry writes about how this property logic was exerted on the bodies of Black women when it came to medical experimentation.[59] Enslaved women served as the template for medical knowledge developed about the female body, but this was done at an enormous cost to their bodies through painful, tortuous experimentation, by a doctor who carried the knowledge he gained with him to practice on wealthy white women in the northeast. Those wealthy white women were treated with discretion and sensitivity to their pain, two characteristics that were distinctly lacking from the experimentation to which enslaved Black women were subjected by the same doctor. When it comes to extractive economies in the United States, those economies have not only been practiced on the land; they have been practiced on bodies governed by the logic of property.

This logic of bodies as property is also present in the shape that incarceration takes in twenty-first-century America. When the Thirteenth Amendment abolished slavery in the United States, it did so with an exception. That exception is that enslavement may be used as punishment in the case of incarceration. Once slavery ended, the legal terrain of the U.S. South was aimed at criminalizing Black Americans.[60] These laws resulted in new constraints on the mobility and freedom Black Americans could have.

As Michelle Alexander points out about the years following the Civil War,

> Nine southern states adopted vagrancy laws—which essentially made it a criminal offense not to work and were applied selectively to blacks—and eight of those states enacted convict laws allowing for the hiring-out of county prisoners to plantation owners and private companies. Prisoners were forced to work for little or no pay. One vagrancy act specifically provided that "all free negroes and mulattoes over the age of eighteen" must have written proof of a job at the beginning of every year. Those found with no lawful employment were deemed vagrants and convicted. Clearly, the purpose of the black codes in general and the vagrancy laws in particular was to establish another system of forced labor.[61]

In the twenty-first century, incarceration disproportionately affects Black and brown Americans. The War on Drugs, for example, was designed to wreak havoc on Black communities because that is where the "war"—complete with militarization, surveillance, and orders to "assume the position"—was waged. The racial disparities that continue to characterize American existence can be noted in most every area of social, political, and economic life in the United States. Such disparities are linked to histories of land theft and removal.

It is clean water and sanitation advocate Catherine Coleman Flowers who demonstrates how punishing the law can be in relation to Black homeowners. The problem Flowers investigates is the lack of sanitation services in Lowndes County, Alabama. Noting that this problem is something that exists across the United States, Flowers paints a very vivid picture of the health hazards related to a lack of sanitation services by visiting and describing homes with raw sewage pouring into the yards or homes that were close to ponds meant to capture sewage from septic tanks. Residents of Lowndes and other Alabama counties risk their health, experience debilitating illnesses, and struggle to afford the repair costs to fix broken or faulty septic tanks while living in poverty. Then, those rural residents of Alabama—most of whom are Black—are threatened with incarceration when they cannot afford to solve the septic issues that sometimes are a result of public officials' failures to address this infrastructure problem with radical public health implications.[62] More than anything else, criminal punishment for being too poor to afford a septic tank, a situation that can end with the resident losing their home or their land, is representative of just how far being Black and poor in the U.S. South is criminalized.

The Politics of Space in South Africa

Questions of rights cannot be easily separated from questions of land in South Africa, nor can the question of the decriminalization of same-sex sexuality be easily separated from the anti-apartheid struggle there. LGBTI activists were visibly involved in the anti-apartheid struggle, influencing the shape that the groundbreakingly rights-inclusive constitution of South Africa ultimately took.[63] At the same time, the tendency among white-dominated organizations formed to advocate for lesbian, gay, and transgender rights was not only to fail to challenge the politics of apartheid, but, ultimately, to collude with the racial logics of apartheid.[64]

South Africa was the first country in the world to include sexual orientation as a protected category in nondiscrimination law.[65] Even as Gevisser and Cameron were putting together their celebratory text chronicling "gay and lesbian lives in South Africa" (the volume's subtitle), they note the tenuousness of gay and lesbian rights in the country. South Africa was still defining its identity as a country not subject to white supremacist political rule, and the constitution was (at that moment) an interim document. As such, "an unpopular clause on sexual equality" could be "jettisoned in order to salvage other aspects—like land rights or economic equity—considered more important to reconstruction and development."[66]

Gevisser and Cameron's framing of "gay and lesbian rights" or "sexual equality" as in competition with issues of land and the economy offers us the opportunity to reflect on what it might mean for those rights to be in competition with issues of the widespread and pervasive land deprivation and economic inequality that preoccupy Ngcukaitobi.[67] On the one hand, gay and lesbian rights might register as something that affects only those who are *unaffected* by the issues of land deprivation and economic equality. Gevisser and Cameron note as much in naming their impetus for compiling *Defiant Desire*, a collection meant to highlight the experiences of a diverse range of lgbtiq South Africans: "What has passed for 'the gay experience' [in South Africa] has often been that of white, middle-class urban men."[68] Unlike "land rights or economic equity," rights—in this case gay and lesbian rights—will cost nothing in terms of the redistributional responsibilities of the government, leaving the vast economic inequalities of apartheid largely intact.

Because "citizenship under colonialism and apartheid was mainly a history of exclusions," part of the project of democratization has been "promoting national identity based on allegiance to constitutional principles and adherence to a culture of rights."[69] During the decade following the adoption of the constitution, same-sex sexuality was decriminalized, several additional protections were added, and same-sex marriage became a legal reality in the Civil Union Act of 2006.[70] Despite the enormous policy wins of the constitution and the policy-changing legal decisions that followed, the failure of the law to change lived realities is one that queer bodies in South Africa intimately know. This is partly because rights advertised as universal must actually be claimed in the context of "deeply rooted cultural norms," such as heterosexuality, and "those who are not heterosexual may experience gross levels of alienation from citizenship: legal, social, cultural and religious."[71]

Claims to citizenship on behalf of queer and trans people in South Africa "are actively denied legitimacy in dramatically discriminatory ways."[72] This denial of queer and trans citizenship manifests most dangerously in violence, especially against Black queer and transgender people, which continues in South Africa despite constitutional guarantees of nondiscrimination. Gay and lesbian South Africans can get married, but depending on where they live, they may feel unsafe, to the extent that for some Black lesbians a relationship to potential and actual violence characterizes their sense of "being lesbian in South Africa."[73]

The Politics of Space in the U.S. South

Same-sex sexuality was criminalized in the United States for longer than it was criminalized in South Africa. Histories of organizing around rights for queer and trans people followed very different trajectories in each country. A near-universal banning of discrimination was codified in South Africa's constitution in 1994. South Africa was the first country to prohibit discrimination on the basis of sexual orientation in the world.

The U.S. constitution was written at a time in history when personhood was only understood to belong to white, property-owning men.[74] Amendments to the constitution were added as each group of people outside of the original holders of personhood struggled toward, and won, their rights. Because of the separate historical battles that each of these groups waged for their own rights, struggles for rights in the United States have often been advanced in the form of identity politics. Often, the connection between different struggles against oppression are minimized when struggles are presented singly in the form of identity politics. (Black feminists, particularly, have stressed the need for intersectional approaches to confronting oppression.) In this sense, the civil rights movement in the 1960s was thought to address racial discrimination, and the struggle against homophobia is thought to have emerged only with the Stonewall Riots in 1969, after which it achieved extremely limited legal success until decades later. For example, decriminalization of same-sex sexuality was not achieved in the United States until 2003. The story of LGBT rights in the United States beginning with a timeline initiated by the Stonewall Riots is only a partial one. Stonewall was an important moment for the mobilization of queer people, but queer existence and activism extends back in time far before the moment of Stonewall. Therefore, at least until the explosion of the phrase Black Lives Matter into public discourse in the past few years in a U.S. context, these struggles have been framed as temporally distant from one another—racism having been "solved" through a series of legislative changes in the 1960s and LGBT rights being seen as the newest front in a struggle for rights in the United States. As the national gay publication *The Advocate* once suggested, "Gay is the new Black: the last great civil rights struggle."[75] Identity politics in the United States has resulted in civil rights being thought about temporally and separately (according to identities) in the United States.

At the same time, it is also true that many of the most significant moments for legal change in recent memory were during the civil rights movement in the United States. The U.S. South was both the impetus for and the target of laws that affected voting rights and employment nondiscrimination. During the time I was doing fieldwork, there were a number of important anniversary years for civil rights–era legislation. One of those pieces of legislation was the Voting Rights Act of 1965. This legislation was meant to address the informal barriers to suffrage that met

Black voters in the U.S. South when they tried to vote. Poll taxes, so-called literacy tests, and other burdens that were placed on Black voters—but that did not affect white voters—were no longer allowed under the Voting Rights Act. It required states to report any change in voting policy they intended to implement. Southern states were particularly guilty of instituting policies that disadvantaged Black voters, so those states were under higher levels of scrutiny, according to the act.

At the time that these laws, meant to address racial discrimination, were passed, same-sex sexuality was criminalized in the United States, so sexual orientation and gender identity were not protected categories in U.S. federal nondiscrimination law. That changed in June 2020 when the U.S. Supreme Court decided that Title VII must be interpreted to include sexual orientation and gender identity in the protected category of sex. Given the court's conservative leaning during the presidency of Donald Trump, this was a surprising decision, but one that no matter how the history is told, followed nondiscrimination as a principle that applied to lgbtiq people in South Africa by two and a half decades.

Earlier, in 2013, the U.S. Supreme Court had dismantled the Voting Rights Act *and* the Defense of Marriage Act (DOMA).[76] These decisions resulted in disparate outcomes for different demographics in the United States. The dismantling of DOMA was a step toward the achievement of what national LGBT organizations in the United States had been calling "marriage equality" because it removed a federal ban on same-sex marriages. At the same time, the dismantling of the Voting Rights Act resulted in the cessation of federal supervision over changes in voting laws made by individual states. Because issues such as gerrymandering and the requirement for formal identification tend to have disproportionate effects on communities of color, these had become major concerns for advocates of racial justice. In 2015, I participated in a march to memorialize/celebrate the signing of the Voting Rights Act into law. By the time we celebrated the fiftieth anniversary of the Voting Rights Act, it was no longer a substantive piece of legislation, having been gutted by the Supreme Court.

While the dismantling of the Voting Rights Act in the summer of 2013 eroded some of the civil rights achievements of the 1960s, the court's decision that same summer to dismantle the DOMA made the achievement of marriage equality an inevitability. The question was no longer *if* same-sex marriage would be allowed in the United States, but *when*. In these two cases, two populations in the United States were treated as if they were distinct, mutually exclusive groups. The court seemed to suggest that rights had already been achieved by one group (southern African American voters)—asking with their decision: Was the Voting Rights Act really necessary anymore? Another group would now be getting their turn: marriage would be redefined just enough to let it remain viable as an institution. Gay people weren't asked how they felt—or if they were aware—that the Voting Rights Act was no longer law, and Black Americans were most likely to be portrayed as deeply religious and in organized opposition to same-sex marriage. This disparate treatment of petitions presented by these two groups continues. In the summer of 2020, when employment nondiscrimination protection became a reality for lgbtiq people, another case before the court that dealt with unqualified immunity for police officers was decided in favor of the officers. Police brutality has been very visibly framed since the death of Michael Brown as an issue that disproportionately affects Black men, even though Black women, transgender, and gender nonconforming people also experience escalated levels of violence from police personnel in the United States. The message from the court seems to be that while for some groups civil rights can continue to expand (LGBT people, presumably imagined to be white), other groups already have enough rights. As Michelle Kelsey Kearl observes in relation to media coverage that pits marginalized populations against one another, "The echoes of racism and heterosexism, both historical and contemporary, will continue to trouble the coalitional possibilities for civil equality."[77] These challenges in forming coalition work were something spoken to by organizers in the South in many different organizational structures.

Queer Landlessness

What I'm framing as queer landlessness here both takes a different form from and is inextricably interwoven with other ways populations have been alienated from their relationship to land. Queer alienation from land is different because it was not required by the state for queer people *as* queer people, though certainly indigenous queer people (in both the U.S. South and South African contexts), Black Americans, and other multiply marginalized queer people experienced forced removal and theft of their land by the state and/or white settlers. Though many pressures, including legal ones, shape the lives that queer bodies live, there have not been mass removals of queer people as queer people. There are ways, though, that the family formations and gender structures of Black and brown people were rendered strange (considered "queer") by white colonial institutions. Cartwright provides this reminder: "As European settlers colonized the lands that would become the United States, they dispossessed Indigenous peoples not only of land, but of kinship systems and gender formations."[78]

What I'm calling queer landlessness—the alienation I understand to result from the discursive impossibility of queer life in out-of-the-way places—is a qualitatively different kind of landlessness because it is often framed as the result of "opportunity" or increased mobility. For white queer people, a relationship to alienation of the kind I am proposing comes primarily through their queerness, while for queer communities of color, that alienation has a double edge—cutting through race and sexuality. As Cartwright notes, "While some white Americans depart from white gender and sexual norms, white Americans as a group have not systematically had their kinship systems dismantled or been structurally forced into ways of life that render their households or their pleasures pathological."[79] John D'Emilio explains this kind of mobility as a special opportunity afforded to (especially white) queer folks (who would have described themselves in a variety of different ways) with the emergence of capitalism.[80] D'Emilio's argument is that changing economies in which individuals sold their labor *as* individuals in order to earn their own livelihood was an opportunity especially beneficial for queer people. However, D'Emilio's argument goes beyond this claim. D'Emilio also argues that this changing economy *produced* "gay" and "lesbian" as the kind of categories that we understand now: individuals who identify themselves and each other by their same-gender desire and seek one another out in communities they form to be in closer proximity to one another.

D'Emilio's argument is not only one about histories of identity formation and changing economies; it is also *deeply spatial*. It is the city as destination for queer identity formation that allows this argument to work: "In divesting the household of its economic independence and fostering the separation of sexuality from procreation, capitalism has created conditions that allow some men and women to organize a personal life around their erotic/emotional attraction to their own sex. It has made possible the formation of urban communities of lesbians and gay men, and more recently, of a politics based on a sexual identity."[81] Alienating queer people from the land through stories about the inhospitability of their homes to their queerness has been seen as something done to benefit rural queer individuals by directing queer desire toward metropolitan centers. Queer people are told that in metropolitan centers they will be less likely to live in isolation, to have to hide who they are, and to suffer the indignity they will likely meet in oppressive rural locations. In such promises offered by the allure of metropolitan queer life, alienation is framed in only one way: alienation from others who share similar sexual practices and desires.

Eli Clare, a queer crip scholar writing about the intersection of queerness, disability, and Clare's own rural home, complicates this framing of alienation with a reflection on what it means to be alienated from the land, our bodies, and other parts of ourselves that do not meet the expectations prescribed by the fairly narrow parameters of queer metropolitan life. Clare describes the relationship between a certain amount of affluence and queer identity being reinforced as the hegemonic version of what "queerness" is because of how dominant conceptions of (white, affluent) queerness are located in urban centers. In this framing, class and place are inseparable and Clare's discomfort at events and gatherings that cost "too much money [for] not enough food" reinforced that "class differences I felt in my bones amounted to my being a country bumpkin."[82] Clare describes this kind of alienation as "exile":

> Occasionally, I simply feel as if I've traded one displacement for another and lost home to boot. Most of the time, however, I know that it is life-blood for me to live openly in relative safety as a dyke among dykes; to live thousands of miles away from the people who raped and tortured me as a child; to live in a place where finding work is possible; to live with easy access to books and music, movies and concerts, when I can afford them. But I hate the cost. I hate the kind of exile I feel.[83]

There is no illusion in such a reflection that out-of-the-way places constitute idyllic homes for queer people. There is simply an awareness on Clare's part that "queer identity... is largely urban" in the narratives about what something that constitutes "queer identity" is, but that identity is comprised of much more than the metronormative narrative allows.[84] The metropole suggests (in odd concordance with homophobes in our own contexts), that the only option for us is to live in exile from our geographical homes. Others in our own contexts rely on the images broadcast from the metropole—in popular media, television, internet, and other mainstream sources of visibility in order to interpret lgbtiq people in their midst. Many of the organizations I worked with and spoke to in order to write this book have been suggesting and modeling other ways of being in relation to the geography of home—making home "queerer," wherever those homes are. In order to do that, though, they have had to work against the metronormative narrative that suggests what they are doing is not possible.

Rural sexualities scholar Mary Gray describes the position this metronormative pressure puts people in when they decide to stay in their out-of-the-way homes. In Gray's ethnography of communities of young queer people in Kentucky, Gray frames queer visibility not as a strategy of the youth Gray spends time with, but as a "demand" that emanates from the metropole, shaping both how rural populations view queerness and how queer youth have to navigate *being* queer in their rural homes. In order to "lay claim to LGBT identities," young queer people have to "confront the politics of gay visibility... that define and shape the recognition of LGBT-identifying people in popular culture and public life."[85] Gray demonstrates how young queer people in Kentucky

> create belonging and visibility in communities where they are not only a distinct minority but also popularly represented as out of place. To do so, they must lean on the structures of rural life, particularly the dynamics of class, gender, race, and location. In equal measure, they must also use mainstream and new media representations to piece together what counts as an "authentic" LGBT identity and integrate these depictions of "realness" into rural settings.... LGBT-identifying youth and their allies use their status as "familiar locals" as well as tenuous access to each other, public spaces, and media-circulated representations of LGBT identities to rework the boundaries of public recognition and local belonging. They rally these resources not to combat isolation from their senses of self, but to weather the demands a politics of gay visibility poses outside of cities.[86]

Familiarity, then, within the context in which they live and the people who share that geographical location with them, is a more productive strategic resource in out-of-the-way places than one premised on a queer visibility that would remove rural queer youth in Kentucky from the fabric of their communities and their homes. This is especially true because the primary difference between the "country" and the "city," as identified by Gray, is not the country's refusal to be a home to queer people, but its lack of queer infrastructure. Whereas it is possible to access community centers, LGBT health services, advocacy organizations, and spaces for socializing based on the presumption of a common identity in the comparatively better-resourced city, queer youth in Kentucky often find themselves meeting and socializing in places shared with their broader communities, such as churches, coffee shops, and Walmarts.

WILL LESBIANS GET LAND?

In a text about the limits of human rights frameworks to translate the promise of rights into lived realities, Makau Mutua uses South Africa as a case study to demonstrate the gap that is at the heart of Mutua's critique of human rights. Failures of resource redistribution in incredibly unequal societies are at the center of the limits of human rights frameworks. Mutua says it like this: "It is not possible to address the demands of the black majority and create a state that respects the gamut of human rights without correcting the gross imbalances and injustices related to land."[87] South Africa's constitution "stands as a monument in the world."[88] In terms of the way the constitution articulates its conceptualization of human rights, "the magnitude of its vision and ambition is unprecedented."[89] Yet, the program of land reform in South Africa has been extremely limited.

Failing to redistribute land during or shortly after the transition from apartheid to democracy left the apartheid conditions of land ownership in South Africa intact.[90] The right to vote and the many other rights advanced in the constitution do not go very far for many Black South Africans, given that "just before the end of official apartheid, whites own[ed] 87 percent of the country's total surface area, even though they constituted only 15 percent of the population of South Africa."[91] Black South Africans were denied the right to own land "until 1991 when the Land Act of 1936, which reserved most land for whites, was repealed."[92] Though "blacks did not fight for democracy so that whites could continue to own 87 percent of the land," the South African government website's page dedicated to issues of land indicates that only 4 percent of the land in South Africa is privately owned by Black South Africans.[93]

Because of the radical inequalities in resources held by different racial groups when the new rights-based constitution was instituted, Mutua argues that the constitution "gave no more than formal and abstract rights to [Black South Africans]."[94] Because white South Africans already owned a disproportionate share of property and wealth, "the rights-based state, with its independent courts and multiple rights commissions and watchdogs, provides a golden opportunity to protect most of their privileges and legitimize the results of apartheid."[95] Ultimately, "the government has failed to institute a meaningful land reform program; virtually all land remains in white hands although the few blacks with access to funds can now purchase land on the free market."[96]

With the changing political landscape in South Africa, land expropriation has been a topic that every political party has been forced to address. The Economic Freedom Fighters (EFF) is now the third largest political party in the country.[97] The EFF has leveraged that platform to insist on a conversation about expropriation of land without compensation, for the purposes of redistributing it to indigenous

Africans, from whom it was originally taken. While the African National Congress (ANC), the party that has governed South Africa since Nelson Mandela became the first democratically elected president of the republic, remains the ruling party in South Africa, the EFF pushed the issue of land reform skillfully and strategically into the public discourse of South African politics. As Al Jazeera reported in 2018, land "has become a party political issue for the first time, and people are aligning themselves with parties based on their position on land."[98]

The ANC and the EFF do not agree on which land should be expropriated and what that process would look like, but President Cyril Rhamaphosa has directed the government to initiate a process of land redistribution.[99] While land is generally thought of as a rural issue, and has been framed by conservatives (especially) as something that would affect white farm owners disproportionately, that is not necessarily the case because "apartheid kept Black people out of the cities."[100] Any attempt, therefore, to redress the losses of apartheid would have to keep that reality in mind. Failure to redistribute the land has affected those whose housing is already the most tenuous "across these three spaces, the cities, the farms, communal areas" where "we see a process of black people being pushed off land and left in much more vulnerable and insecure positions."[101]

The Commission for Gender Equality (CGE) has introduced a program called "One Woman, One Hectare" in order to ensure that there is some gender parity in the redistribution of land and that single mothers (especially) are not made even further economically vulnerable through the process. The need to address gender in any program of land distribution is a reality, since, as noted by Mutua, "the position of women, especially black women, remains marginal."[102] Knowing about the importance of land redistribution and the CGE's program, and anxious to know what claims to land lesbians would have in the unfolding process, a facilitator raised this question at an event addressing political parties in Cape Town.[103] The facilitator had heard that lesbians would not be granted land in the process of redistribution and asked the representatives of the political parties and the CGE present to clarify what the details of the program entailed for lesbian women.

The CGE representative in attendance at the event spoke to the intentions of the program to advance gender equality in the land redistribution process. The CGE representative also spoke to the complexity of addressing issues of language when it comes to concepts like "family" and the multiple ways that term has been defined through different historical traditions, patriarchal contexts, and now, in light of a constitution meant to expand equality further than in most countries.

The representative referenced "a document that we [the CGE] have tabled in the Parliament: one woman, one hectare" and described it as "clashing with the approach of the minister of rural development and land reform." That minister, the representative claimed, was using the language of "one family, one hectare." Ngcukaitobi provides context for where this language of family originated and how it was interpreted heteronormatively at the time of its origin: "The Bill recognised 'the sanctity and inviolability of the home as the right of every family.' Everyone, regardless of race, should have the right to 'own, buy, hire, lease and occupy land' or any other form of property, with restrictive laws being repealed."[104] This Bill of Rights proposed by the ANC was written in 1943 and at that time the debates about suffrage, land ownership, and even formal membership in the ANC itself were focused on the sole barrier of race as something that was excluding African men from full citizenship. Even though women had begun organizing under the auspices of their own organizations, they were not yet acknowledged as leaders, members, or subjects deserving of suffrage and citizenship rights.[105] African men had not yet extended their own desires for autonomy beyond themselves as heads of family units. This logic appears in the "one family, one hectare" language introduced by the minister of rural development and land reform. It is language that the CGE attempts to undo in asserting "one woman, one hectare." However, for lesbians, the question is not only what is a family, but what is a woman?

The multiple histories of the land that is currently called South Africa trip the CGE representative up as the representative attempts to think through the conflict in approaches between the minister of rural development and the CGE: "Now, if we look in the history of South Africa, or in the—let me say not—apartheid—but the history of South Africa, the majority of people that are owning land, based on our history, are men." While recognizing competing histories and competing definitions of "family," "ownership," and perhaps other competing terminologies that would affect this process of redistribution, the CGE representative settles on an assumption of common patriarchal understandings of who should be responsible for the land, and how those responsible for such land should acquire or "own" it. This has major implications for the lesbians in the organization that have organized the event, should they choose to pursue the option of acquiring a hectare. Will they be recognized as women? Will their family formations (enshrined as legally binding by constitutional understandings of equality but heavily contested in other domains) be recognized as families? When the minister of rural development says "one family, one hectare" and the CGE says "one woman, one hectare" but lesbians in South Africa face both discrimination in their attempts to access their legal rights and violence in response to their ambivalent relationships to womanhood, how do they get their hectare?

Referencing a common patriarchal understanding of how land ownership works across these competing histories, the CGE representative continues, "The procedure for land distribution . . . was that you're either a man or a wife of a man—not a wife of a wife, understand?" The representative maps out the implications of patriarchal understandings of land ownership for lesbian women by saying, "Now, that's where the challenge is. Because if you look traditionally . . . they say a wife to a man. Now, if you are a gay, you can have land, but if you are a lesbian, it could be difficult because you will come as if you are the wife of a wife . . . so that's where the issue is. Now, if you look at the family in terms of land reform—what is a family in South Africa? It's a male, a female, and children. You understand?" At this point in the representative's response, something very interesting happens. The reference to competing/contradictory histories of "family" in South Africa collapses into apartheid definitions of family. Those definitions resulted in distortions of the meaning of family for Black South Africans in order to access what little property was available to them under the apartheid regime of racial segregation. The example is one involving heterosexuality. The representative says that if the government entities in charge of redistributing land "say a family" then they "will ask the marriage certificate to get the land, which was the same thing that was done by apartheid in those years. To get a house in New Crossroads, Gugulethu, or Langa, you will have to have a wife, then you can get a house. That's why my grandfather married his sister. They got a house in New Crossroads. My grandfather married his sister so he could get a house."

The implication here is that patriarchal, heteronormative (and apartheid) definitions of family pervert even heterosexual relationships, especially when white supremacy demonizes Black sexuality and separates families by turning men into laborers and women and children into people who are left behind. I am not suggesting that the CGE representative is articulating the only possibilities for land ownership under an evolving process of land redistribution. Instead, I'm interested in the terms that are up for negotiation in this process. What a family *is* is something that is under negotiation. The constitution defines family in a particular way. According to the representative, there is another story about how family in South Africa is more commonly understood: "a male, a female, and children."

Apartheid spatial and labor policies resulted in a perversion of sexual and familial relationships. While this excerpt draws from an anecdotal account foregrounding the concern of one individual attending a community meeting, the pressure that migrant labor separating families exerted on African people is well known. The requirement that domestic laborers live on the premises of their "employers'" homes in a tiny room without their families; the requirement that mine workers live far from their families with only a couple of days per year to visit at home; and the reality that both parents traveling far to work often meant that children were left with grandparents all contributed to a fragile sense of what family could be for Black South Africans.

The renowned South African writer Sindiwe Magona illustrates this better than most empirical descriptions could in a short story from the collection *Living, Loving, and Lying Awake at Night* called "It Was Easter Sunday the Day I Went to Netreg." In the short story, Magona tells the tale of a young girl who meets a lover. The lover is working as a migrant laborer, and the girl (who also narrates the story) becomes pregnant by him. In the story, Magona explains how familial relationships were disrupted by the separation of families through labor coercion: "The zones, euphemistically called Single Men's Quarters, are barracks used to house African men forced to leave their wives and children in the village when they get 'permission' to come and work in the cities. That most of these 'migrant' laborers were very much married bothered government policy-makers not at all. It could not. The white, highly specialized and learned officials had yet to grasp the simple fact of these men's being human too."[106] In helping the girl negotiate the pregnancy, her mother accompanies the girl to meet the man who impregnated her. The story ends with a punch in the stomach: the girl has become pregnant from a consensual sexual encounter with her own father. Neither the girl nor the man knows they are related until she brings her extended family to meet him because he has promised to marry her. This revelation demonstrates how relationships between lovers, family members, and others in communities shaped by the unnatural demands of migrant and domestic labor were distorted by the architects of apartheid. The CGE representative who tells the story above about a grandfather having to marry his sister is a common expression of the power of apartheid to distort familial relationships.

Some have argued that migrant labor, especially that on the mines in South Africa, resulted in a freedom of expression for same-sex loving men, who were able to enter into "marriages," partnerships, and sexual relationships with one another in the homosocial environment of the mines.[107] Such relationships certainly are documented, but the distortion of heterosexual relationships and family that facilitated the conditions within which they occurred are a reflection of the intensely limited opportunities for human contact and intimacy available for men who worked as migrant laborers, which is a tricky thing to frame as freedom for same-sex loving.

Leveraging the Law

In 2020, the South African Civil Union Act of 2006 was amended in response to a campaign that the Black lesbian organization Free Gender had been mobilizing since 2016. In 2016, Free Gender launched a campaign called "Troubling the Civil Union Act." The year was significant, as it marked a decade of legal same-sex marriages in South Africa. What Free Gender had found, first through anecdotal evidence of their own members' experiences, then through more focused research, in conjunction with researchers and other nongovernmental organizations, was that Black lesbians were some of those who were least likely to be able to access the Civil Union Act in their own communities because of a provision (section 6) that had been included in the original law, allowing Home Affairs personnel (employed by the state) to refuse to conduct their marriages for religious reasons. A person who was denied their marriage certificate/ceremony at Home Affairs could arrange for a private religious official to solemnize their marriage, but there is a cost associated with seeking private services, while marriage through Home Affairs is publicly available as a government-provided service. The discrimination inherent in a provision that allows state officials to deny queer people services available to everyone else most specifically disadvantaged queer people with the fewest financial resources.

Free Gender's campaign was aimed at removing that provision. The removal of section 6 of the Civil Union Act would mean that no more same-sex marriages would be inaccessible because of the personal objections of Home Affairs employees. In an interview, the founder of Free Gender, Funeka Soldaat, identified two reasons why this campaign mattered for Black lesbians in Khayelitsha and other townships in South Africa: "When you go to Home Affairs ... it's a happy time for you.... And secondly... there must not be ... a loophole that will make people to start practicing their homophobic attitudes.... We can't really have any space that will make people to see a way of trying to discriminate people, so that's why... for me, it's like just to scrap the section totally." When Funeka describes the problem Free Gender's campaign addressed, Funeka is less concerned with the fact of the marriage not taking place than with how the refusal of services enables homophobic attitudes and behavior. Free Gender's primary concern as an organization is violence experienced by Black lesbians in their communities. For Free Gender to take on marriage as an issue worth their time and energy, there had to be a connection to the experience of lesbians within their communities. Amplification of homophobia, not access to marriage, was the connection between lesbians' experiences in their communities and section 6 of the Civil Union Act.

None of the popular media sources chronicling the adoption of the Civil Union Act Amendment 8 (which abolished section 6) mention the Black lesbian organization based in Khayelitsha as being behind the mobilization to remove this discriminatory section from the Civil Union Act. I followed the work of Free Gender between January and July 2016, accompanying members of the organization to meetings and information sessions about their collaboration with the Legal Resources Centre to bring forward the challenge to section 6. The campaign itself was launched to a public audience as part of the Khumbulani Pride program in 2016 with a presentation by Mazibuko Jara, who had been involved in the passage of the Civil Union Act in 2006. Jara delivered a history of the act in isiXhosa to an isiXhosa-speaking audience in Khayelitsha. This is the meeting I described recording and "transcribing" in chapter 2 of this book. At the time, I was not aware that I was witnessing political education that would ultimately result in a change to South African law. Free Gender's position, though, was that section 6 was disproportionately affecting Black lesbians outside of the city center and had become a serious issue of service delivery for Black lesbians, on whose behalf Free Gender has always mobilized.

Marriage was not the most important issue at stake in this campaign. The site of discrimination for the affected stakeholders was the denial of their legally promised right to marry. However, marriage legislation was the tool Free Gender used to leverage their larger goal of safety and security in their communities. The issue at stake for Free Gender was discrimination within service delivery in the country. If Black lesbians could not access what more affluent, white queer people could access, how could this not be an issue taken up by Free Gender? Marriage through a local Home Affairs office in your community heightens your visibility as a couple and as queer people. If Black lesbians can be refused marriage—something that is purportedly available by law equally to everyone in the country, what government services could Black lesbians not be refused?

Free Gender confronts violence against Black lesbians on a daily basis. The organization's object in this campaign was not to win something called "marriage equality" in U.S.-based efforts for advocacy. Marriage equality for same-sex couples had purportedly been part of the law for a decade in South Africa before Free Gender took up the issue.[108] Returning to the question of land for lesbians, Free

Gender insisted on their legitimacy and legibility as *family*—a concept that for Black South Africans had been so distorted by apartheid law and practice that the fictional scenario in Magona's story is not implausible. Labor conditions that alienated men from family life could very realistically have resulted in a father unknowingly impregnating his own daughter and, as a participant present in Free Gender's discussion noted, a grandfather might marry his sister in order to access a house. If recognition as family is necessary for acquisition of land, Free Gender pushed the law to respond to its promise by not allowing "a loophole that will make people to start practicing their homophobic attitudes."

In both the beginning and concluding examples in this chapter, the potential relationship between queer bodies and the land does not translate well. The idea of lesbian farmers was equally unfathomable to Rush Limbaugh, right-wing conspiracy theorists, and liberal commentators mocking the generation of conspiracies that Limbaugh amplified. Neither of these perspectives imagined that queer farmers might already exist. To both conservative and liberal commentators who wrote about this event, it would take a coordinated government effort to infiltrate the conservative stronghold of rural America with queer farmers. The incomprehensibility of queer farmers was exactly one of the things Leslie, tasked with coordinating the LGBT summits, characterized as a perception driving the purpose of those summits: to connect queer and trans folks already living in rural areas to the services offered by USDA. People in rural areas are, after all, most likely to desire the services, funds, resources, and support of USDA programs. Of course, as Thomsen notes, when discussing coverage of the summits, the one thing that was missing from this commentary was any discussion of what actually occurred at the summits themselves. Nor was there any mention of what rural queer individuals might have gotten from or contributed to the summits or their local communities. In commentary around these events, there was never any curiosity about life as it already exists for rural queer Americans. The question of possibilities for rural queer life had already been settled: if they existed at all, they were seriously foreclosed by violence, antagonism, and misery.

As far as lesbians getting land in South Africa, the question had not been settled and no one at the meeting where this question was raised had answers about how land would be claimed by lesbians. The government platform of "one family, one hectare" was already contested by the CGE, whose platform was "One Woman, One Hectare," but Free Gender had concerns beyond the terminology governing the claims to land. One of those concerns was around the ability of Black lesbians living in townships at the periphery of South African cities and in rural areas to self-determine their relationship to family. If lesbians could be denied marriage by government agencies, and marriage was supposed to be legally available to them, was it realistic for them to expect to be included in the negotiations over land expropriation? They had called this meeting with representatives of political parties to see who understood their concerns and how they should exercise their votes in relation to the party that would advocate on their behalf. Black South Africans had had such a tenuous relationship to property ownership since colonization, and queerness already has an "unAfrican" connotation on the African continent. Therefore, it was necessary for lesbians to assert their claims to land as part of ongoing struggles about how land would be redistributed.

The planning of rural LGBT summits with the assumption that queer bodies inhabit rural space in the United States and the assertion of Black lesbians that they have a right to land in South Africa demonstrate that lgbtiq people are part of the struggles that unfold over land in their contexts. LGBT(I) struggles for rights, safety, and mobility cannot be separated from the struggles over land that unfold around them. Histories of exploitation, struggles over land and resources, and state-enforced racial divisions that continue to have a social and political life of their own are all issues that shape the conditions in the specific places where queer people live.

CHAPTER 4

Welcome to Modernity

"This Ain't Asheville"

In 2012, in one rural county in North Carolina, a small group of concerned folks gathered to talk about an amendment to the constitution being proposed in their state. The amendment was Amendment 1, which would be a constitutional ban on same-sex marriage in North Carolina. Every meeting I attended in North Carolina in 2015 involved discussion of this amendment. Even meetings outside of the state where North Carolinians were gathered involved references to and discussions of the battle over Amendment 1. To me, this preoccupation with Amendment 1 indicated how traumatic the experience had been to organizers on the ground. That trauma was not just about the adoption of the constitutional amendment banning same-sex marriage. The trauma extended to how the campaign against Amendment 1 had played out and how organizers had felt limited in their ability to shape the narrative in their own state.

Even though the decision on same-sex marriage was on the very near horizon at that point, it was not possible to talk about LGBT advocacy work in North Carolina for this research without talking about Amendment 1. This is partly because of the central argument in this book: the most compelling political struggles are the ones that happen at home. Organizers in North Carolina had been consumed by the fight against Amendment 1. Some of them were burnt out. Some of them talked about mistrust and resentment that would take years to heal. Most of them attributed that mistrust and resentment to the larger picture of the best-funded and most visible campaign against Amendment 1—the Coalition to Protect All NC Families—being led by someone from another state and the fallout from different decisions taken by different organizations about how to engage with that campaign. The small group of individuals I mentioned at the beginning of this chapter, however, had come together and formed a new organization in their county in order to respond to Amendment 1. They were not alone in finding camaraderie and solidarity in the face of enormous opposition. They were also not alone in facing vocal backlash and ugliness when they advertised their intention to meet.

I asked Ethel, a white married fifty-something-year-old lesbian, about the protestors who had gathered outside of one of the organization's meetings.[1] Location, political orientation, and possibilities for queer life were conflated in the response of protestors to the organizing efforts to confront Amendment 1 in this rural North Carolina county: "I think her sign said, 'This Ain't Asheville,' and [my friend] . . . said what does it mean or something. She said Asheville is the gathering of gays. That's how she put it." Ethel went on to talk about how people in the area responded to the coverage of the event: "They showed that part of it on the news. So, it really got a really wide viewing and then folks in [our county], some of them were like, 'Oh, you made us look really bad.' [My friend's] like, 'I didn't put the words in your mouth.'"

In order to speak in support of or in opposition to LGBT rights or issues, speakers position themselves in relation to and demonstrate an awareness of the map of good and bad places to be gay. In the excerpts above, not only did the protestors, who are also neighbors of the organizers, reference Asheville as "the gathering of the gays"—putting it on the map of "good" places for queer life, they were aware that when their remarks were captured on camera, they "looked really bad" to an audience who saw the clips when they were circulated more broadly. There is a clear awareness on the speaker's part of a political contest with consequences that resonate beyond the speaker's own location. On the one hand, the protestors articulated a desire to distinguish their county as a place that is not a "gathering of the gays," but on the other hand, they did not want to "look really bad" to an audience outside of their county.

The nuances of spatial politics can collapse under state or regional homogenizations. As much as the individuals in the rural county that created a gay and lesbian advocacy organization for the first time in their county spoke about that county very specifically in relation to neighboring counties, the participant quoted below moved from a Midwestern state far north of North Carolina to the place characterized above as "the gathering of the gays." The reputation of Asheville had not reached Michigan, where Manuel, a young gay organizer of Puerto Rican descent whose specific interest was in the intersection between religion and sexuality, was living.[2] When Manuel decided to move to Asheville, members of Manuel's congregation issued a warning: "When I left my church in Detroit to come and move to Asheville just for my job at [a regional LGBT rights organization], that Sunday, I preached my last Sunday in Detroit, and I'm in the line where everyone is leaving and they are like, great message, blah, blah. And, I'm not kidding, probably ten of the old ladies said, you better be careful down there. They are going to kill you." The church Manuel was leaving had a history of participating in mass actions during the civil rights movement of the 1960s and, according to Manuel, some of the people who traveled from the church to participate in actions, such as the march from Selma to Montgomery, were killed. Clearly the South remained a terrifying place in their minds. Part of that terror articulates itself in response to a perceived intolerance and deadly hostility to queer bodies and LGBT rights work expressed in the phrase "they are going to kill you."

Discourse to Go

As I traveled the U.S. South and then South Africa, many differently located speakers articulated the work of LGBT(I) rights in terms that reference the United States and its dominance as a queer cultural center. Mark Gevisser, a white South African journalist who has written about LGBT(I) rights in South Africa for decades, for instance, was part of the curriculum at the summer school hosted by the University of Cape Town each January. Gevisser was, at the time of my fieldwork, previewing the argument from a book that has since been published as *The Pink Line: Journeys across the World's Queer Frontiers*. The argument in the book is that a "new" global conversation is animating LGBT(I) advocacy and activism.[3]

Speaking at the summer school, Gevisser claimed that "ideas of gay love, of gay families" are "not just in the United States," yet at the same time identified the United States as the source of such ideas, which are then projected in the form of TV programs and foreign policy objectives. Gevisser commented that gay cultural productions can be seen not just in America, but in "Nigeria or Nairobi":

> I mean these shows are seen all over the world because of satellite TV. You can be sitting in Nigeria or Nairobi, and you can be watching *Modern Family and Will & Grace*.

Observing that some world leaders were then engaged in "something that the gay activists do," Gevisser noted that the political posture of some multinational corporations were aligned with those world leaders, drawing special attention to the doodle that Google

> put on its homepage on the day of the Sochi Olympics, basically saying "f-ck you" to Russia. Saying we believe in a set of values, a set of rights, and it's a real problem if you don't. That's interesting in this world that it's actually multinational corporations as well as other actors who in the United States, like human rights activists, who are putting these messages into the global arena. The other thing that's happening at the moment is that human rights advocacy has become a foreign policy objective. So, it's not just something that the gay activists do. Something that Barack Obama does. . . . Something that David Cameron does.[4]

Though "you can be sitting in Nigeria or Nairobi and . . . watch[] *Modern Family* and *Will & Grace*," those who "believe in a set of values" that have "become a foreign policy objective" are situated in a very specific place. They are "multinational corporations as well as other actors . . . in the United States." They are Barack Obama and David Cameron. They put "these messages into the global arena. When these parties say "f-ck you" to Russia, it becomes "a real problem if you don't" join them. In this way, then, getting on the map has everything to do with geopolitical relations of power that have the capacity to move out-of-the-way places even further off of the map if they don't acquiesce to the "foreign policy objective" defined by multinational corporations and other actors in the United States.

Listening to Gevisser in January 2016, you would never have been able to imagine that Donald Trump would become president of the United States in less than a year and that transgender rights would become one of the most hotly debated legislative topics for the foreseeable future in the United States. From a critical location off the map, a key question for this discourse is: Which comes first? The "foreign policy objective" erasing state sovereignty and solidifying global dominance among former colonial powers and the United States, or believing in a "set of values" that is also a "set of rights"? Given that the latter is often a tool for accomplishing the former, I don't believe that the answer to this question is as clear as those who say "f-ck you" to Russia suggest it is.

Not every speaker and certainly not every activist I encountered adhered to the U.S.-generated script of what LGBT(I) rights work should look like. Some resisted it; some leveraged it strategically; some navigated it in order to secure funds, rolling their eyes after the grant applications were submitted. The two people who seemed to accept and enthusiastically perpetuate the U.S.-generated narrative about the global dynamics of LGBT(I) rights without any reticence were both white, cisgender gay male journalists. They both framed the global terrain around LGBT(I) rights as a "new Cold War" where the political lines around same-sex sexuality rearticulate the political lines drawn between capitalism and communism in the mid-twentieth century. In this rather stale rehashing of "world powers" politics, Gevisser accepted and declared as given that getting married, glamorous transitions (Caitlyn Jenner was trending at the time), and corporate endorsements and sponsorships of "Pride" are inherently unproblematic signs of a move toward liberation for lgbtiq people. The result of such discourses about LGBT(I) rights is that "progress" takes on very specific spatial associations: "On the one hand, you've got . . . the cosmopolitan intellectual who is embracing an inevitable process of globalization. On the other hand, you've got . . . a fearful provincial who's trying to protect his children from the consequences of this process because he thinks they are bad."[5]

Gevisser was not the only person who spoke this way. In 2014, a colleague at my institution had invited BuzzFeed journalist and international LGBT rights correspondent Lester Feder to give a presentation. Feder's presentation was advertised as a talk that would "explore how anti-democratic regimes have used homophobia as part of an agenda to de-legitimate the global standards on human rights."[6] These two presentations, one in Cape Town and one in Buckhannon, West Virginia, are to me representative of a globalized narrative about how LGBT(I) rights and attitudes are characterized by international journalists. These journalists could easily be described as belonging to Joseph Massad's "Gay International" because of the way their narratives advance American exceptionalism through the framework that some places are "good" places to be gay and others are "bad" places to be gay.[7]

For Gevisser, the "cosmopolitan intellectual" versus the "fearful provincial" is a formulation in which what results from globalization is increased exposure to

Will & Grace, Modern Family, and *Time* magazine covers. Other consequences of globalization, such as exacerbated wealth disparities and increasingly militarized borders, disappear from view. The first reference Gevisser makes to LGBT(I) rights within the context of "a quite extraordinary global conversation" is same-sex marriage. Same-sex marriage is established as the top of a hierarchy of "rights." Gevisser later describes a "really interesting piece of research done by the Pew Research Center" that correlates greater acceptance of "homosexuality" with "secular and affluent societies": "Now, note this isn't about marriage. This is just about acceptability, which is a lower bar than marriage."[8] However, when Gevisser discussed violence in this talk, the violence that queer bodies experience is attributed to lower levels of acceptance of same-sex sexuality and gender nonconformity, not the absence of access to same-sex marriage. The logic of "acceptability" as "a lower bar than marriage," regardless of how inconsistent that logic was with actual experiences of violence among lgbtiq populations, was not isolated to Gevisser, or, for that matter, Feder.

Many participants described South Africa as a place where same-sex marriage is available by law *and* as a country where violence against lgbtiq people is an ongoing and urgent problem. One panel discussion I attended as part of a schedule of Alternative Inclusive Pride (AIP) events in Cape Town was designed to raise questions about what the most relevant issues for lgbtiq people were in that moment. The facilitator, a young transgender activist of color, briefly contextualized LGBT(I) advocacy work in the country by saying: "So, for a long time South Africa has been mobilizing alongside many other parts of the world for same-sex marriage to become legalized and that was the end all and be all of the struggle for the entire LGBTIQ community—transgender people . . . were thrown in there just in passing. Almost being lumped together—that the one struggle has now been—the sexual orientation struggle, it's about being in same-sex relationship."[9]

The rest of this discussion was very interesting—including perspectives from several activists who felt alienated by Cape Town Pride but who worked hard to carve out space for queer and transgender people to feel at home in their own communities in Cape Town. Caitlyn Jenner's name was on everyone's mind—partly because Jenner was receiving international attention and partly because, as so many activists pointed out, Jenner's transition was so different from what being transgender for them might look like. Not being celebrities, not being American, not being incredibly wealthy meant that Caitlyn Jenner's story of transition was so "foreign" that it was in some ways not even recognizable to them. The bigger concern, though, was that the incredible publicity around Jenner's transition meant that Jenner's story risked making their own stories unintelligible to their friends and family. The work of translating their experiences to family and friends became more difficult if those family and friends had only a single point of reference for what it meant to be transgender and that point of reference was a wealthy, white celebrity in America. In South Africa, publicly subsidized transition care *is* available to transgender people, but the wait list for eligibility for that care is so long that transgender activists have a joke among themselves that if they have a child, they should register that child for gender-affirming surgery as soon as the child is born so that if the child needs to transition, the child won't have to wait decades for care.

In the context of interviews, participants spoke about "amazing legislation" and "brilliant policies" that position South Africa as a "land of milk and honey" for doing the kind of work they do, especially from the perspective of international funders and activists working in other African countries. Pete, a Black lesbian who founded an organization focused on LGBTI equality and is active in politics, articulated how easy it is to "become so relaxed" when "you've got the laws."[10] Because of a strong history of post-apartheid legal advocacy work, David, an advocate of color who represents an international organization in Johannesburg, concluded, "on paper this country could not get better."[11] In these conversations, there is a sometimes unspoken (sometimes explicit) suggestion about which countries *could* get better. Even though protective legislation for lgbtiq people in South Africa predated similar legislation in the United States, the reference to which countries could get better was not a reference to the United States or anywhere in Europe. The countries where "what people are asking for are very, very basic rights that everyone should be entitled to," according to David, are other African countries. Speaking specifically to the Southern African Development Community (SADC) region, David demonstrates a logic wherein acceptability "is a lower bar than marriage":

> So, the rights that people are asking for throughout SADC is not same-sex marriage. It's not even civil unions or anything of the sort. It's about please give us access to the rights that we're entitled to as human beings. And so, that's where the conversation is in our region. In South Africa, depending on where you are, the conversations differ because some people are saying I have the right to get married to my spouse, to my partner, to my, whatever—we get it. But for most people the conversation is still I should be free from violence, I should be safe in my own home, I should be able to go to the clinic when I am beaten up.

In this example, for people in the SADC having the right to be "free from violence," "safe in [one's] own home," and able to "go to the clinic when I am beaten up" is more pressing than the legalization of same-sex marriage or even civil unions. David communicates that such rights are much more basic and fundamental. However, David goes on to indicate that lgbtiq people in South Africa do not have an expectation of safety, freedom from violence, and access to services either, even though same-sex marriages are legal. While speaking to a rural context in South Africa, Andile, a young Zulu-speaking Black gay man, suggests that marriage is something other than the "many problems we are facing right now": "So, with that, it's not a big issue at least here. We don't talk of things like, not that we don't want to talk about them but it's just—there are so many problems we are facing right now to be dwelling on pretty things like marriage."[12] Through a logic of universal rights, where acceptability is a "lower bar than marriage," marriage can be understood as a "pretty thing." It is important to ask how marriage could be a higher bar than acceptability—if it is possible to have the legal recognition of marriage but also be subject to violence that is a result of not being accepted. How can marriage be such a high bar when acceptability seems much more difficult to ensure or secure? Many speakers identified the answer to this question by referencing the gap between policy and implementation of policy, as Xolani, an isiXhosa-speaking gay man, does in this excerpt from an interview: "It's still like although our constitution allow us that ok being gay is acceptable in the constitution . . . it's still a problem because if right now you go to the police station, we are experiencing stigma and discrimination, go to the clinic, you're experiencing stigma and discrimination, schools—kids, the learners are still bullied at the school. The people who are working in those industries are still having attitude because of using this—using the term that our tradition and culture does not allow us, you know?"[13]

One of the things that becomes most evident in a discussion of legal rights in South Africa is the way that rights theoretically available to all are available differently "depending on where . . . you're located." David, who has experience working in several different southern African countries, speaks to this: "So, depending on where in South Africa, where you're located, what community you're from, where you live, those conversations are incredibly different. And that is part of the complication of South Africa and countries, to be very honest, like Botswana and Namibia where you have an extremely wealthy middle class. Depending on where you are in those countries, the law and how you access your rights are just very different from other people. So, we have to deal with those differences and those nuances within the community."[14] "Where you're located," then, has to do with complex histories of colonialism, geographies of racism, and class-based exclusions. "Where you're located" also has an enormous amount to do with whether you can access what's been promised to you through a constitution or a specific law like the Civil Union Act of 2006.

Liza, a white cisgender activist who had founded a transgender advocacy organization, raised the issue of family formation and the different shapes it has taken historically among racially marginalized communities in South Africa during a discussion at an AIP event in Cape Town.[15] Liza spoke to the way that some relationships are recognized and celebrated through the Civil Union Act and other relationships are not legible, even though their existence has a long history: "So, who can really get those things that's promised to us? Long before . . . all of those things, how often did it happen that your lesbian couples in rural areas and townships by default . . . have to raise the children of the sisters. So, they long had already this kind of like complex different kind of family household settings. But it was never acknowledged—they never got support either from subsidies and the government." Same-sex marriage through the Civil Union Act is the kind of "acknowledgement" that means "support . . . from subsidies and the government." Though "complex different kind of family household settings" have long existed, they have not been on the map of "support . . . from subsidies and the government."

Some South African activists wondered whether it was worth getting married when their families might "not even accept it," which suggests that marriage is not a higher bar than acceptability for some lgbtiq people. Marriage can be guaranteed through the law, but acceptability is something that is negotiated within families and communities. If families and communities are potential sites of violence for lgbtiq people, acceptability in those contexts is critical to the safety and security of lgbtiq people in a way that state-sanctioned marriage may not be. Kian, a Muslim religious leader and gay activist and organizer, spoke about the ambivalence many people feel about marriage because it seems tangential to their more immediate and more important concerns about families and communities:

> I think at the time when we spoke about marriage a lot and we got the sense that most gay people were—either because they felt that there was a lot that they had to go through in order to get married, and would the families even accept it even though they're struggling with accepting them in their identity—is that even possible? . . . A lot of people still felt that homosexuality somehow is still a sin, but that God would forgive them for that, and so, why should I still go and get married? And then there were just a few who felt like, agh, I'm already in a relationship and we've been together for five years, so it's almost like a marriage—why should I still go through all the drama?[16]

Marriage is something that some of the constituents of Kian's organization felt was unnecessary—"why . . . go through all the drama?"—and yet, their engagement as a religious community *has* involved expanding the parameters of what marriage can be within the imaginary of their community. Struggles with relationships, sexuality, family, and religious beliefs show the complexity of navigating homo-antagonism. Marriage here is not a "higher bar" than something called acceptability. Instead, legal marriage as a right in this discussion is peripheral to questions about how families would "even accept" same-sex sexuality. Marriage is legally available, but in some ways, it is undesirable if it means having to "go through all the drama."

The tensions between what is legally available and what is rarely possible to guarantee for queer and transgender life in any context are striking. Hegemonic discourses of LGBT(I) rights, which often reduce their interest to a scenario wherein "the more gay and lesbian rights are affirmed in some parts of the world, the more they are being denied elsewhere," do not account for the tensions and layers of complexity outside of a polarized account of rights where some people, communities, and/or nations are "pro-gay" and some are "anti-gay."[17] The material here shows how a reductive framework that relies upon dividing up every space into "cosmopolitan intellectual[s]" and "fearful provincial[s]" reproduces consequences for those queer bodies who share the geographical space of the "fearful provincial." Queer and trans lives are wrapped up in fierce contestations over their existence at the margins of both heteronormative cis-centric existence *and* the globalized gay cultural productions that are often indicative of the achievement of LGBT(I) rights.

On the Map: "On Paper This Country Could Not Get Better"

The idea that "on paper this country could not get better" can permeate South African activists' sense of their own country. Some described both their deep frustration with their own country and their sense that things were worse in every other African country. While the sense that things were worse elsewhere usually came up in relation to other African countries, the idea of things being worse somewhere else was not limited to the African continent. Pete described traveling to Russia at a time when an anti-homosexuality law was being discussed and "approved" in that country.[18] Pete acknowledged that being from a country like South Africa means that you feel that "you should be safe everywhere you are," so that "hostile environments" come as a surprise for which you may be unprepared:

> So, as I arrive it was the day they approved the law. As I land I received the text and I'm like thinking do I hop back on the plane or do I just do what I have to do here? So, I did what I had to do there but I mean the point is that you know, you end up being in hostile environments and also maybe unconsciously you know because of where you come from, you're thinking you know, you should be safe everywhere you are ... but then I think because the moment you also leave your country you're also talking now of universal human rights, which should also be observed.

On the one hand, South African activists know that South Africa is not "safe" for many lgbtiq people. On the other hand, mainstream language around guaranteed rights in South Africa and the vibrant civil society sector that won so many of the internationally coveted policies pertaining to lgbtiq people can give even seasoned activists a sense that "you should be safe everywhere you are."

Similarly, activists working on a wide range of issues in South Africa, from hate crimes and violence against lgbtiq people to issues of transgender health and inclusion in policy decision making, to access to service delivery for lgbtiq people, spoke to the way that South Africa being "on the map" of progressive LGBT(I) rights legislation had serious consequences for funding LGBTI rights work. South Africa was sometimes characterized as an "anomaly" because of its "brilliant policies, amazing bylaws" that coexist with violence against lgbtiq people. These participants spoke about the way that the legislative achievements for LGBTI rights in South Africa translate into the assumption on the part of funders that money should be spent elsewhere, particularly in countries where work can be done to improve the law.

Asa, an isiXhosa-speaking transgender woman who works on transgender health issues for rural South African populations, described the impression of South Africa as that of a "land of milk and honey."[19] Though "anybody ... who has ever been to South Africa will know that is not the reality," Asa spoke of an impression on the part of donors that funding should be directed elsewhere. Because of the way that countries are positioned on the map based on their legislative terrain,

South Africa may not register as a country that warrants investment. According to most participants, funding rubrics often value concrete and measurable changes, such as changes to the law, over changes in contexts or communities that cannot be so clearly and easily evaluated. I don't mean to suggest that LGBTI rights work is not funded in South Africa by major international funders. It is. However, funders and advocacy organizations both know that different issues become priorities for funders at different times. One thing that Asa was communicating was that there was an expectation among some funders that work funded in South Africa should address regional issues as well—issues affecting other African countries.[20] The sense that work that is funded should be measurable came up in several interviews in both South Africa and the U.S. South. However, only South Africa ever appeared on the map because of its progressive legislation for LGBT(I) rights. The U.S. South has never registered as a site of progressive legislation with the capacity to facilitate the possibility of queer life.

The material from participants in contemporary South Africa suggests that their activism plays out within the discourse of being on the map and living off of it. At the same time, activists in the U.S. South live in the country with which these values, cultural productions, and language about queerness are most strongly associated, globally speaking. Yet, the terrain these activists navigate is decidedly off the map and tends to show up for funders as either a place where nothing is possible or a frontier where a "vast desert of nothingness" requires the civilizing presence of metronormative values.[21]

The Making of the Map

Before turning to the "vast desert[s] of nothingness" that some activists and organizers felt was used to characterize their contexts, I want to turn to the making of a map that is used to indicate "good" and "bad" places to exist queerly. If modernity can be characterized by technological advancements and industrialization, the accumulation of wealth accompanying and facilitating such advancements was built upon the violence of forced removals from land and the decimation of entire populations of indigenous peoples (see chapter 3).[22] Similarly, the scientific knowledge that we have come to associate with the advancement of modern societies is premised on a history of eugenics and human experimentation on those denied their personhood in early scientific practice.[23] Instead of scientific knowledge eliminating the logics of eugenics and freeing human beings from bias and backwardness, it was put to use in the service of eugenics logics and the kinds of categorizations that entrenched the idea of the gender binary and heterosexuality as natural.[24]

Yet, contemporary understandings of modernity also encompass human rights norms that have to do with freedom from persecution.[25] Persecution in these understandings of human rights is often framed as intolerance of essentialized concepts of identities. In other words, persecution is a response to someone's religious beliefs, political affiliation, sexual orientation, racial identity, or some other personal characteristic associated with a group affiliation. Persecution is one of the few legal justifications for crossing borders and seeking a new home for those who do not have the financial means required to chase their dreams through the costly bureaucratic maze of securing legal documentation, a new place to live, and a new life across national borders.[26] Persecution is often framed as emanating from a place of "traditional" norms that are incompatible with modern life. And yet, modernity would not have developed the way that it did without the mass removals, enslavement, and dispossession of "colonized" by "colonizer." In other words, even as traditional norms are often framed as the source of persecution (especially gender- and sexuality-based persecution), the violence of colonization, eugenics, and the gender binary paved the way for modernity. At the center of the concept of human rights exists this fundamental tension between the "protection" of the individual as one who possesses rights and the simultaneous erasure of the communities in which that individual is embedded in the interest of "progress."

Silvia Federici, Sarah Franklin, and Colin Johnson have something to say about the connections between industrialization, land, and agricultural technologies.[27] They also have important things to say not only about the politics of modernization through industrialization, but also the spatial politics of modernization. By most definitions, to be modern means to be (among other things) disconnected from land. Metropolitan centers are far from provincial terrain that has been left "unimproved." Modernity is built upon the assumption that "progress and economic gain" is improvement.[28] As Franklin, a historian of science, writes, in an exploration of the relationship between agriculture, industry, biotechnology, and empire, an "ethos of improvement that saw the Highlanders forcibly banished from their ancestral homes, and often left to starve, was based on enclosure of land as private property and the use of livestock animals to increase its profitability."[29]

The stories about the Highlanders that were used to demonstrate how much better used their land would be by sheep are taken from the same template as the story told about Appalachians being removed from their land because it would be better used as public land available for private development (see chapter 3).[30] In the interest of "progress, humanity, and even nature" and "like the native inhabitants of Britain's colonies, the Highlanders were depicted as primitive, savage, and illiterate tribal peoples in need of rescue and improvement. Their land was unproductive, their way of life ancient and irrational, and they were being saved from themselves by being forced to leave their harsh way of life behind, along with their squalid homes. Ironically, it was more 'natural' for sheep to inhabit the Highlands than the Highlanders themselves because the sheep made better use of it, in the sense that they were more efficient—meaning simply that they emerged as more economically profitable."[31]

These politics of removal, of efficiency, of industrialization are wrapped up with things that seem antithetical to human rights, such as eugenics logics and the criminalization of same-sex sexuality that circulated in the world before, throughout, and after World War II. As ugly as the politics are, the implementation of the Highland Clearances was even uglier: "Possessed of a 'rage for Improvement,' [Lord]

Stafford began forced clearances on his estate in 1807, legally evicting his tenants at will and then burning their homes, forcing them to flee leaving their crops, animals, and possessions behind. Many emigrated to the colonies, while others were offered uninhabitable coastal property where it was imagined they might earn a living from fishing."[32] In a consideration of the centrality of agricultural technologies to the "science" of eugenics, Johnson, a rural sexualities scholar, does not suggest that either cities or rural areas are innocent of investment in eugenics logic. Johnson describes a political economy in which both rural and metropolitan ideologies are imbricated in a process of disseminating information aimed at structuring sexual norms and practices toward racial and gender conformity. In literature and films about "personal and sexual hygiene," metropolitan ideologies of "racial purity" and rural agricultural technologies of animal husbandry converged.[33] "Urban social reformers" disseminated their ideas about "being well-born," "the right kind of life," and "social evils" through societies, committees, and publications.[34] In this scenario, it is not the metropole that is "advanced" in its politics or its technologies. Rural animal husbandry practices provide the "technologies" in these "modern" materials. To be modern, in this story, means to subscribe to eugenics logics as the means to improving the species. To be modern, in this story, also means to subscribe to and perpetuate "compulsory heterosexuality," valuing reproductive sexuality, and viewing any other expression of sexuality as deviance.[35] Perhaps it *is* the metropole that is modern and "progressive" in this story, but modernity and progress are defined through their affiliation with the racial purity, white supremacy, and heteronormativity bound up in the pursuit of empire.

The Making of the City

Modernity is not only a time but a place. Space and time are not isolated from one another in discursive projections of what modernity means. Instead, they are mapped onto one another. To be *modern* means to be associated with the metropole. The rural is situated in the past in the spatial politics of temporally bounded geographic space. "The horror of the rural and its status as a closet for the more socially 'intelligible' forms of queerness are evident in" representations of rural areas and the Global South and in the amplification of stories of violence against queer people in those locations.[36] The story about how the city facilitates queer life goes something like this: "Across both understandings of convergence, bodies are placed in new relations with one another via the circulation of capital. In the instance of urban centers, patterns of use and exchange orient people in space: crowds coalesce on city streets, communities concentrate in neighborhoods, and strangers bump into each other on sidewalks and public transit. Urbanization is a corporeal experience that has enabled the development of public cultures among sexual minorities."[37] And yet, the city is not the metronorm. Cities have been structured along fault lines of race, class, nationality, ability, and gender. While rural areas can generally be characterized as having fewer resources for lgbtiq people to access, the reality of those resources in the city cannot be characterized only by their abundance. *Where* and *how* resources are concentrated and distributed and to whom they are available in urban areas is also part of the story of community centers, educational and advocacy materials, health care resources, and shelter for queer and trans people in cities. Zooming in on metropolitan centers, it becomes clear that resources are available much more readily to some parts of the queer populations in those cities than others. In fact, American gender and sexualities scholar Myrl Beam, writing about the hegemonic shape of LGBT rights organizations in *Gay Inc.*, demonstrates the way that different queer metropolitan populations are framed as "donors," "recipients," or "advocates," and each population is given or denied access to decision-making power in relation to their access to power and influence.[38] As I argued in 2013, well-resourced communities and individuals are better able to buffer themselves from the violence of homo- and trans-antagonism; those with fewer resources are less able to afford and access such a buffer.[39] This is true inside and outside of the city. Beam tells a devastating story of how locating queer resources in city spaces facilitates the sense of inclusion for some (usually whiter and wealthier) queer bodies and facilitates the criminalization of other (usually Black and brown, poorer, and less gender-conforming) queer bodies. Service delivery initiatives sort queer bodies into those who "donate" and "volunteer" and those who "need" services or are "clients" of organizations.[40]

Metronormativity then, is a *narrative* of what the city is. Scholars of queer life like Beam, Eli Clare, Dean Spade, and others have demonstrated that the narrative of easy queer existence in cities is not felt equally by all queer populations in those cities.[41] For some, the city is a site of unmitigated surveillance. While the sense of invasive surveillance for queer folks is usually most closely associated with rural areas, what Mary Gray's participants demonstrate is that in a community where everyone "knows you," the suffocating familiarity of rural communities is something that can also be leveraged in pursuit of safety and mobility (see chapter 3).[42]

Sexual and gender identities beyond heterosexuality and cisgender identity have such immediate connections to modernity and the metropolitan that the one (identity) can easily stand in for the other (space). The easy association between non-heteronormative expressions of sexuality, trans expressions of gender, and the metropole obscures answers to the question "What does queer practice *look* like? It is at this point in which the metronormative valences of queer visibility foreclose the possibility of imagining queer country."[43] The presence of nonconforming gender presentations in rural and farmland areas seems to be an inconvenient reality in this narrative.

Scholar of space and sexuality Clare Sears demonstrates that the establishment and policing of gender norms was central to the making of cities as sites for the expansion of capital. In other words, in order for cities to become sites of modernity, they had to become sites of "civilization" and "order." To become civilized and ordered, cities produced legislation that policed (sometimes violently) mobility by enforcing normative gender expressions and racist immigration laws, rather than allowing people to live freely and openly as themselves. Using San Francisco as an example, Sears maps the way that cities used anti-cross-dressing laws to police racial and gender norms. This policing persisted into the latter part of the twentieth century, even in areas of San Francisco known for the flourishing of queer life, like the Tenderloin district.[44]

Sears describes cross-dressing laws as "foundational city codes ... central to the project of modern municipal government."[45] In addition to establishing gender normativity as a component of regulating modern space, cross-dressing laws "extended beyond the policing of normative gender to impact the "social meanings of city space, race, and citizenship." Sears continues: "In particular they crossed paths with federal immigration laws to limit the terms of national belonging and construct a gender-normative nation. Far more than a local government order that created a misdemeanor offense, cross-dressing law represented a specific strategy of government that constructed normative gender, reinforced inequalities, and generated new modes of exclusion from public life."[46]

Colorado is another state where Sears chronicles the enforcement of gender normativity as central to expanding the reach of capital. Nuisance laws, the same type of law that generated the cross-dressing prohibition, were first used to police property destruction by protecting private property rights. As municipalities that imagined their beginning as frontier mining towns grew into aspirational city centers, it became imperative for them to subscribe to the kinds of norms that would allow wives and "ladies" (in the case of San Francisco) and tourists from the East Coast (in the case of Colorado) to see them as "civilized" enough to live in and visit.[47] As Robin Henry, contributing to the discussion of rural sexualities, explains: "Where earlier mining communities ignored aberrant sexual behavior in order to attract as many people as possible to their towns, mine owners now understood sexual behavior had the potential to threaten the stability and growth of their company."[48]

Cities are now understood to be havens for queer life and the site of a range of gender expressions. However, cross-dressing laws regulating "illegible bodies that threatened the cultural imperative of verifiable identities in an anonymous city" were central to the formation of the city as a site of modernity.[49] Colonial centers and city centers have been integral to establishing norms that govern sexuality and gender. These norms have been and remain critical to establishing citizenship. Citizenship is central to establishing access to rights, even rights framed as universal. As Sears documents in the example of San Francisco, municipal cross-dressing prohibitions established which kinds of bodies could occupy public space without being harassed. Colonial centers then took those norms and exported them to their colonies. The erasure of gender diversity, then, started in the city and was taken *from* the city to the world through colonization. Liberation did not travel with colonizers, but gender norms did.

Off the Map: "This Vast Desert of Nothingness" and Violence at a Distance

The discursive investment in policy and law as a rubric for rights takes different shapes. George, a white gay man who is the director of a statewide LGBT rights advocacy organization, described the process of the U.S. South being written off the map through an interaction with a national LGBT rights organization.[50] The national organization was promoting a mapping project they had done to "draw attention to the states" in the form of "all different types of legal recognition." George was approached by the organization to feature this map on George's organization's website. George refused. The description of the encounter illuminates how assumptions about place and what "counts" as progress get mapped:

> They're a national organization. Their research really has to do a lot with effective messaging, doing research on legislation. Several years ago, they started a new project. Again, their goal was to draw attention to the states, to the state-based work, trying to focus some of the attention, less attention on what happens in DC.... So, they release these series of maps that looked at all different types of legal recognition, and because they only looked at something that had passed on the statewide level, we ended up with this vast desert of nothingness in the South. They asked us if we would put the map on our website and I said no. They said, "Why? We don't understand. We put a lot of time and effort into these maps. These maps are designed to help you," and I said they don't because what it does is it reinforces this self-fulfilling prophecy that change cannot happen here in the South and in fact change happens here all the time. Some of it is taking different shapes.

The national organization described here wanted to document LGBT rights–related policies as the result of state-based advocacy work at the state level. Because their attempt to make such work visible relied on mapping state-level policy, it resulted in a "vast desert of nothingness in the South," which was an erasure of the work that "happens ... all the time" and "takes different shapes" by the organization that refused to put the map on their website. While it was not possible to win advocacy campaigns at the level of the state legislature because of the dominance of Republican legislators, several organizers noted the work they had done building networks with other organizations that might have overlapping or even separate interests in municipalities, counties, and other entities, like individual school districts. Elaborating on the "different shapes" such work might take, Jack, a white gay representative of a national organization representing state equality organizations noted: "[This state equality organization] has gone district by district and now has a majority of the students in the state protected with enumerated policies—that's a huge win that affects the lives of a lot of students but is not something that anyone really notices when they're looking at kind of the bigger picture of the state."[51]

The kind of work described above is not legible in the map of statewide policy change because it was achieved not through law at the state level but through a different strategy rooted in going "district by district" to ensure that "a majority of the students in the state" are "protected with enumerated policies." This work is work that takes place off the map. Even so, state governments recognize the threat of networks of municipal nondiscrimination protections. When North Carolina became nationally notorious for the hotly contested "Bathroom Bill"—the law that *Politico* described as "the ... bill that ate North Carolina"—the effort behind it had been an attempt to undo municipal equality ordinances.[52] The bill was introduced immediately after the city of Charlotte adopted an ordinance protecting transgender individuals' rights to use the bathroom that aligned with their gender identity. State-level bills aimed at policing transgender bathroom use or claiming to "protect" religious freedom frequently have a less discussed element within them: they seek to strip autonomy from local bodies like municipalities and county commissions.[53] Not only does state policy in these examples say where transgender people can and cannot use the bathroom or on what grounds discrimination is or is not permissible, the state (through these policies) also prohibits municipalities and county commissions from deciding otherwise in their own districts.

It is important to note that though the coverage in the *Politico* article makes it seem that municipalities are simply by their nature more progressive than state governments by virtue of being cities, queer and trans advocates have worked hard at accomplishing locally based municipal protections as part of a concerted strategy of winning locally where it has been impossible to win at the state level. Municipalities do not have these policies by accident but because advocates and organizers have pushed hard for their adoption. These are the kinds of internal political battles that do not register on maps that project the U.S. South as a "vast desert of nothingness" where conservative interests reign without contestation.

Historically, the U.S. South has not been a place where national progressive organizations see "winning" as a possibility. This is informed by and informs the discursive position of the South as an out-of-the-way place. Cynthia, a Black lesbian activist who has done intersectional work organizing in the South for decades, was clear that these attitudes were not specific to the dynamics between national and local LGBT rights organizations but were instead about the way the South is understood to fit into the rest of the country:

> The first time I ran into that was when I moved here in '82 and we were having some major elections only to find out groups like the National Organization for Women [saying,] "There's not one need to put anything in the South. Nothing's going to happen there." I mean, you have groups like NOW ... saying that. That would give you a clue of just the attitude. It's almost like, well.... The South is what it is—it's always been very conservative. It's what it is. But to be totally written off like that—"Well nothing's going to happen. We're not going to put a dime into North Carolina." That was coming from the women's groups, other

groups. And with the queer movement, I mean, this recent thing about the South being all of a sudden rediscovered or discovered—I feel like we're a bunch of— let me just get this out—like that thing around Amendment 1, we're just a bunch of dumb shits that don't know what to do. That was the most offensive thing, and it was just amazing, well, we don't know nothing.[54]

According to Cynthia, the South is an impossible context that has been "totally written off" as a space for progressive organizing or policy work from the perspective of national organizations when it is not being suddenly "rediscovered." Even if "the South is what it is," Cynthia expresses frustration that national organizations decided "nothing's going to happen there." Cynthia reads the "vast desert of nothingness" identified by George above differently than organizations who think "there's not one need to put anything in the South." Living in the South taught Cynthia and other organizers that "the South is what it is—it's always been very conservative," but it also taught them different ways of engaging with advocacy and activism directed at making queer and trans people safer in their homes and communities that do not rely on strategies originating in the metropole.

The erasures recounted by the participants above take other forms as well. George speaks to how positive stories that should have national significance get very little coverage when they are based in the South.[55] George also speaks to the effect of neglecting such stories because national media believe "that can't possibly be true":

Certainly, up until very recently, so much of the stories—that when national media would want to do a story on the South, it was basically this theme of how could you possibly live in the South, because life has to be just awful for you.... I think this is really telling that when [one of our legislators] was elected as the first out Black lesbian in any state legislature in the country, why wasn't that a cover of *The Advocate*? It was a little blurb, and it was a little blurb about hey, Victory Fund does it again. There was another organization, there were the people that recruited her, the people that helped to recruit her campaign, they ran her campaign, the transgender people, the African American people, the people from her neighborhood, and her personality and her skills.... I mean that's how she won. Why wasn't that more of a national story? I think that it's because people are like well... that can't be possibly be true.... No, that can't possibly be true.... I think also that there is still this ongoing, perception that it is harder and slower here for queer folks.... It's usually a perception that it's either not much going on or that it's super scary or super slow.

The sense of things being "super scary or super slow" for queer and trans folks in the South means that "the first Black lesbian in any state legislature in the country" does not end up on the "cover of *The Advocate*." The "little blurb" that tells the story of this political victory credits a national fund sponsoring LGBT political candidates, the Victory Fund, rather than the specific local efforts that resulted in the candidate's election.

How stories like these are told perpetuate the "sense of danger" in the South outlined by Stacey below. Stacey, a married white lesbian advocate and political representative, is the founder of a regional LGBT rights advocacy organization in the U.S. South.[56] Speaking to a new interest on the part of funders and national organizations in what is happening in the South, Stacey suggests a range of ways in which national organizations and funders engage and are engaged in the space of LGBT rights work in the region. One of those ways is through a sense of opportunity because "there's sort of a romanticized sense of the danger there." Stacey also speaks to the ways that this perception of violence functions both as an opportunity for would-be interventionists and as a warning that locally based activists should not be doing this work: "I think the misconception is that if you do this work, especially in smaller towns or rural communities, you'll get shot. Or harassed.... There is, I think, a myth that if you're out in small town Mississippi, you know, you make yourself vulnerable to immediate violence. There's that." The suggestion that it is too dangerous in the South to do the kind of work that Stacey's organization does on a daily basis has material implications. National organizations have used the reputation for danger in the South as a way to raise money, take it elsewhere, and to suggest that it is better for the work to be done far away. Criticizing a national organization with a pervasive presence, Cynthia speaks to how this extractivist model works:

> In fact, the reason why the Equality Federation had to start their own—because all the money was going out of the state. These dinners don't leave money in the state. Every penny goes up to DC, and I know how it works 'cause I worked there for three and a half years. Now, the rationale is this: If we do a dinner in your state, we'll bring in some high-profile, wonderful, you know, well known—every penny we take out of your state, we'll put it back because we'll have the influence on Washington that has federal policy. No. No![57]

The Equality Federation is a network of state-level LGBT rights organizations that advocate for equality in their states. Most of these organizations follow the formula of "name of state" plus "equality" or "equality" plus "name of state." In West Virginia, our statewide organization, which is a member of the Equality Federation, is called Fairness WV. Resources removed from the South also make it difficult to do work that needs funding to continue. The extractivist pattern of fundraising on the part of national organizations contributes to keeping the South off of the map of positive legislation in relation to LGBT rights. The lack of positive legislation at the state level, translating into the "vast desert of nothingness" in the example above, also contributes to other impressions about the capacity of people who are doing the work in the off-the-map region of the United States that is the South.

The Authority to Speak: "This Isn't Possible Everywhere"

The use of the law as an international measure of progress has positioned both the U.S. South and South Africa very uncomfortably in relation to stories about progress and LGBT(I) rights. South Africa has the kind of legal protections for LGBTI people that register favorably in barometers of LGBTI equality. However, the level of violence against queer bodies in South Africa is a clear indictment of strategies that rely on the law to accomplish safety and bodily integrity for queer populations. In interviews, participants responded with the assumption that no matter how bad the context felt for doing this work in South Africa, the law ensured that it was better to be doing LGBTI rights work and maybe even better to *be* lgbtiq in South Africa. My interest is not in the accuracy of this assumption as much as it is in how it functions discursively. Garth, a transgender director of a queer and trans advocacy organization in South Africa, characterized South Africa's discursive position in relation to the rest of the continent by saying, "Like if you can't do like the queerest thing here then don't even think of planning it in Kenya or somewhere else. . . . Despite there being extensive backlash [here], the backlash of violence, the backlash of hate crimes."[58] South Africa is characterized here by both legal protections and potential for backlash. Potential for backlash in Kenya means "don't even think of planning it," but because of legal protections in South Africa, it is possible to plan events and actions "despite there being extensive backlash."

However, the law is not always reliable because of the unevenness of its implementation. Asa, director of a queer and trans advocacy organization in the Eastern Cape, speaks to the relationship between the law and reality in South Africa: "In South Africa, at least I know when somebody violates me on the street based on my gender identity—I might not—but at least theoretically I have a legal remedy. Right? In practice I might not."[59] Asa locates the law in the realm of the theoretical. The potential for Asa to be violated on the street is not theoretical. The "legal remedy" is qualified before Asa even articulates it. "I might not," Asa says, even though queer and trans people in South Africa are supposed to have a legal remedy. Asa qualifies the legal remedy a second time by saying, "In practice I might not," after characterizing it as "theoretically" available because of the protections against discrimination the law is supposed to afford lgbtiq people in South Africa. Garth identifies the work it takes to invoke the theoretical remedies described by Asa:

> Even sometimes when the law is not perfect, it's still existing. Like the challenges around the gender marker, we can all complain et cetera, but there is a law, and it does work, and it takes time and requires extensive advocacy, but it works and where it doesn't work, we can act on it and make it work. So, I think that's the difference to a country that, like Uganda where they just changed the birth registrations act to say that if you change your gender or your name it's completely illegal. You would be considered a noncitizen. So, where both are not even possible. So, I think there is, we are realizing or at least I'm teaching the team to realize that if you can't do it here in Africa then you can't do it anywhere.

Because there "is a law" that "does work" but "takes time and requires extensive advocacy," South Africa provides a space of more possibility than anywhere else in Africa. Sometimes there are difficulties with the law. While for Asa, the law can exist "theoretically" as a remedy, Garth says that even "where it doesn't work, we can act on it and make it work."

Similarly, David discusses coming out as a tool that advocacy organizations can utilize. However, coming out "isn't possible everywhere": "But I do think that local communities or local LGBTI people coming out has been one of the most powerful tools. This isn't possible everywhere because if you come out in some countries, you are either going to be arrested by the police or worse by the community because in the community you are then going to face mob justice." South Africa is not identified as a country where coming out isn't possible, but the country *is* identified by David as a place where "more lesbians [are] killed than all the other Southern African countries combined" and by different speakers as a place where there would be "extensive backlash . . . of violence" and "of hate crimes" for living as a visibly queer person and/or planning and hosting events focused on sexual orientation and gender identity advocacy. In many accounts of South Africa, activists indicated that coming out is considered possible because of the legal protections that exist there. The reality that such "coming out" could be met with similarly extreme violence whether or not there are legal protections places enormous confidence in the law. There did not seem to be questions about whether or not such confidence in the law was warranted, if it does not prevent or deter violence.

Zethu Matebeni, reflecting on the "constant challenge and negotiation between realising one's full identities and withstanding the risk of being violated or criminalised," recounts an example that speaks to why I question whether confidence in the law is warranted.[60] Matebeni was attending a lesbian-focused conference in Mozambique, where same-sex sexuality is criminalized, and recalls that the experiences articulated by lesbians in South Africa were "shocking and unimaginable" to participants from other countries, even countries where same-sex sexuality is criminalized.[61] Participants from Mozambique "had never heard of violence towards lesbian and gay people or criminalisation of same-sex acts, although the latter were still in their Statutes."[62] The latter part of this statement seems to suggest that participants confessed an ignorance of their own laws, but there is another way of thinking about this admission of not knowing on the part of such participants. The reality is that though same-sex sexuality remained criminalized in many African countries after the end of formal colonization in the shape of penal codes inherited from European colonial law, such laws were rarely enforced. Obviously, this is not universally true, and there are many countries where laws have been strengthened to oppress lgbtiq people, but for some queer and trans Africans, not having rights did not translate into the violence and backlash South African speakers in this section anticipate in African countries outside of South Africa.

The excerpts in this chapter are all from speakers who appeal to the map of "good" and "bad" places to locate themselves in a narrative about LGBT(I) rights. Though these speakers are located in a variety of places, their credibility is constructed through access to and negotiation of the discursive map of "good" and "bad" places for lgbtiq life. Regardless of the diversity of their actual contexts, their use of spatial discourse enables their capacity to name themselves in relation to the map. They find themselves either on the map or off the map, and they strategize based on how they are located in relation to the spatial discourse of sexuality.

As metronorms exert their pressure on the spatial politics of sexuality, out-of-the-way places are pushed farther and farther out of the way. Each out-of-the-way location references a place that is farther out of the way, about which it is able to say, "Even if there is violence (or other consequences), at least it is possible to do x, y, z thing *here*." The suggestion attached to such statements—explicitly or more subtly—is that in an even farther out-of-the-way place, even modest activist goals would not be possible.

Through the lens of rights, same-sex marriage is enshrined as a policy goal—something that puts a country on the map. But for queer and trans people, especially ones at the margins, acceptability, safety, and mobility are much harder to access than the map of "good" and "bad" places to be queer would suggest. There is nowhere in the world where acceptability, safety, mobility, and love for queer people is so taken for granted as to be "a low bar." I explore the reality that acceptability, safety, and mobility is not a low bar in chapter 5 by focusing on advocacy work that is done in metropolitan city centers in South Africa and the U.S. South. Even though the metronorm governing queerness is generated in New York City, Cape Town has been called the "gay capital of Africa" and Atlanta is sometimes referred to (in a bid to attract queer tourism) as "Gay-lanta." These major metropolitan areas outside of the metronormative centers governing queerness both rely on their reputation as welcoming to queer people in order to locate themselves on a map that would improve their reputations in a world that increasingly commodifies queerness. Yet, the different experiences of differently located queer populations in those cities demonstrate that living in a city is not enough to guarantee rights, mobility, safety, and acceptability for queer people.

CHAPTER 5

Metronormativity as Alienation

A Penis at Pride

In February 2016, Alternative and Inclusive Pride (AIP) disrupted Cape Town Pride for the second time.[1] The standoff looked like this: a group of multiracial, but mostly Black, activists blocked the road in front of a giant blue penis float. Without a path through the blockade, the penis float was stalled, ejaculating its "tweet-activated" confetti until the activists once again allowed the float to move forward. The activists from AIP turned around and started to *lead* the very march they/we had come to disrupt.

The months leading up to the Pride march and its disruption had been full of attempts to demonstrate the race and class divisions inherent in a celebration (of Pride) planned by white men who disregarded the call for dialogue demanded by Black lesbians from the city's periphery. The original theme for the 2016 march was "Colourblind." The organizers did respond to calls to change the theme.[2] Presumably, they did not want to appear to be racist. However, when it came to their authority to define what Pride meant for lgbtiq people in Cape Town, they did not feel it necessary to consult with anyone else.

The event after the march took place inside a fenced outdoor area, with an entry fee for admission. The march was marketed as being for everyone. The cis- and homo-normativity of the giant penis could have spoken for itself, but I believe the designers of the float describe it even better: "We The Brave is a new sexual health initiative aimed at men who have sex with men. We needed to stand out at Africa's biggest LGBT event, Cape Town Pride. So we came out in all our glory with a tweet-activated float designed for maximum exposure."[3] In case there was any ambiguity in terms of what the designers intended, We The Brave campaigners tweeted additional descriptions of the float, instructing attendees at Cape Town Pride to "tweet at us to make our #cockfloat blow it's load with glitter!"[4] In anticipation of a Pride event in Durban, We The Brave tweeted: "Having made an appearance at Cape Town, our giant dick float will be at Durban Pride this year!"[5]

The possibilities for describing the float seem only as limited as language describing penises, erections, and ejaculations, but the We The Brave campaign page on the website of the Ivan Toms Centre for Health, which is based in Cape Town, is clear about who the campaign serves: "Are you after a Bear that bares it all in a dark club? A Muscle-Mary with a penis as firm as his pecs? A Twink who takes it from a-top? A Drag Queen who dares to enter a darkroom? An After 9 who likes to give it from behind? A Sugar Daddy seeking out his next candy crush? A Ladyboy with the parts to please? Or just a regular guy who likes guys?"[6] The launch of this campaign, geared so specifically toward the demographic the white male organizers of Cape Town Pride were accused of solely catering to, begs the question of whether or not they were simply baiting AIP by changing the theme of Pride from an emphasis on "colourblindness" to a march behind a giant tweet-activated penis that became the centerpiece of the entire event. This conflation of maleness, masculinity, the penis, and male same-sex sexual desire and activity guaranteed that Black transgender activist Sandile Ndelu's desire that "every single facet of me is recognized on the streets of Green Point" could not be realized within the confines of this campaign.[7] While the organizers of Cape Town Pride responded to criticisms of their event with claims that they did not see race or gender, their embrace of a campaign that would only reflect the desires of a limited segment of Cape Town's lgbtiq community meant that their exclusivity was showcased in all its phallic "glory."

The Universal as Specific

In chapter 4, I argued that the creation of cities as centers of capital relied upon practices such as forced removal and alienation from land for rural and indigenous populations. I also argued that the enforcement of binary gender norms, most associated with areas outside of the city, were central to the creation of the city as a site of modernity. Subsequent to the enforcement of such norms, cities have become associated with freedom of expression and progressive values, while rural areas have been most closely associated with the policing of norms that prevent freedom of expression.

This chapter addresses the functioning of the metronorm *within* cities that project themselves as centers for queer life and tourism. To demonstrate how metronormativity functions to alienate different queer communities from their homes, I use examples from cities that have reputations as "queer tourist destinations" or centers of queer life. I want to be clear that metronormativity is not exclusively damaging to those outside of the metronorm in out-of-the-way places; it is also damaging to those who live at the periphery of the city center and those who are consumed by the city center through their vulnerability to housing insecurity, poverty, gentrification, and the violence of policing.

Much human rights work, including LGBT(I) rights work, operates through a deployment of the "universal" in relation to rights. Universal models have won their hegemony through the influence of policy, the media, funding, and research.

However, the way that sexuality and gender expression has been pathologized, written into law, viewed, and "treated" cannot be unraveled from the colonial history that resulted in anti-sodomy laws exported from colonizer to colonized in the first place. The "homosexual" as a particularly modern metropolitan subject was produced in the discursive formations of nineteenth-century colonial medical, scientific, and legal categories regulating gender and sexuality in conjunction with urban migrations that were both temporal and geographical/spatial/cultural.[8] Nigerian gender scholar Oyeronke Oyewumi refers to the binary gender categories through which colonialism unfolded as "bio-logic."[9] While same-sex loving people were not a construction of colonial knowledge, the "homosexual," as a category of person with particular characteristics identified and pathologized by colonial knowledge, was.[10] To neglect the meaning of this history and the way it informs contemporary global realities is to neglect the "fields of power and knowledge" within which all contemporary geographies are situated.[11]

The city itself was built with gender norms at the center of what constituted "civilized" behavior in the form of ordinances against cross-dressing, as I argued in chapter 4. Contemporary concepts of what constitute properly "gay," "lesbian," and "transgender" subjects of rights originate from a particular place and time but affect the way that rights-focused projects proceed at a global scale. A range of respectabilities have been won through appeals to "sameness" (or gender normativity), but these "prizes," such as legal recognition of same-sex relationships, entry into mainstream visibility, corporate and state or municipality sponsorship of mainstream metropolitan Pride festivals, and some political currency, have come at an enormous "price."[12] The costs of assimilation to white, affluent, able-bodied, hetero-become-homo-norms are most frequently paid by those who are already the most vulnerable to multiple kinds of violence from racism, classism, trans-antagonism, and other antagonisms that cannot be so readily named.[13] South African gender and sexuality scholar Graeme Reid traces the shape that such normativity has taken when conceptualizing and framing what categories of sexual and gender identities even mean:

> "Gay" has come to imply gender normativity, which had its early roots as a reaction against popular perceptions (and psycho-medical discourse) that tended to cast homosexuality and effeminacy as synonymous. [Anthropologist David Valentine] also identifies an emphasis on "sexuality", rather than gender, as a central tenet of the gay and lesbian political movement in the United States (and elsewhere in the Western world). This is the basis for legal and social equality—in which sameness is stressed, both in terms of gender normativity in same-sex relationships and in relation to heterosexual counterparts, where the only substantive difference is seen to exist in the realm of [sexual] object choice.[14]

I contend that the universal gay subject of rights (championed by Mark Gevisser and critiqued by Joseph Massad) alienates queer people from their own contexts. I am not the first person to have asked questions about how this works. Robert Lorway's ethnographic work with an LGBT(I) rights organization in Namibia prompted this question: "What are the consequences when international interventions... try to save and protect LGBT people from discrimination with programs that treat their sexualities in isolation from the local conditions in which they are embedded?"[15] This chapter suggests that the local conditions in which queer and trans people are embedded exist not only in rural places, but also inside cities with deeply contested histories of racialization, class stratification, and many other intersecting factors that shape experiences of city life for queer and trans people who live in them. The metronorm not only alienates rural queer populations from their homes, it also alienates those inside of the city who do not have access to the privilege and insulation from violence afforded through whiteness, affluence, and adherence to gender norms.

Erasure by Metronorm

The application of metronormative frameworks to a range of geographic spaces denies the complexity of the interaction between space and sexuality. In a study of organizing work in Namibia and South Africa, American scholar Ashley Currier uses "visibility" and "invisibility" as the frame for interpreting the meaning of advocacy work in two southern African contexts.[16] Currier asserts that "visibility confers intelligibility to individuals and objects in Western systems of thought."[17] However, Currier does not account for what "visibility" might mean in philosophical and epistemological traditions subsumed by "Western systems of thought," even though Currier's research is located in a space peripheralized by those systems of thought. Currier cites voices in the Global North who are critical of visibility because of its potential to be an "end point" for LGBT(I) advocacy work, and Currier is very clear about the meaning of "(in)visibility" without considering the limitations that may be inherent in the very terms set by "visibility" and "invisibility" as a conceptual frame when applied to peripheralized geographies. Currier views choices that activists make around their engagement with a range of issues as an embrace or refusal of visibility, which flattens the complex strategic choices that activists all over the world make. Actions are then sorted as advancing visibility or choosing invisibility, which allows for only a limited reading of the agency, coercion, pressure, strategy, politics, and negotiation that activists manage on a daily basis.

American scholar of rural sexualities Mary Gray, working ethnographically in the U.S. South, problematizes metronormative models of advocacy in the United States because their "politics of visibility needs the rural (or some *otherness*, some *place*) languishing in its shadow to sustain its status as an unquestionable achievement rather than a strategy that privileges the view of some by ending the vantage point of others."[18] Refusing to rely only on visibility as a measure for how freely queer lives are lived allows a more nuanced understanding of the shape that queer life takes outside of the borders established as "good" for queer life by metronormative narratives of queerness. Carly Thomsen goes further, detailing the specific ways that visibility as a measure of anything beyond adherence to metronormative organizing campaigns is practically useless—when it isn't actually harmful in the lives of the individuals Thomsen speaks to and writes about.[19]

As Nigerian blogger and writer Sokari Ekine and Kenyan activist Kagendo Murungi demonstrate in their contributions to the anthology *Queer African Reader*, which was also co-edited by Ekine, there are other ways of conceptualizing queer activist and organizing presence in locations outside of the metropole.[20] Several authors in the collection are explicit about the harmful implications of being *visibly* associated with Global North LGBT rights organizations and their internationalizing structures through the requirement that they privilege identity-based strategies. These authors argue for strategies that would link them more closely with the work that is happening in their own contexts. Sometimes work with more relevance in national contexts (Kenyan, Ugandan, Tanzanian, Ghanaian, Zimbabwean, South African, for instance) but distanced from "global gay" campaigns is capable of confronting homo-/trans-antagonisms or working to dismantle heteronormativity without provoking the damaging and counterproductive association with "foreign" domination that feeds into the accusation that same-sex sexuality and gender variance is "unAfrican." This accusation is a significant burden impeding the work of LGBTI rights organizers on the African continent. An insistence by international funders located in the Global North that advocacy work happen within the framework of LGBT(I) rights leaves limited space for activists in out-of-the-way places, especially places where same-sex sexuality remains criminalized, to negotiate their own contexts in ways that may have the most resonance with other people who live there, confronting homophobia in the local context but not winning the splashy headlines that international funding organizations want to see and use to measure "success" or "visibility." As Ekine writes, "Framing the narrative in terms of rights creates tensions with other civil society and social movements. Queer Africans are not just queers, they are people who live their lives in the same ways as everyone else and as such our struggle needs to align itself with other social justice movements such as those of and for rural women, shack dwellers, climate change, land rights and so on." The reality Ekine describes is that queer people share the spaces where they live with the heterosexual people who live there, as well. Both the internal politics of those spaces and the external associations that characterize them are shared with queer and trans people's heterosexual neighbors. Those dynamics are rarely navigated alongside funders based in metropolitan centers. This reality, as described by Ekine, was something that emerged not only in the South African context, but in a U.S. context as well. The issues people are navigating vary from space to space, but those issues are not navigated by queer and trans people in isolation.

Thomsen reflects on associations with context and perspectives about those associations, too, while asking interview participants how they imagined they would be seen by queer people or advocacy organizations in New York, for instance. This was a funny question to some participants, many of whom had ready responses, even though a few confessed to never having thought about how others located far away considered them before.[21] Responses to the question indicated that the imagined city-dwelling-gay-rights-advocate inhabited a world that was different from the world inhabited by Thomsen's Midwestern interviewees. This difference did not come down to one place that was homophobic and another place that was not, but the imagined difference (in both directions) was a clear indication that Thomsen's participants shared something in the context in which they lived with cisgender heterosexual people who lived there that they did not share with the imagined gay rights advocate. That shared space is the space of context. Responses to Thomsen's question might have been playful (and funny!), but when someone else's story about where you live is *the* story about where you live, there can be material and political consequences of the reality they imagine for you.

Queer people everywhere are "not just queers"; they are also embedded in the needs and struggles, joys, and sufferings of their contexts. It would be very difficult to argue that queer Africans who have created coalitional networks or embedded themselves within movements addressing a range of social issues, even while refusing to privilege an identity-based rights framework, are not visible. Instead, the model proposed by Ekine and Murungi is one that is responsive to context rather than the demands of external actors such as transnational nongovernmental organizations (NGOs) and funders based in the metropolitan centers of the Global North. Rural sexualities scholar Colin Johnson is also critical of identity-based approaches required for visibility in a consideration of rural histories of sexual dissidence in the United States because "when identity is invoked as a category of historical analysis, there is always a hazard that the vagueness of that concept will be filled with unspoken assumptions about what it does or does not mean to possess an identity—assumptions that are necessarily conditioned by our own historical circumstances."[22] It certainly is possible to organize around identity, but existing in one's identity while organizing around intersectional issues or even issues that affect queer people *and everyone else* in their context is not invisibility.

To demonstrate the colonizing and alienating effect that the globally dominant model of the universal gay subject of rights exerts, I turn to transnational sexuality scholar Ryan Thoreson, whose ethnography of the International Gay and Lesbian Human Rights Commission (IGLHRC)—later renamed OutRight International—tells a story about how organizations based in the United States with partners and offices in other global locations operate. This text, written about Thoreson's experience as an intern conducting research, provides a glimpse into the relationships between organizations advancing a version of LGBT rights that is proudly and unapologetically universal and the specific contexts where their transnational interventions are launched.[23]

The story Thoreson tells serves as an apologetics for a universal human rights model launched from the metropole into diverse global spaces. Thoreson draws on critical literature to suggest that examining the center (where power is concentrated) is a crucial way to learn about processes of marginalization but in the end concludes that IGLHRC deserves to exist because it is doing the best that it can as "a small NGO with a large mandate but relatively little power."[24] Being such doesn't prevent IGLHRC) from emphasizing the importance of its existence, however.[25]

One director of the organization interviewed by Thoreson speaks about the role that IGLHRC played in "catalyzing the African LGBT movement": "I think we played a really important role in catalyzing the African LGBT movement. A lot of the convenings around which people started getting a sense of themselves and their power and their potential, I think, we convened.... Convenings don't always have concrete outcomes, but I think they are spaces in which people develop political community, and know each other, and know where to go for help, and develop a sense of what the possibilities are."[26] The assertion that "a small NGO with a large mandate but relatively little power" situated in New York City could be a central player in "catalyzing" a movement for an entire continent is an extraordinary claim.[27] Such a statement is also highly contested by those who themselves founded organizations, worked in their individual capacities, or mobilized their communities in their own countries. Some of those same activists, who also formed cross-continental links with other individuals and groups on the African continent in order to further their advocacy work and built a network of support across the continent, would not credit IGLHRC for "catalyzing" their work.[28]

The suggestion that "convenings don't always have to have concrete outcomes" is indicative of a double standard that exists in relation to accountability for "a small NGO with a large mandate but relatively little power" and locally based organizations and activists.[29] According to Thoreson,

> IGLHRC's professionalization and compliance with U.S. financial regulations also made some expenditures untenable. Brokers could disburse money to third parties to support activist work, but receipts were required to account for all money wired abroad. This made it difficult to send money to activists who did not have bank accounts, or to fund urgent needs that could not be documented—for example, informally paying an official to help an activist recover a confiscated passport. MoneyGram requires that recipients present state-issued identification, which was particularly problematic for transgender brokers who lacked access to accurate, gender-affirming documentation or activists trying not to draw attention to their ties with Northern LGBT groups.[30]

It would be possible to characterize IGLHRC's "untenable" expenditures as a failure of imagination. In chapter 6, I tell the story of an organizer who created a way to organize with local chiefs, even though, as the organizer noted, it is not standard protocol to include a budget line for "beer with chiefs." If gender-affirming documentation is a barrier to many things for transgender individuals, it seems odd that IGLHRC would opt to conform to U.S. legal norms that reinforce that barrier rather than imagine ways to address and dismantle the barrier in order to provide more immediate assistance to transgender individuals and organizations with even fewer resources and much less influence than an organization with a global reach like IGLHRC.

Though Thoreson claims to want to know how power operates by observing a transnational LGBT rights organization based in New York, Thoreson's work takes on the assumptions of the logic that drives the organization's work in order to understand it. IGLHRC's slogan, which claims it advocates for "the rights of everyone, everywhere," provides some suggestion of how debates around issues of rights are framed through the lens of universality by such organizations. Thoreson argues that "in divisive debates about gender, sexuality, and law, proponents and opponents of LGBT human rights have vested interests in reifying claims in particular ways. Proponents frame LGBT rights as straightforward issues of dignity and fairness, insisting universal human rights must be extended to and enjoyed by all. Opponents construct these rights—and, typically, LGBT populations—as foreign, contrary to local morality and custom, and inexorably shaped by global power disparities."[31] The suggestion that these two positions are the only ones that exist is not only reductive; it also ignores the intersecting issues faced by queer and trans people in their contexts and the messy, complicated shapes that politics take in those contexts, as well.

To many involved in these "divisive debates," there are only proponents and opponents of LGBT rights. However, to thinkers like Massad, layers of complexity are obscured by such a simplistic dichotomizing of perspectives.[32] The tendency of the "human rights framework . . . to transform widespread exclusion and mistreatment into discrete problems with identifiable culprits and technical solutions" leads Massad to think about how the arrest of some gay men in Egypt was influenced by a "vilification campaign" that was strengthened by the "Gay International."[33] Massad demonstrates a complex dynamic of power playing out between the Gay International and "the press and conservative Islamists":

> Indeed, the vilification campaign against these men intensified precisely as a result of the actions of the Gay International and the Western politicians whose support it solicited. During the hearings, the prosecution frequently referenced the Gay International's campaign, pledged to defend the "manhood" of Egypt against attempts to "violate" it, and wondered what would become of a nation who sits by idly as its "men become like its women" through "deviance." The press and conservative Islamists have begun to call for explicit laws criminalizing same-sex practice. The Gay International and its activities are largely responsible for the intensity of this repressive campaign.[34]

Viewing the place itself and the people who live there as the source of "opponents to LGBT human rights" fails to examine an aspect of that opposition Thoreson names as central: its foreignness. To reinforce the charge of foreignness by continuing to promote values associated with "America" or other "gay places" without translating the needs of local queer people as a part of the texture of their local contexts is to perpetuate the alienation of queer people from the places they/we call home.

"Gay Cape Town"?

Thoreson is not the only author to adopt the assumptions of the globally dominant model of the universal gay subject of rights in a supposed effort to critique that model. In a study of what the author calls "gay Cape Town," another transnational scholar of sexuality, Natalie Oswin, attempts to determine whether there is a globalized gay identity projected from the Global North or a distinctly "African" mode of expressing queer existence. The observation with which Oswin concludes an examination of "gay Cape Town" is that there is neither "an imposing Western queerness or a resistant African homosexual culture" in the city, a conclusion that Oswin is able to make for two reasons.[35] The first of these reasons is that Oswin writes about such discursive formations as if locating them would require them to be static and free of each other's influence. The second reason is that the places Oswin looked for African resistance are all dominated by legacies of whiteness, which renders African resistance unlikely, at the very least. "Gay Cape Town" is itself something that exists in the imaginary of whiteness only.[36]

An awareness that "the local" as positioned in a globalized world is full of hybridities shaped by contestations between internal and external power dynamics and characterized by their own political, economic, and historical realities should be the *entry point* for inquiry, not a conclusion. As anthropologist Anna Tsing maintains, "out-of-the-way-places" are "distinctive and unequal subject positions within common fields of power and knowledge."[37] To suggest that it is possible for either a totalizing global hegemony to displace local people's agency *or* that a "pure" local essence can exist untouched by global influence disregards the "common fields of power and knowledge" in which all locations are situated. Oswin acknowledges the naïveté of the ethnographic inquiry but still discounts the capacity of locally mobilized work to confront what is most dangerous to local queer existence with locally grounded and generated solutions.[38]

Oswin suggests that though "the study of different expressions of queer politics and cultures" does matter, "it runs the risk of romanticizing local heterogeneity and overstating its political efficacy."[39] Oswin's study is a clear example of how authors who are not deeply familiar with a context can misrepresent the shape of that space. Rather than flattening out-of-the-way places, for instance, South African sexualities scholar Graeme Reid spends time in "small-town" South Africa. While Reid discloses naïveté on the very first page—confessing "I expected to find gay people living in secrecy and fear and dreaming of migrating to the cities"— Reid's sense of the context develops in conjunction with and in response to the community in which Reid was situated over the course of the research.[40]

Reid contextualizes both the legacy of meanings of same-sex sexuality forged in Western contexts and the way that "small-town gays" negotiate their own contexts. "Small-town gays," Reid observes, insist on their value in their own contexts. Reid discusses the way they mobilize femininity to "be accepted into society and integrated into local communities as women."[41] This embodiment of femininity interacts with localized gender norms and understandings of sexuality: "By respecting gender norms, effeminate gays become the social equivalent of women who can enjoy solidarity and a degree of protection, but at the same time also experience the vulnerability of women. Their feminine self-presentation and their social designation as women enable their boyfriends to have sexual relations with them as straight men."[42] The point here is not to suggest that the gays in small-town South Africa are living a more authentic version of sexual and gender identity than the metronormative model. The point, instead, is that dynamics of gender and sexuality that do not conform to the universal model of LGBT(I) rights may open possibilities for negotiating one's existence in one's context that are otherwise foreclosed, especially when the universal model is interpreted as foreign. There is another point, as well. If small-town gays are living a life where they share vulnerabilities with women in their own contexts rather than the vulnerabilities of gay men living a life closer to the universal model of gay identity in a city somewhere else in the world, queer and trans advocacy models based on the universal model of LGBT(I) rights are not going to address the needs and vulnerabilities of small-town gays in Ermelo, South Africa, or the needs of lgbtiq people in multiple other contexts. The remainder of this chapter demonstrates that not only is a universal model of gay rights inadequate for small-town gays, the universal model of rights does not respond to the intersecting needs of Black lgbtiq people in Cape Town or Black lgbtiq people in Atlanta, Georgia, because the dominant set of values attached to that model is shaped by whiteness and legacies of exclusion based on racism, classism, xenophobia, and ableism.

Disrupting Gay Cape Town

Cape Town is unlike any other city that I have spent time in for the purposes of my research. In terms of narratives about the possibilities for queer life, the closest analog to Cape Town in the U.S. South is Atlanta or New Orleans, but those cities are not known internationally, in the way that Cape Town is, as "the gay capital" of an entire continent. Atlanta and New Orleans might be oases of queer acceptance in the U.S. South, but they would be eclipsed by New York City in any discussion of globally recognizable cities where queer life can thrive.

Cape Town has a thriving queer district at the edge of the city center complete with bars, clubs, retailers, and even a gay church, which the Ugandan gay activist David Kato marveled at upon discovering.[43] What does Cape Town's "gay village" look like to those who share a history of forcible removal from city centers across South Africa? What does it mean for the most reliably safe space you could frequent as a queer person to be a forty-minute drive from your home? What does the forty-minute drive mean when you do not have a car? As queer South African scholar and activist Zethu Matebeni observes about the (in)accessibility of Pride to those who live at Cape Town's geographical and economic margins, "the last taxi or train to the township would leave before the actual Pride after-parties really begin."[44]

The Black lesbian advocacy organization Free Gender argues that no, Green Point may as well be in another city entirely from Khayelitsha, where the Black lesbians locate their activism. When they are not organizing against homophobia in Khayelitsha, Free Gender members spend their activist energy confronting racism in the queer activities dominated by white gay men in the part of Cape Town that is far from where they live. In Green Point and in the city center, Black queer and trans people have historically been excluded from full participation in activities centered on a queer identity that, according to the universal model of gay rights, is *the* important identity they share with other queer people in the city. In order for Black lesbians, especially impoverished Black lesbians living in Khayelitsha, to claim the benefits of queerness in the "gay capital of Africa," they must travel far from where they live, leaving behind their familiar surroundings only to endure racism from white queer people who enjoy more mobility, more access, and more wealth. After they have done all of this, they may be asked to leave, having wasted money, time, and energy to travel an hour to the place the universal model of gay rights says they should most naturally belong.

The disruption of Cape Town Pride activities engaged in by Free Gender is not an ahistorical protest. Black queer people in South Africa have been engaging the racism of their white counterparts for decades. Founder of Free Gender Funeka Soldaat describes some of these actions in a chapter about Black Lesbian organizing in Cape Town by discussing the way that activists protested the policing of entry into queer clubs in Green Point, Cape Town's gay village.[45]

While the white male organizers of Cape Town Pride claim that it is the Black lesbians of Khayelitsha who are "racist" and who refuse to participate in planning Cape Town Pride—after all, everyone was invited to participate in the planning—multiple realities of life for queer folks who live in the townships prevent any meaningful engagement with Cape Town Pride as it is currently structured. The organization of the event, in its current form, reflects the apartheid architecture of the city. The distance for Black lesbians to travel to participate in evening planning meetings is too far; the taxi fare too expensive; the night too dangerous. The sense of disgust that Khumbulani Pride planners feel about the party environment of Cape Town Pride as they continue to bury members of their own community who are killed in horrific acts of violence is palpable in their refusal to participate in the white-dominated Pride party that takes place in the Green Point gayborhood. So, while the white men who claim to invite "everyone" to participate in the planning of Cape Town Pride have the financial capital to live in the city center or an affluent suburb, the ease that comes with reliable and safe transportation, and the proximity to the locations where they always choose to hold planning meetings, this is not the case for the Black lesbians involved in the planning of Khumbulani Pride.

Beyond these practical negotiations facing Black queer individuals who want to attend Pride or contribute to its planning is the reality observed by Matebeni: "The city was not meant for Black people."[46] Apartheid architecture meant that "the Black subject had to give evidence of his or her economic usefulness to white families or employers" in order to have any mobility at all. In the twenty-first century, "white lesbian and gay people . . . enforce a different kind of racist segregation of Black lesbians and gender non-conforming people during Pride."[47]

I preface an exploration of the ethnographic material with my observations of what it is like to interact with Green Point in order to think differently about city life for queer people who do not share the privilege of whiteness, wealth, and mobility characteristic of the planners of Cape Town Pride. Khumbulani Pride is a direct response to metronormativity as alienation. The organizers speak to the distance between their realities and the realities of the white gay men who dominate the planning of Cape Town Pride.

A metronormative perspective of Cape Town would see Khayelitsha, at the periphery of the city, as only ever hostile to queer life and Green Point as only ever welcoming of queer visitors and residents. Andrew Tucker, for instance, has written about queer life in Cape Town in the book *Queer Visibilities: Space, Identity, and Interaction in Cape Town*. Tucker's project is descriptively accurate, but the organization of the book, moving through Cape Town's apartheid architecture from the center of the city among white men outward to its peripheries among "coloured" men, then finally among Black (Xhosa) men, neglects the spatial politics of sexuality beyond what can be explained through a metronormative discursive position.[48] Tucker's observations, for example, that white gay men, as a group, remain unpoliticized, that coloured men, as a group, created a kind of visibility for themselves in conjunction with apartheid regulations through cross-dressing, and that the raced and classed position of Black African gay men's lives means that they face a set of distinct and compounded issues in multiple city spaces (both in their own communities and in the gay village) are an accurate enough mapping of the racialized legacies of apartheid Tucker reads in participants' responses. However, the gaze of the text centers whiteness and positions the author and the reader in the center of the city looking out, surveying the apartheid-designed landscape and taking its designations for granted.

The structure of Tucker's text reifies assumptions about African responses to same-sex sexuality that could be worked with or understood differently if the township at the periphery of the city or Black queer men's experiences were the lens through which Tucker read queerness in Cape Town. Had Tucker moved from margin to center, the complexity of queer African lives might have been a starting point for understanding queer life in Cape Town and in South Africa. These complexities demand an intersectional analysis that cannot be separated from the way that the apartheid infrastructure of the city shapes queer and trans people's access to housing, transportation, employment, sanitation, water, and economic security, all of which shape their proximity to violence, a violence that is held at bay in Green Point by the infrastructure that supports queer life there and the privilege of expendable suburban wealth that can purchase safe transportation and accommodation at most hours of the day and night.[49]

Tucker instead begins at the center of the city, which is also the center of whiteness, power, and capital in Cape Town. For Tucker, Black African same-sex sexuality is at the periphery of queer South African experiences. Similarly, by positioning Khayelitsha (for instance) at the periphery of the geographical boundaries of the study, life for queer people there is the worst, not by virtue of the indignities of apartheid-structured life that has never been redressed, but (according to the rubric of places written onto and off of the map) because Khayelitsha's residents are more homophobic. A view from the center also misses the way that queer existence in Khayelitsha (for example) is embedded in negotiations with family and community. Queer individuals do not exist outside of these relationships in their communities but negotiate them instead in their daily lives.

From the periphery of Khayelitsha, the Green Point suburb with its gay bars, clubs, and restaurants appears as a closet, whose doors open or close more or less easily depending on one's race and access to capital. This is an idea I was first introduced to by Thiyane Duda at "Queering Africa III: Queering Cape Town," a symposium curated by Matebeni, and it is a different way of seeing the part of Cape Town reputed to be most gay-friendly. A closet is not generally a gay-friendly place to be. Instead, it contains queer desire and restricts its expression to a small, isolated, and hidden space. Queer existence in Green Point is not negotiated with broader community or kinship networks but is in fact its own area of the city, cordoned off by the limits of its imagined boundaries. The view from Khayelitsha is very different from the view from Green Point, and not only in the ways that the metronorm might imagine.

When I volunteered with Free Gender, which is based in Khayelitsha, Funeka and I, along with two or three other members of the organization who would fit in the car, attended many evening meetings. Without access to the car I had rented, we would not have attended those meetings. However, according to participants, evening meetings persist as a norm in the LGBTI advocacy sector. This suggests that the risk Black lesbians face using public transport (and the general inaccessibility of other kinds of private transport) in the evenings and after dark does not always register in the scheduling considerations of LGBTI rights organizations situated in, or closer to, the city center.

Other activists, too, spoke to issues of accessibility that arose when meetings are held in the evenings in town. For Liza, a white cisgender organizer who lived in the center of the city, the logistical challenge of being able to get to town safely and reliably affected the dynamics of those involved in planning committees for events, such as Cape Town Pride, which were theoretically meant to represent and incorporate all lgbtiq people in Cape Town: "We always tried to have a staff member of [our organization] going there, but I mean it's really also hectic because the meetings are always in the city."[50] Narratives about the accessibility of Pride were often connected to the unreliability of transportation to and from the event. The question of transportation and its link to the accessibility of events and meetings where decisions were taken for an entire sector or an entire movement could not be untangled from the demographic makeup of those making influential decisions and those who registered as constituents.

Kian, a Muslim religious leader and gay organizer, speaks to this by discussing the accessibility of Pride for different demographics of people who live in different locations at the periphery of Cape Town: "So, we also got talking to other organizations and the issue of accessibility came up. How accessible is pride to people in the Cape Flats, for example? And people coming from subeconomic areas. [Pride is] still predominantly white."[51] For some organizations in rural areas in

South Africa, questions about safety and accessibility were about a specific site of transportation. The elaboration of the taxi rank as a site of violence for queer, trans, and gender nonconforming people by some participants located in an advocacy organization in the predominantly rural South African province of the Eastern Cape helps to contextualize concerns about the relationship between transportation and accessibility outlined by participants located in Cape Town in the excerpts above. Asa, an isiXhosa-speaking transgender woman and founder of an organization, speaks to the decision of this organization in the Eastern Cape to focus an intervention on taxi ranks.[52] The environment in the taxi rank is rooted in the violence of masculinity that structures relationships between transportation and access:

> One problematic space that we really have in [our province] is the taxi rank. The taxi rank has always been predominantly about men, masculinity, and heterosexuality. In my life living in [this province] ... up to this year of my life I've never once heard of a gay man who is driving a taxi. I've seen women ... on this very ... popular taxi route here. I've seen two women, and I would be very interested to hear how they engage.... The people who suffer violence at the taxi ranks are sex workers: those are women issues. The lesbians who are gender-nonconforming: those are women issues, the transwomen. So, in a sense we are all at risk for violence.

If the taxi is simultaneously one of the most common modes of transportation in South Africa *and* a site of violent gender policing, the mobility of a range of different women, feminine-presenting, and gender-nonconforming people is seriously curtailed when they must rely on it. If the space also allows for a public policing where onlookers sometimes participate in the violence, rather than diffuse it, it becomes a site of terror for those who rely on it for transportation, which means that their access to a range of things is limited by alienation from transportation or violence for insisting on moving freely in public space as others (cisgender men) do.

Because the lives of lgbtiq people cannot be separated from struggles and issues faced by members of their broader community, whatever is happening in the broader community also affects lgbtiq people, as members of their communities, which cannot be reduced solely to their identities as queer people. In a public space in a South African township where we talked about community, Kayla, an isiXhosa-speaking Black lesbian and one of the planners of Khumbulani Pride who was approaching a decision to retire from leading an organization comprised mostly of young people, described why it is important to do work that connects queer experiences and realities with the broader conditions affecting life in the community: "So that was really, really crucial for me to work with civil society and also people to know that some of the things that's affecting them—those are the things that's also affecting me. I mean, if there's no water in the community, it's also affecting me, regardless of who I am. That was crucial for me that we have to take all those struggles seriously."[53]

Commitments to home are complicated, though, and come not only from a sense that home is shared with community and family members who are not lgbtiq-identified, but a keen awareness that sharing home is what can intensify violence for lgbtiq people who live there. Kayla acknowledges this fraught reality by speaking about the source of violence for lgbtiq people in their own community: "And also, looking at the issue of hate crimes and homophobia—it's not done by gay and lesbian people. It's done by other people. Those people that we are keeping them away from us. So, for me, it was very important—in the struggle of dealing with homophobia and hate crime, to include the people that are against LGBTI people in order that they have to understand gay and lesbian people are just people. They are human people. The only difference is how we feel." If Pride is in Green Point, far away from the source of violence located in Kayla's community, the growth and change that Kayla wants to see happen in that same community will be difficult to accomplish. Queer and trans life will be associated instead with the white-dominated activities in the part of the city most closely associated with queerness and/or Pride: Green Point.

The association of queer existence with "town" (or "the city") and other places beyond town that are not home complicates lgbtiq people's relationships with home for many reasons. One of these reasons is that the events celebrating queer life, confronting homo-antagonism, or bringing awareness to hate crimes would happen far away from where these concerns are most relevant to planners of Khumbulani Pride. What it really means for Cape Town Pride to be isolated to, and therefore associated with, the city center or the suburb of Green Point is that the sites where Khumbulani Pride is located are still shared with antagonistic heterosexuals without the antagonism being addressed. For Black queer township dwellers to attend Cape Town Pride in Green Point means to go party with other queer people, with whom you share little else other than your queerness, and then go home to the fear of violence in your own community from "the people that are against LGBTI people."

Working with some of those involved in the planning of Khumbulani Pride, which is situated in different Cape Town townships in order to bring awareness to violence against lgbtiq people and Black lesbians especially, highlighted for me a vision of a Pride that was meant to evolve over time from being an event for lgbtiq people who felt that they existed in isolation to one that moved outward to their communities. Pride could then happen in and for communities so that lgbtiq people could be "visible in our communities." This visibility as a kind of presence is important not only in designated metropolitan areas where metronormative iterations of queer visibility are considered acceptable or even, to some extent, desirable, but in the places where families and neighbors also live. Xolani, an isiXhosa-speaking gay man who has spent a career working with a major nonprofit in Cape Town and is one of the members of the planning committee of Khumbulani Pride, speaks to the importance of holding events where Black queer and trans people live in order to challenge the narrative that same-sex sexuality and gender diversity are a Western or foreign thing:

> It's important we have Khumbulani Pride because Cape Town Pride is not inclusive in terms of involving the communities because everything is happening in town. What about our communities? People's families, you know? We need to be exposed or to be visible in our communities, you know, not only in town because now they will see like this is a white thing, not for everybody, but for gay people, you know. Because they are saying that this is a Western thing. It's not African. It's because everything is happening in town. Why not do things in the community where there are people and people, they can just learn something—different things, from LGBTI people.[54]

Within the racialized architecture of apartheid that forcibly removed anyone who was not categorized as white from the city center, the association of Pride and LGBTIQ people more generally with "town" conveys the message that Pride events are "a white thing, not for everybody, but for gay people." The conflation of "gay" and "white" plays into the already intractable narrative that "this is a Western thing. It's not African." Xolani is clear that the source of these messages is the location of such events "in town." If communities are engaged from within, "people who are against LGBTIQ people" will be more likely to learn that LGBTIQ people are already their community members, families, and friends.[55]

"For a Lot of Folks, It's Better in Atlanta, but It's Not Better for Everyone"

Elsewhere, I have written about Pride disruptions in both Cape Town and in New Orleans, Louisiana. The discussion of New Orleans, strongly based on the compelling work of BreakOUT!, is in Matebeni and Camminga's collection *Beyond the Mountain: Queer Life in Africa's Gay Capital*.[56] For the members of BreakOUT!, life in New Orleans means dissonance between the decadence advertised by the city and the criminalization they experience as queer and trans youth of color. While many were celebrating the legal victory of same-sex marriage in the United States in 2015, BreakOUT! launched a campaign that asked, "How can we walk down the aisle when we can't walk down the street?"

When BreakOUT! was invited to serve as a Marshal for the New Orleans Pride parade but decided they could not participate because of increased police presence at the event, the organization set the terms for the safety of its members in a city where they face ongoing threats of criminalization for "walking while trans." The visibility inherent in a marshal position would not only make individual members of the group vulnerable to profiling and harassment from law enforcement, it would also be a risk for the entire organization—their members could be profiled, arrested, put at risk of physical violence, or incarcerated.

New Orleans, described on its own tourism website as "an oasis in America's South" for lgbtiq people, is a city that markets itself as a gay travel destination and overall destination of decadence for travelers.[57] However, Louisiana, the state in which New Orleans is located, was listed by the *Rolling Stone* magazine as one of the five worst states for lgbtiq people to live in in 2014, based on a lack of legal protections, violence against queer and trans people, and the enforcement of the state's archaic anti-sodomy statute.[58] In 2020, Louisiana ranked thirty-first (of fifty) on a list compiled by USA Today's "24/7 Wall Street" section, based on its lack of legal protections for lgbtiq people and its public acceptance of queer and trans people lagging behind other parts of the country.[59]

Atlanta, Georgia, is another city that is often viewed as a metropolitan exception in the otherwise "rural" South. Atlanta is a city similar to New Orleans, in that it is a metropolitan center inside a state that is otherwise considered part of the "deep" South, with all of the conservative political connotations that accompany that imaginary.[60] Like Free Gender (and the larger AIP network) at the periphery of Cape Town, queer residents of Atlanta, too, have established their own alternative Pride space. The event is called Southern Fried Queer Pride (SFQP). Rather than drawing on metronormative, corporate-sponsored Pride models, the event is structured around a radical and intersectional model of Pride that cannot be purchased with corporate dollars.

The organizers describe the event this way: "Southern Fried Queer Pride (SFQP) is a queer and trans Pride festival in Atlanta celebrating the robust and vivid Southern queer community that exist amidst the Bible Belt, the Deep and Dirty South. Deep fried in the activism and radical heart of our forequeers, SFQP aims to provide a weekend of full-flavored community and intersectionality, without all the corporate and capitalist additives that taint modern day Pride festivals across the nation."[61] Just like Cape Town, Atlanta has a story about what kind of city it is, what kind of city it is for Black Americans, and what kind of city it is for queer people. Unlike Cape Town, Atlanta is a city that has strong associations with Black political power. As I write in 2024, Atlanta is embroiled in a political contestation over a proposed "Cop City"—a massive police training facility.

SFQP organizers draw on the legacy of Black political power when they describe how they want their festival to fit into Atlanta's social economy. Avery Willis, a representative from SFQP interviewed by a Georgia radio station, discussed the reasons that SFQP exists separately from the mainstream Pride celebrations in Atlanta, where the "faces that you see are more white faces or cisgender faces, and it's very easy to feel a little lost."[62] Willis identifies a legacy of Black and brown queer creators to connect to: "Atlanta is such a home to Black ingenuity and Black creation and art, and we wanted to make sure we are showing ourselves in the same way."[63] SFQP does not appeal to the universal model of identity-based rights in order to celebrate and cultivate queer community. The festival locates itself very specifically in the cultural landscape in which it finds itself, prioritizing intersectional perspectives on what it means to be in Atlanta, what it means to be in Georgia, and what it means to be in the South. Some participants in my research, too, spoke powerfully about the legacy of Black cultural and political power that is part of the allure of Atlanta, making it a special place (if a sometimes infuriating one) to draw on the kind of legacies referenced by SFQP in materials publicizing their events.

Hal, a Black gay man who does organizing work that focuses on building power among Black gay men, spoke movingly about what it means to be from Atlanta. For Hal, "the possibilities of Blackness in Atlanta" were demonstrated by "so many examples of what Blackness could look like, in terms of physical appearance, in terms of personality."[64] Hal adds, "I always tell people, I don't have any angst around being Black, like I don't have that." Hal feels that Hal might have such angst almost anywhere else. The possibilities for Blackness in Atlanta were so rich, however, Hal's parents moved from New York to Atlanta "to escape racism":

> I grew up not being the only Black kid in my honors classes. That's what it means being from Atlanta for me. Like every Black kid I knew they had this narrative. I was the only Black kid in my AP [Advanced Placement] class. That wasn't it at all for me like because that's what it means to be from Atlanta. I grew up, always with the Black mayor, always with the Black principal, always the Black teacher.
>
> I mean my parents moved to Atlanta to escape racism in many ways. They moved to the South because they were living in New York in the middle of the busing crisis and there's a hideous racism that we never talk about. My mother tells us a story of Atlanta. She tells us a story. They come to Atlanta in 1971 and she talks about how they were leaving New York, and everybody is white, all the pilots are white, the flight attendants are white. Everybody is white white white white white in New York. They get to Atlanta, the pilots are Black, the flight attendants, and everything is so Black. . . . My parents they always held that like they always believed that Atlanta is where you can be . . . a Black person. They really believe that.

Accounts of Black gay men in Atlanta suggest that the city does not always live up to its promise, however. As I attended an event in Atlanta, comprised almost exclusively of Black gay men, I was surprised to hear the men use the phrase "especially in Atlanta," a phrase I had not anticipated hearing. I asked Hal about this in an interview. Hal had organized the event as part of a series hosted specifically to prompt conversation among Black gay men. The event was not exclusively attended by Black gay men, but they made up most of the attendees. Hal spoke to me about why Atlanta was complicated for Black gay men. Atlanta was home for Hal, a home Hal loved, and a home Hal felt "saved" by from a more insidious kind of racism that saturates other American cities like New York City.

At the same time, Hal spoke to the way that Atlanta is a city that promises much more than it can deliver to the constituency of Black gay men who had been in the audience of the event:

> I think part of it is that people don't expect to be let down as much as they are here. The presumption is that Atlanta is the Black gay Mecca. That Atlanta is the place to be for Black gay men and once they get here . . . I think they're often very disappointed and disillusioned by the lack of infrastructure to support affirming Black gay men spaces. It's like you know the streets are paved with gold, like, and so I think they're not prepared for the other parts of the alienation, the

loneliness, but I don't think those are issues representative of Atlanta. I think that Black gay men in most metropolitan cities have very similar struggles. It's a sense of being completely surrounded like you're in a sea of Black gay men but you also feel disconnected at the same time. I think that some of that is part of Atlanta, like the modern world. I think that people feel very disconnected in general, but I think when you're in a marginalized community, I think it's more intensified.

More generally, participants often perceived, or spoke about, Atlanta as a metropolitan city of exceptionalism in the South. Jerome, a Black transgender representative of a national organization working in one of its regional offices, spoke to some of the perceptions of Atlanta that result in Atlanta being spoken about as an exception in the South: "It's something about the number of universities, higher ed. institutions, big businesses, and folks coming in, both tourists and residents that make it different than other cities in the South."[65] Because of Atlanta's metropolitan reputation, when Jerome spends time in southern communities outside of Atlanta, attempts at connecting with rural folks around a shared southern experience sometimes meet resistance: "I hear that a lot when I give workshops and trainings in rural areas where I'll talk about the South just a little bit as like a shared, a monolithic shared experience often, because it's the South, and then people say, 'No you live in Atlanta.' So, I think even other southerners outside of Atlanta have that same view, like this is a big city."

What it means for Atlanta to be "a big city" through the eyes of queer and trans residents of color is that the city is plagued by historical divisions that persist into the present. It is Atlanta's status as a big city that is the source of incredulity when Jerome tries to express a sense of shared southern experience with people in workshops and trainings. The presumption is that life is better for queer and trans people in big cities. If Atlanta is a big city, experiences that queer and trans residents of Atlanta have could not be shared by residents of rural Georgia. Things must be better in Atlanta through the lens of attendees to Jerome's workshops and trainings. George, a white gay man and director of an advocacy organization, spoke to the assumption that queer and trans folks think life is better in Atlanta: "For a lot of folks, it is better in Atlanta, but it's not better in Atlanta for everyone. I mean it really is living in multiple worlds and multiple realities all at the same time. A lot of it does, to no great surprise I don't think, fall along lines of race, class, privilege, educational status, what neighborhood you live in, what are your family connections. So, for a lot of folks it is better in Atlanta, but it's not better in Atlanta for everyone."[66] The reality of multiple worlds in one city was not limited to group differences in race, class privilege, educational status, or neighborhoods people live in, but also impacts the infrastructure of organizing that different groups have been able to do in Atlanta.

Hal spoke about the different experiences that Black gay men and white gay men have had when it comes to trying to build an infrastructure of organizing and community building that will be sustainable for them:

> I think white gay men were able to establish institutions that were sustainable. I think that also had implications for the ability to be resilient and the ability to survive. They were able to establish these institutions that are still sustainable. Then also were places that held their culture, there were places that held norms and the wisdom. I think this is really important, the importance of institutions as a source of resilience and cultural restrictions and those kinds of things. You know even though Black gay men, even though we were able to establish some groups and . . . some community building in the world making amongst ourselves, we didn't have access to the kind of resources that make that kind of institutional sustainability possible.[67]

The narrower resources available for Black gay men to build sustainable infrastructure that would allow them to be resilient in the face of crises like HIV/AIDS did not only not "match the impact of HIV on our communities," they could only be used to respond to HIV in Black male populations, which foreclosed the opportunity for funding to organize in other ways as Black gay men. This availability of funding only to address HIV/AIDS for Black gay men is double-edged. In 2022, the rates of HIV/AIDS in the United States were highest in Atlanta. There is a crisis around HIV/AIDS in Atlanta that largely goes unaddressed in national discourse.[68] At the same time, the availability of funding that connects Black men to that crisis and sees them only through that lens means that Black gay men have a heightened vulnerability not only to HIV/AIDS, but to being pathologized through the very funding mechanisms that are meant to address the public health issues affecting them as Black gay men:

> In Atlanta . . . I think that there were a lot of resources available to . . . Black gay men in the HIV context. There were not these many resources available to convene Black gay men outside of HIV contexts. We are in a post-HIV moment where . . . Black gay men don't experience HIV as central to their existence, and I think it's not to say that it's not significant, it's not to say it's not critical, it doesn't have a huge place. But the place isn't central, like it shouldn't be the starting point. It should be one issue among many. I think those are the kinds of conversations, but I think we just haven't figured out how to talk about that, like how to talk about what place does HIV hold in our collective community building? How do we talk about it, how do we think about it now in 2014?

George, too, who has done HIV/AIDS awareness and prevention activism work for decades, speaks to the gaps between perceptions, realities, and knowledge about the relationship between HIV and Black gay men: "When studies came out last year that looked at the extremely high HIV infection rates amongst young Black gay and bisexual men, it also showed that safer sex practices were more prevalent in Black gay men than in their white or Latino counterparts."[69]

Part of what Hal identified as building infrastructure would have allowed Black gay men to drive the narrative about their lives and experiences from their own perspectives rather than see those narratives co-opted and turned into stories that pathologize them and their sexual desires and practices. The organizing that Hal has done around Black gay men being able to build community, and through building community to build power, looks like this: "I think it just looks like when sort of on one hand often creating our own narrative, so not just being responsive but being able to tell the story about Black gay men in our own way, and sort of like having that be the conversation."[70]

In Atlanta, the type of racialized histories central to the erasures felt and identified by Hal and George remain a part of the spatial architecture but can also be traced through legacies of policy designed to keep formerly enslaved people from accessing opportunities to build wealth and political power. Jerome talks about this as a history that interested Jerome specifically, as someone who had moved to Atlanta but had also lived in many different places.[71] Jerome recounted living in multiple different cities in the United States, growing up in St. Louis, spending some time in the Bay Area, and living in New York City before living in Atlanta. Jerome's sense of what distinguishes Atlanta from some of the cities in other regions of the country in terms of its architecture of racism is that while many cities in the United States might have anti-loitering, anti-panhandling, anti-vagrancy laws "on the books," in Atlanta, "they are enforced":

> They are enforced in Atlanta. So, what that means is . . . you don't see street performers on the train, you don't see them . . . even vendors, street vendors, food trucks, the little ice cream guy. . . . I'm thinking a little, just tiny carts that are pushed around—none of that happens in Atlanta because we have a very strict—what would you call it. . . . I call it anti-entrepreneurial. You need to have a particular, like, startup capital, a particular store front, a particular clientele even to have a business here. You can't just set up a food truck. In fact, because of that we had a thing called Food Truck Park where a bunch of folks who have food trucks have pooled their money and just, they go to an area that's sort of a vacant lot. You don't see them sort of up and down Peach Street like you might on Wall Street.

Jerome ties these contemporary realities of laws policing who is visible in public spaces back to "the making of this city, which was built off the cotton industry."

> Rural areas around Georgia and other parts of the South that were picking cotton were sending it to Atlanta to be manufactured. So, you have a lot of mills . . . Ironically a lot of these old mills are now turned into condos. So, you can see this whole history unplay if you drive around the city. There was a group of Black folks who came to Atlanta after the Civil War to look for work. There were laws set up as part of the Black code, to prohibit them from being in the city at all. So, what the law said was, "You need to have a permit from a former employer or a current employer." Now of course the . . . slave masters are not going to give them a permit. . . . Those are some of the earlier laws that lead us to what we see now in this century around people being creative with finding capital and with finding ways to live.

Jerome understands these laws that criminalize people for being in public space without "permits," "employment," or expendable income (to purchase an apartment in a gentrified former mill space, for instance) as "more of an alibi to criminalize LGBT people and especially folks that are read as such: read as queer, read as trans."

The area where Jerome's organization is situated is not "part of the gayborhood," but it is "in part a haven for folks who live on the street" because "we have the largest housing shelter right here." The shelter houses five hundred people, but people are required to leave at a particular time in the morning: "People who sleep have to leave there by . . . I think 8 A.M. So, once 8 A.M. comes droves of folks who have no home and have no income are just wandering the street either finding income or finding work however they can or maybe trying to keep themselves alive. So, they are interacting with sort of more middle-class and wealthier queer people that are mostly white." According to Jerome, the close vicinity of the LGBT advocacy organization, a large homeless shelter, and a business district of the city result in "all three groups interacting in the same neighborhood."

The most vulnerable of the queer and trans people in the city find themselves in close proximity to residents of the shelter who are not queer or trans, which makes the dynamics in that neighborhood "complicated." Jerome explained that "there are the people that are on the street because of poverty issues . . . then there is also a whole group of trans women that also stay in the shelter who are harassed by the white folks who are both the . . . straight and the gay people, white gay folks who are in this neighborhood." Black trans women being harassed on the street by white gay business owners or residents of the city of Atlanta is not something that features in the story of "Gay-lanta," just like racism in Green Point is not something that would feature in advertisements for Cape Town as the "gay capital of Africa." However, the reality is that the metronormative narrative of the mobile queer or trans individual finding the freedom to be who they are in welcoming big cities alienates some queer and trans people in those cities. With the mobility that comes with wealth and whiteness, it is possible to buy comfort and some level of safety, but without those things even the metronormative narrative of the city's welcome disintegrates for multiply marginalized queer and trans people.

The need to confront homo- and trans-antagonism in a person's context *and* racism, xenophobia, ableism, and classism in LGBT spaces means that home is layered with complications for queer and trans people of color in rural areas *and* in big cities. Discourses that frame cities as the ideal location for queer expression often gloss the architectures in those cities that are built from legacies of colonialism or histories of white supremacy. In Cape Town, Green Point can function as a place where queerness is contained but is also far away from and inaccessible to Black lgbtiq people who live at the periphery of the city and for whom public transport is unreliable, dangerous, or inaccessible. In Atlanta, the reality of the prevalence of HIV/AIDS shapes the opportunities that Black gay men have to build community and political power, even in a city that is closely associated with Black political power and the civil rights struggles for racial justice of the 1960s.

Perceptions of the habitability of queer life are calibrated by a discursive rubric for what counts as the achievement of LGBT(I) rights. Both Cape Town and Atlanta are cities with a reputation for queer habitability. These cities are places that queer and trans folks in other African countries (Cape Town) or in rural areas in Georgia or other parts of the U.S. South (Atlanta) might feel they should go to live comfortably. LGBT(I) advocacy and organizing in places considered both on and off the map of queer habitability, however, reveal the tensions in what it means to do work that centers queer lives.

While Tucker describes Cape Town with assumptions that align with the perspectives of the city center, Free Gender raises serious questions about those norms as norms structured around the dominance of whiteness and class privilege.[72] Even though metronormativity now tells a story of queerness having its home in the city, those either at the city's periphery or consumed by the city's vast inequalities are best positioned to see the city's exclusions. There are also multiple ways to view the rural and peri-urban environments that are the sites of activism for the participants in this book. One of the ways to view these sites is as "home." Home as a place that is off the map of queer habitability is a place as complex as the cities described in this chapter, and work in those out-of-the-way homes is the work to which we now turn.

CHAPTER 6

Queer Organizing in Out-of-the-Way Places

"Patient with a Crisis": Destructive Urgencies and Persistent Commitments

One of the ways metronormative practices become most apparent is through the urgency characteristic of an approach described by Joseph Massad as "missionary."[1] Garth, who is the transgender founder of an organization that works on transgender representation in the media in South Africa, spoke to a dynamic around urgency that Garth found troubling. Garth described urgency as something that justifies the colonizing presence of researchers from one place who "arrive" in another place.[2] Looking out from the metropole in the direction of out-of-the-way places, "the more urgent you appear, the more functional you are."[3] Garth tells another story:

> In fact, that interpretation here is the opposite. It just means that you've never been patient with a crisis that we've been dealing with for beyond our life, before our birth. So, I think there is sometimes those clashes, I mean sometimes I just "delete request" because this is not going to work. Purely from the point of view that there is still this notion that people want to come and do something. So, they want to come and report on or they want to come and do something about something. And I just think, don't you have problems in your own country? . . . But I think the idea of like trying to understand the space here and to respect that space has been very difficult for organizations here because sometimes we have to push back and push back very hard to ask people to back off.

Urgency in Garth's account belies an inability or unwillingness to recognize and commit to confronting historical injustices that have staying power. For Donna Haraway, "staying with the trouble" is necessary to sustain cross-species survival and build more livable futures.[4] This is the type of sustained commitment that will be required to address not only queer and trans antagonism, but the deeply intersecting inequalities Makau Mutua identifies as realities that are ignored and obscured by the prioritization of much human rights work.[5] Working for the transformation of all kinds of inequalities from housing insecurity to hate crimes to addressing the structural causes of poverty takes a kind of commitment that urgency cannot often sustain because it means working against entrenched historical factors from the normalization of capitalist exploitation to the architectures of racial segregation. A view from the periphery foregrounds the persistence (or in Ann Stoler's terms, "durability"[6]) of crises. In queer activist work at the geographical periphery, being "patient with a crisis that we've been dealing with for beyond our life, before our birth" communicates not only an awareness that "crises" are not new, but also a recognition that because violence is ongoing, work against violence requires sustained commitment. This is the kind of sustained commitment that cannot afford a fizzle following the initial urgency.

I want to be clear that in writing critically about urgency I am not suggesting that violence, harm, and death of queer people is not an urgent issue. It is. The organizers I spoke to, however, seem to have a sense that folks who bring a sense of urgency from outside of their contexts to address a single (or even multiple) isolated incident(s) do not understand what it means to have to live in the same community. Survivors of violence have to live in the same community with the family of the perpetrators of that violence and sometimes even the perpetrators of the violence themselves. Addressing violence can take the shape of addressing the aftermath of violence against a person. Garth's organization tells the stories of individuals who have been subjected to violence. In the telling of those stories, there is a hope that the organization's efforts will translate into better community dynamics for queer and trans people in those communities in the future.

Whether responding to or working to prevent violence, any attempt to build safer communities for queer and trans people requires building relationships. Relationships cannot be built with urgency at the center because they require staying with the trouble. Violence against queer people is an urgent issue, and it is one that the people quoted in this chapter respond to, process, grieve, rage against, and go out to address again. However, when arguing against the urgency that characterizes the missionary impulse to do something that does not center the knowledge of those who have been living with and fighting against a problem for a long time, organizers identify a cost associated with outside urgency to their long-term possibilities at home. One specific challenge in trying to resist the urgency of missionary intervention is the reality that outside influences (often in the form of larger organizations) can have access to more resources.[7] This uneven distribution of resources means that the story of "home" is often vulnerable to co-optation by missionary urgency.

Garth also speaks to the way that urgency has implications for how issues affecting lgbtiq people are represented. Because of the spatial politics of sexuality, stories about violence against lgbtiq people also tell a story about the communities in which lgbtiq people, who have experienced violence, live, especially if those places are outside of the metropole. Garth discusses this in relation to Garth's own work:

> Because in most cases the person you're reporting about is deceased. So, you have to kind of find ways around that narrative that speaks to, I guess the dignity of that person. What are those kind of issues, versus a media story that says someone's head was cut off and their genitals were—you know? So, to really extract a sensationalism and to really ... focus on the assertion that this person lived a life that was out, lived a life that was not a secretive life at all and to connect that to like family, community, and context in a sense.

Dehumanizing narratives driven by a tone of urgency create not only a spectacle of a person's death, refusing the person their "dignity," they also create a spectacle out of the person's "family, community, and context." Such spectacles distort the narrative of visibility prioritized by some American thinkers.[8] Though Garth suggests that the individuals memorialized by the work of Garth's organization were living openly and visibly in their communities, the spectacles created suggest that their death is a direct consequence of their visibility. The suggestion that their death was the consequence of visibility obscures the very visible life that the person lived, and instead becomes evidence against the possibility of living visibly in the person's community.

These narratives unfold as if hate crimes do not happen everywhere in the world and as if the person who was killed was the only person living openly, visibly, *queerly* in their context. Though hate crimes target individuals, the effects of a hate crime are not isolated to the individuals who experience them. The impact of violence encompasses the individual *and* the relationships within which that individual is embedded. Work on hate crimes at the level of policy may not reflect those relationships, and the law does not provide the support required to sustain families and communities through the trauma of a hate crime and the process of following it through the courts that is often required in order to pursue some measure of justice. Janet, a white lesbian with an interest in religious support for queer and trans individuals who has been doing LGBT advocacy work in Cape Town for several decades, has helped victims of hate crimes from across South Africa navigate the legal process of court cases.[9] Janet does this sometimes in a professional capacity and sometimes after establishing personal relationships with families who are pursuing cases in the courts:

> These crimes don't only impact on the person that they happen to. They impact on the family, they impact on the LGBT community in that area, and the community at large. It's long work, it's tiring work, it's emotionally draining work, it's expensive work. Although hate crimes, there are funders out there that fund [responses to] hate crimes, they're predominately funding the high-level stuff.... It's not easy to go through the justice system, it's a lengthy process. It's a process that can be extremely intimidating and it's one where you are having, if you've

survived it and not been murdered, you are facing your perpetrator and in our courts your perpetrator is just right on top of you.

If only "high-level stuff" gets funding, the "lengthy process" of supporting a survivor and/or family and community through extensive interactions with the courts is neglected and can become untenable for those who have less access to resources and who may be traumatized by violence or loss. If advocacy remains at the level of policy, it may not "filter down to the police officer behind the desk and the state prosecutor in the court that this is something to be taken seriously." In fact, when advocacy around policy is prioritized over every other kind of advocacy possibility, access to that law and policy, in addition to access to a range of other things, might be neglected.

Many organizers located in out-of-the-way places described sustaining queer communities or beginning their own organizations with their own funding, driven by their conviction that organizing could not be neglected in their communities, whether larger organizations felt the need to invest in them or not. This conviction was one they embodied even at the expense of various strains on their own personal relationships and at significant financial cost to themselves personally, when they had the resources. Kayla, founder of a grassroots organization in the Western Cape in South Africa, speaks to the need for the organization to exist before there was any access to funding:

> You see ... when we started the organization ... it never came to our mind that we have to have money for the organization to survive. The only one thing that was on our mind was to organize ourselves and to show ... our visibility in our communities. That was the first thing, and the second thing was also to say [the] killing of lesbians is not OK. And then, all of that will end ... being ourselves, being part of participating effectively in our society as—openly as gay people. And, also, to—I mean to be just ourselves. That was the main thing. So, for us, when you look at that, it didn't need funding. You see. It just need ourselves to do that. And then again, I think, as we do our work and then we are funded. Oh, OK, sometimes we have to go to ... a court in [another area that would require transport]. And again, it didn't bother us because we know people, they see what we are doing. So, you just write a letter saying that or you make a call, for example, [to individuals who support us and] say, "Hey, guys we are going to court tomorrow, and we don't have transport money to go to court, so we need to go to court." And then they just do that. And then we come back. And then we don't need anyone to give us funding money to go there. And if we say when we go we'll be there for the whole day and, also, we'll need food ... we approach someone else, and say we are also going to need food. And then they give us money for food. And that's all. The following day, nobody is going to harass us [for reports and paperwork] while we are busy doing that.[10]

Kayla describes the work that is necessary in the community as being self-evident. It should not have required funding to "organize ourselves" by "being ourselves."

Even then, just organizing themselves to say that "the killing of lesbians is not OK" did require some material support in order to get them where they needed to go and in order to sustain them with food while they were there.

Even without salaries or administration costs or other kinds of organizational costs, "getting there" required assistance. Kayla recognizes, though, that seeking formal funding places constraints on the organization that would "require them to respond to a funder" instead of doing the work that they "have to do." Remaining independent of funders would allow them to say that "if we say this week we are going to do this, nobody is going to change that." Kayla's organization found a way to sustain themselves by cultivating and relying on an economy of friendships with people who could "see what we were doing" and would offer the kind of support that resulted in "nobody . . . harass[ing] us while we are busy" doing what they themselves needed to do in their community.

When participants at larger organizations not embedded in local communities noted "successes" in their work, it was often because they had taken context seriously in a way that allowed them to engage with a range of actors within the spaces where they were working, rather than seeming to "come in" and "go out, with no follow-up." For example, one participant spoke about a community-based intervention in an area where there had been a hate crime. The strategies for addressing violence in a community setting that Andile, a young Zulu-speaking activist, speaks about employing below are strategies that rely on knowing how power operates in the community.[11] Andile also had to engage authority figures and community members in a way that emphasized their roles *as* community members in order to have a conversation that resulted in reincorporating a traumatized member back into the fabric of that same community:

> There was a lesbian-identifying lady . . . where she was victimized and I think her ex-partner was killed because she was a lesbian and raped and killed. So, my director . . . gave us a task: What can we do [there] for us to change the mindset of the guys there? So, we told her, let's have a soccer tournament since it was 2010, so soccer was very vibrant. So, we said we're gonna have our soccer tournament with the opening game. . . . So, yes, we got a group of guys, they brought in their kids. We said, this should be a group of guys, the soccer players, but it should be their kids coming to play, so they could teach their kids about LGBTI. We got a few drag performers to come to the township, but for us to do that, we first had to engage with the chiefs. So, we came in that way and we workshopped the chiefs. We got them into a tavern, like a bar, which is in the township . . . sat them down, bought them beers, sat them down and we talked about these things, and things changed. Things changed, and mostly we managed . . . and she lives very happy in the same township and so, it's things like that where we changed the people who have the power over people first and talking their language. . . . We have to talk to people in their language and in their level. So, yeah, that's the challenge we've been having, especially [with funders]. [Funders] think that mostly in our developed country, everybody knows English. Yes, the people in

the room might all know English but they might not want to be engaged with you in English because, firstly, you come in as a gay man. Secondly, you're coming in with something which they think it's foreign, and then you're going to be talking it in English.

Not only is the language of funders laden with foreignness, it is also difficult to imagine a line item in a funding organization in New York City being approved as "beer for chiefs." Based on Ryan Thoreson's account of the International Gay and Lesbian Human Rights Commission (IGLHRC)'s relationship with organizations on the African continent, in fact, approval for such a line item would be virtually unimaginable.[12] However, Andile is clear in this example about what facilitated the success of this event and allowed a woman who had been "victimized" to continue to "live very happy in the same township" where the "mindset of the guys there" had "changed." Emphasis on conversations, a focus on building relationships, prioritization of the language that a community itself prefers to speak, and understanding that there are multiple ways to approach a problem resulted in Andile's organization providing a queer person the tools they needed to feel safer in their community.

The foreignness of the language of LGBT(I) rights can also cause miscommunications when its meanings are not established before conversations about those rights are facilitated. David, who works for an international organization in an office based in Johannesburg, speaks to the role that language can play in misunderstandings among audiences who may use a set of vernacular terms to refer to lgbtiq people and concepts that don't register in the colonial English lexicon of LGBT(I) rights language:

> And so, our language is imported, the language of LGBTI is an imported language. If you go into communities and you talk about lesbian, gay, bisexual, transgender, and intersex people, often they have absolutely no idea what you're talking about, but they know they don't want it. And so, my experience recently in Malawi with a group of religious leaders was, you know, we talked for an hour about LGBTI people, how we should respect them, the Bible, all of it. All of it. And one of religious leaders stood up and said, "You know what . . . one day when we encounter these LGBTI people, we will treat them well." So, I then realized that I was talking to them about LGBTI and they were envisaging something really foreign. So, I had to go down to the activists who—none of them were out. So, we had to call a pause to the session, take the activists to a very safe space and say, "I know you have discomfort with it, but what in the local languages are the words to describe lesbians, gay, bisexual, transgender, okay?"
>
> So, most of them I can't pronounce, but it doesn't matter—we'll write them down. I take the flip chart back into the room, and I say, "I really apologize, I got it all wrong, I just assumed that we all understood the same thing. But the people that I'm talking about aren't aliens from another world. They're actually right here. They're in your community. I'm sure they're in your community. They're part of your congregation. And often we refer to them as—" and I just

go through this whole list. And you could see the lights coming on because [they said,] "Oh, that is what you are talking about. Why didn't you say that to begin with?" I said, "Because these words are so negative. They're so loaded," and the religious leaders agreed. It's true. These are very negative words. There are very few of them that are neutral in our language, and so, and so then the connection was made.[13]

In David's example, the foreignness of the language of LGBTI rights compounds the perceived foreignness of lgbtiq people. Though sexual and gender nonconformity pre-exists colonialism, the foreignness of the "the language of LGBTI" stems from it being "an imported language" that undermines the relationship of familiarity that may otherwise exist between lgbtiq family members, neighbors, and friends.[14] Participants speaking about the lack of indigenous localized vernacular to describe sexuality and gender indicated that the colonizing Anglocentrism of LGBT(I) rights language can create a barrier to the translation of their identities and experiences to their local communities. Of course, there is also evidence that indigenous concepts of gender provide creative conceptual frames for communicating sexual and gender diversity better than any English terminology ever could.[15] I argue that the damage of this label of foreignness cannot be underestimated in contexts where the primary objection to sexual and gender nonconformity is in fact its perceived foreignness.

When David insists on bringing the vernacular terminology for sexual and gender nonconformity into the space, the conversation shifts from one that is vague and full of tolerance that may as well have been about "aliens from another world" on the part of the religious leaders to a conversation that directly addresses "negative" and "loaded" terminology in the religious leaders' own language. The familiarity with this terminology allows the conversation to move more meaningfully into a terrain where "they're actually right here"; "they're in your community"; and "they're a part of your congregation." Imagine if the facilitator had not been perceptive enough in that instant to sense that something wasn't translating. Imagine having conversations about high-stakes issues. Imagine that these are issues where misunderstandings can mean the difference between life and death for you and your loved ones. Imagine having those conversations in a language that is not the language that feels like home to you.

While it is possible for organizers without facility in the local language to facilitate these conversations, it would be difficult to argue that those who speak the language most fluently would not be better suited to guide these conversations, negotiating on equal footing with other members of their own communities. In this case, though, the organizer sensed that the imported lesbian, gay, bisexual, transgender, intersex, and queer lexicon was not translating and was able to quickly adapt to the situation, radically altering the impact of the workshop. That crucial decision resulted in a much more valuable conversation without the facilitator even being able to pronounce the words that communicated the meaning necessary to have the conversation in the first place. Engaging local and contextually specific terminology for sexual and gender nonconformity moved the workshop into a meaningful discussion that went beyond the vague and foreign character of the conversation that was introduced by the imported language of LGBTI rights. However, much LGBTI rights work is done in colonial languages. This turns those who are most fluent in indigenous languages into "clients" or "constituents" rather than "experts" or "facilitators" in their own contexts.

Andile, too, spoke to concerns about the efficacy of trainings that aren't conducted in the vernacular of their context.[16] Discussing a training Andile was involved in designing, Andile describes questioning the assumption of English as a universal language for LGBT(I) rights funders, organizations, and constituents:

> It's basically designed for the middle-class person that understands a few things and who is going to school, but me—I had to bring it down, I had to unpack it.... Also, I—as an activist, when we're doing a curriculum for [this training] because I always had to question them. There is no vernacular in all of this.... We really have to start thinking about how we use things. I guess in that way I think I was a pain when it came to doing [the training] and making my input.... But I guess it's issues that we don't talk about and with [the training], we have people from different countries. I'm not saying other countries have been submissive to English, but we find my Zimbabwean counterparts are fine with just using English. So, they said no, we are happy with using English. Vernacular would give a problem, but with me, it's different. In the context of the Eastern Cape, there are proud people, all the people—the Xhosa people, the Zulu people are very proud, and should you come with English, you are no more gonna be talked about, whatever you are going to be saying is not going to be taken into heart. They are not even going to think about what you are saying. It's finished.

Andile presents a complex set of dynamics wherein people "are not even going to think about what you are saying" partly because of the foreignness attached to the subject *and* the language, and partly because you cannot "be taken into heart" if your "being there" means speaking a funder's foreign language, giving a workshop, and then moving on. Andile does take into account the accessibility of English for people in rural areas in many different African countries. However, Andile continued with an example where, during a workshop in a rural area, an elderly woman corrected the spelling of a complicated English word Andile wasn't even sure the audience would know. An issue that goes beyond whether or not audiences *can* speak English in these settings, where presumably conversations about desire, intimacy, sexuality, and other internal complexities are under discussion, is whether they *want* to speak about these things in English.

Context as Epistemology

South African lawyer and human rights activist Sibongile Ndashe grapples with the question of what it means to have one's home defined by a "single story" through an exploration of international advocacy organizations' preoccupation with

"African homophobia."[17] In a world where spatial politics did not define the parameters of queer organizing and funding, it would be possible to see every context as sites of "opportunities and challenges of building and sustaining relationships with other movements, local, regional and international," but that opportunity is foreclosed when one context is framed as on the "pro-" side of Mark Gevisser's "pink line" and another context is framed as on the "anti-" side of that same line.[18] This single story of African homophobia is mobilized to undermine the work of local activists and movements in confronting the homo-antagonism transnational activists do not deny exists and to colonize the space for better-resourced outside organizations to justify their mandate:

> The single story is indeed a dangerous story that makes it easier to impose ready-made solutions in the sea of "nothingness"; it makes it easier to undermine local processes because "they are not happening"; and it makes it easier to co-opt individuals and call them local movements in order to gain a foothold in a country. This gives non-African voices the cover to pursue their own agendas and reinforces homophobic elements within society when they argue that homosexuality is part of a Western agenda. Even with the best intentions, foreign interventions often misunderstand local dynamics and politics and can do much more harm than good. More fundamentally, the attempted foreign leadership of the movement's struggle in Africa subordinates the interests of local community to those of external actors, reinforcing entrenched racial divides within the global movement and drowning progressive voices and positive developments.[19]

Ultimately, the work of transnational organizations interested in LGBT(I) rights has been "built on the premise of saving Africans from Africa."[20]

In other global contexts, Judith Butler and Jasbir Puar critique the complicity of neoliberal discourses of gay rights deployed against racialized populations, particularly in immigration practices designed to close European borders to Muslim immigrants from specific parts of the world, especially the Middle East and North Africa.[21] Massad has done this type of exploration with the closest attention to context in the 2007 book *Desiring Arabs*, which explores the existence of same-sex sexuality *and* the construction of its meaning in relation to Arab concepts of civilization. Civilization is something produced discursively by both colonizing empires and by those asserting their autonomy in the face of colonization. Massad engages with discursive histories that frame sexuality in different ways, depending on what the historical moment demands. These processes do not happen free of other contemporary and historical influences, as Massad's detailed exploration demonstrates.

As a counterpoint to a view of out-of-the-way places as "backward hinterlands," Graeme Reid questions the flexibility of concepts of modernity in geographically marginalized locations.[22] In an ethnography of gay hairstylists and activists in rural South Africa, Reid demonstrates links between gay identities, fashion, and modernity, suggesting that the association between "gay" and "fashion" creates the link with modernity because "hair comes to embody social and political change, a form of identification as Africans." Queer bodies then negotiate their contexts in ways that generate mechanisms to produce "public gay space," where "gays are also seen to embody modernity in the form of the ideals contained in the Constitution and the values of constitutional democracy" in South Africa.[23]

The complexity of such negotiations with context cannot be reduced to the homogeneities structured by a debate that dichotomizes the global and local, only considering "a proliferation of 'Western' concepts of sexual identity in the rest of the world" in distinct opposition to "local forms of sexual self-understanding."[24] In this debate, both binary poles are reified, leaving no room for the flexibility and creativity Reid describes in the negotiations of queer life in an out-of-the-way place that is situated in a globalized world: "Thus, forms of self-identification that draw on national and transnational (global) discourses of gay and lesbian identity are increasingly evoked. Gay activism is also an avant-garde practice in this context—a form of self-styling and presentation of a particular 'modern gay identity' that is also necessary in establishing important networks and even in securing resources. Both are aspects of modernity as imagined in local worlds."[25] Reid's approach demonstrates the ways that "small-town gays" position themselves at the interstices of local and globalized meanings of modernity, negotiating their contexts through "modes of self-styling and performance" that "are ways of conceiving and performing the self as 'modern,' with the incumbent advantages and disadvantages—the positive and negative associations with fashion and the ambivalent place that homosexuality occupies."[26]

Much research about sexualities located in out-of-the-way places in the Global South has been preoccupied with the question of whether globally dominant iterations of "gay" or local and particularized versions of "queerness" are most prevalent.[27] Such investigations miss the point, preventing faithful accounts of the operations of power driving the questions. Writing about the legalization of same-sex marriage in South Africa through the passage of the Civil Union Act of 2006, South African gender and sexualities scholar Jane Bennett is clear that the only way to understand legislative change and responses to it is through attention to a "country-specific set of contestations."[28] "Country-specific" concerns are the more primary and urgent questions identified by Bennett as important to populations within any given country (or, I would argue, state or municipality) wherein "equality for women, redistribution of power based in the privilege of race/class, and the meaning of the link between 'the family' and 'the nation' are in constant contestation."[29]

For instance, country-specific movements toward liberation in South Africa resulted in the decriminalization of same-sex sexuality there and constitutional protections against discrimination for lgbtiq people in 1996.[30] Same-sex sexuality was not decriminalized in the United States until 2003. Constitutional protection of lgbtiq people from discrimination in the United States has not been a reality in the way that it has been in South Africa for several decades.[31] Country-specific processes also resulted in recognition of same-sex marriages in South Africa in 2006. Same-sex marriages were not secured as a nationwide legal right in the United

States until 2015.[32] The historical and contextual unevenness here—the global model of metropolitan gay being an American one, while same-sex sexuality remained criminalized and relationship recognition was resisted for so much longer in the United States than in other countries in the Global North, demonstrates the necessity of considering each context in relation to its country-specific political terrain.[33] Such contradictions also demonstrate how unreliable hegemonic narratives derived from spatial politics are in understanding the specificities of context.

The country-specific process by which same-sex marriage became the primary agenda of the best-funded lesbian and gay rights organizations in the United States was not a spatially neutral process either. As explored by John D'Emilio, the marriage equality "wins" in a few states where same-sex couples already had some access to partnership recognition came at the expense of queer folks in the rest of the country, where anti–same-sex-marriage initiatives had become even more deeply entrenched, making it difficult to advance any other kind of "positive" legislation in relation to LGBT rights.[34] D'Emilio calls the campaign for same-sex marriage in the United States "an unmitigated disaster" because it "created a vast body of *new* anti-gay law."[35] Proponents of the universal subject of rights and champions of Gevisser's pink line might argue that the struggle for marriage equality in the United States could not have been a disaster because it resulted in access to legally recognized marriages for any same-sex couple in the country, regardless of where they live. In fact, proponents of the pink line might even argue that since marriage equality activists won marriage, D'Emilio's chapter in an obscure collection by an independent radical press is irrelevant and "outdated."

However, there are other ways to understand the aftermath of the marriage equality battle. Yes, it is true that marriage is now accessible to same-sex couples in the United States. Legal scholar Nancy Polikoff, though, demonstrates the way that emphasizing marriage at the expense of all other relationship forms severely constricted possibilities for protecting families of all shapes and configurations.[36] None of the family configurations Polikoff discusses are configurations that were protected when the Defense of Marriage Act was law, prohibiting federal recognition of same-sex relationships. Only some of the relationships Polikoff discusses are protected by the change in law that legally recognizes same-sex marriages. This is partly because many of the relationships discussed by Polikoff are not premised on romantic affiliations at all. However, to the people in those relationships, they are each other's most important relationship. Therefore, while same-sex marriage expanded the federal financial, legal, medical, and other benefits available to some families, the designation of "family" was still limited to those in romantic dyads. Gender theorist Judith Butler, too, has been critical of a movement-wide focus on same-sex marriage. Butler's concern is less that the definition of family is narrower under the regime of marriage than that a narrowing of the "sexual field" occurs when marriage is prioritized at the expense of any other (political, sexual, legal, health, and financial) need that queer people might have.

For activists in the U.S. South and in South Africa, the tunnel-vision focus on same-sex marriage advocacy meant that the possibilities for their activism were shaped by the decision of funders and larger organizations to focus on marriage advocacy at the cost of any other political priority. Now that marriage equality has been won, it might be difficult for those who prioritized it as a goal to think about what else could have been accomplished with the time and resources poured into advocating for it. However, for activists working in the U.S. South, what was possible for them was held hostage for decades by the fight for nationwide marriage equality.

A focus on the universal rights of lgbtiq people, including a narrow preoccupation with marriage as *the* measure of queer and trans habitability, that does not embody a critique of patriarchy and other dominant structures of power organizing the societies in which lgbtiq people live risks compounding the vulnerability that queer bodies face. To demonstrate how this compounded vulnerability plays out in practice, Robert Lorway describes "self-empowerment" workshops hosted by the organization with which Lorway spent time in Namibia. The focus of these workshops was often learning about terminology for sexual orientation and gender identity generated in the Global North and encouraging attendees to situate themselves within those meanings, "where precise sexual identities were made to fit discrete categories."[37] Lorway found that while more "open" displays of "gender dissidence heightened erotic tensions between young feminine males and local straight men . . . sexual violence usually accompanied these erotic tensions," a subject that was not addressed through workshops that "treat . . . sexualities in isolation from the local conditions in which they are embedded."[38] As a consequence, "most feminine male youths became acutely aware of how to identify 'antigay discrimination,'" but "when it came to their intimate sexual relationships, these youths were unable to explain, challenge, or politicize the recurring forms of sexual violence they encountered."[39] Lorway's examination of participants' "idioms of desire" led Lorway to question how "LGBT rights interventions" disconnected from the contexts in which LGBTIQ people's experiences are embedded "led them along a path toward their own self-exploitation":

> Here I am referring to the following ironic life trajectories of the Rainbow Youth: the pursuit of females to become "like men" in order to escape sexual violence that leads to the intensification of their oppression at the hands of men: the longings for "real men" by young feminine males who yearn for love, intimacy, and social acceptance that ends in their severe physical and sexual abuse; and the fetishization of foreign and local gay elites by impoverished young males in search of greater social mobility and erotic freedom that results in the loss of their bargaining power during negotiations for safer sex.[40]

When young people discussed economic realities that increased their vulnerability for contracting HIV/AIDS or experiencing multiple kinds of violence that could not be explained through the frame of "antigay discrimination," "there was just no 'space' for it to fit within LGBT rights discourses of autonomy and empowerment."[41] It is clear that those who are already most vulnerable to violence and exploitation pay the cost for such failures of universal LGBT(I) rights logics partly because "an identity politics that privileges notions of autonomy and self-determination elides the exigencies of poverty."[42] Massad is clear about this, too, in this indictment of the "Gay International":

> It is not the Gay International or its upper-class supporters in the Arab diaspora who will be persecuted but rather the poor and nonurban men who practice same-sex contact and who do not identify as homosexual or gay. The so-called passive homosexual whom the Gay International wants to defend against social denigration will find himself in a double bind: first, his sexual desires will be unfulfilled because he will no longer have access to his previously available sexual object choice (i.e., exclusively active partners, as in the interim they will have become heterosexual); and second, he will fall victim to legal and police persecution as well as heightened social denigration as his sexual practice becomes a topic of public discourse that transforms it from a practice into an identity.[43]

While both Lorway and Reid identified ways in which embodying femininity can lead to increased financial and social capital for gay men either through increased opportunity in specific professions (hairstyling in Reid's study) or through association with organizations tied to funding opportunities, "for many of the masculine females" in Lorway's study, "prospects of employment vanish, access to social status diminishes, and family relations become disrupted."[44] Though many of the young lesbians with whom Lorway spoke had experienced "unsafe sex with men" due to a "weighty sense of responsibility to their family" either financially or through "the sense of an obligation to have children . . . the fact that many Namibian lesbians were mothers lay silent in political discussion forums" focusing on LGBT(I) rights and issues.[45] The realities, then, for these lesbian women cannot be extricated from the lives of other women living in their communities. An approach that responds to their needs would pay careful attention to contextual experiences of poverty, vulnerability, and gender inequality, including the reality of being lesbian women who are often mothers and sometimes engaged in sexual experiences with men for various reasons.

Kaitlin Dearham, an LGBT(I) advocate contributing to the *Queer African Reader* from Kenya, reflects on the "professionalisation and institutionalisation" of nongovernmental organizations (NGOs) resulting in those organizations generating "programming [that] did not address [the] reality and challenges" of "low-income" women, whose "increased dependence on family for survival" often meant living with family or very close to neighbors.[46] These living conditions meant that their "behaviour was easily policed" in "the form of verbal harassment, physical violence, and rape."[47] These realities affect not only queer women's mobility in their own communities, but also their ability and interest in participating in the activities of increasingly "professionalized" and "institutionalized" organizations, which can be out of touch with the needs and vulnerabilities of some of their constituents:

It can be difficult for these women to participate in NGO-style workshops and other activities for several reasons. Such activities, which are frequently conducted in English, may be inaccessible for those with little formal education; for women who are living with or married to men, the need to attend a meeting can be difficult to justify; and meetings and other activities are often held downtown or in middle-class neighbourhoods, which can be difficult for lower-income women to access because of travel time (as low-income neighbourhoods and informal settlements are mainly located on the outskirts of Nairobi).[48]

Dearham is clear that in "professionalizing" and "institutionalizing" NGO practices, there are many ways the contexts of socioeconomic marginalization in which some queer women live do not register as LGBTI issues, which further perpetuates their vulnerability.[49] In South Africa, Nonhlanhla Mkhize, Jane Bennett, and Vasu Reddy demonstrate how erasures of class differences among lgbtiq people intersect with histories of racial exclusions, which are implicated in "the ongoing life of apartheid cultures, despite the formal dismantling of apartheid legislation," and which shape access to resources, including the availability of public queer space:

While it would be both absurd and counterfactual to suggest that lesbians racialised as white, for example, do not experience homophobia, gender-based violence or hate speech, it is simultaneously true that dominant cultures of "safe space" for lesbian women tend to exclude all but well-resourced women, the majority of whom are white. Thus, clubs and bars in the "Pink District" of Cape Town are frequented mostly by white people.... White lesbians—as a group (not as individuals)—tend to feel "safer" in their sexual orientation than lesbians of any other racial categorization in South Africa.[50]

Lives inflected by multiple, layered historical and contemporary marginalizations are not lives that can be captured adequately in a model of the universality of rights that erases the specificity of those marginalizations or that characterizes marginality as dictated solely by homophobia or transphobia. Similarly, "solutions" to the problems that lgbtiq people face will not be effective if they are aimed solely at the level of knowing the self, empowering the self, and identifying the self through "workshops on sexual and gender identity, self-esteem, body image, and safer sex."[51] Kagendo Murungi demonstrates the practical implications of public association with LGBTIQ identity labels as part of the African diaspora. Murungi argues for the importance of activists being able to self-identify rather than having to claim a letter of the LGBT acronym by considering *both* the risk activists take on in doing this work in contexts where same-sex sexuality is criminalized *and* the politics of the foreignness that are ascribed to these letters in many African contexts:

If we are to destigmatize the defence of human rights for LGBTI Africans, we must first recognise that any African who does so publicly is immediately marked as a homosexual and directly subjected to social stigmatization. This is certainly true for Africans in Africa, but also for those of us in the diaspora. My three-year tenure as Africa/Middle East/Caribbean regional specialist at the IGLHRC made me the only "Kenyan lesbian" easily associated with lesbian and gay rights via Internet searches, which contributed significantly to my duress at the time. This is clearly not helpful in sustaining an effective sexuality-related human rights movement. Ensuring African autonomy in self-identification is therefore critical to this work, and requires the broad implementation of standards for security and the protection of confidentiality.[52]

Murungi sees opportunities within other movements that have more resonance within African contexts for doing the work of destigmatizing and working toward decriminalizing same-sex sexuality, such as "women's work for gender justice," which "is a fine African tradition."[53]

Mapping (and challenging) the discursive formations of marginality in LGBT(I) rights work and queer theory becomes a project to restore the complex subjectivity of those inhabiting these spaces.[54] This restorative approach, focused on the dignity of inhabitants of a region instead of sensationalizing the most painful things that happen in that region, has the potential to "decolonize" and rethink "center-periphery" relationships in the knowledge produced through queer theoretical frameworks.[55]

Often, the very dynamics that allow people to negotiate some mobility in their contexts are viewed as false consciousness, regressive, or—even worse—inauthentic expressions of who they would *really* be if they were only liberated like the "properly queer" neoliberal subject of rights.[56] In reality, though, queer existences are "nested within a broader social world" and cannot be extricated from that world.[57] No one knows that world and can navigate its context better than those who live in it, which is why Murungi is clear that "people-centred human rights advocacy work that protects freedom of expression should permit and encourage practitioners to frame and promote their work as they see fit."[58]

Self-determination of the kind imagined by Murungi, however, is rarely supported by funding or other kinds of resources. One of the obstacles for organizers working in out-of-the-way places was lack of resources. There is no shortage of ways to use resources that are rarely readily available in peripheralized geographies. Heather, a young white queer-identifying person, identifies the challenge of being located in an out-of-the-way place where "there is never a resource." When national and regional organizations are primarily "based in cities," "there is never a training that's specific to . . . how to do this work here, whether it's about supporting queer, whether it's being like a white anti-racist ally":

So after I started [my organization] I went to Creating Change when I was in Houston, and I mean it was like nothing was applicable to here, you know what I mean? Like—I went to trainings on how to support queer youth in the public schools. All of that stuff—like even the trainings that we have around like queer things, like how to work with queer youth or whatever are so focused on urban settings. Like in rural settings in public schools, youth aren't out a lot of times, right? So, how do you support queer youth when they don't feel safe coming out? ... Some of that has come since founding [my organization] but I think just that a lot of different spaces feel kind of frustrating, that this doesn't relate to where I live, and where I want to be.[59]

Though Heather knows that "there are people who are doing it ... people who've been doing it," attending events hosted by national and regional organizations, hoping for resources that never materialize, leaves Heather with the question: "How the hell do you do it in rural conservative Appalachia?" This question, of how to work in out-of-the-way places without the types of resources that might be more readily available in metropolitan centers, is one that organizations based both in and outside of out-of-the-way places grappled with.

The question of resources can also come in other shapes, too. Sometimes a resource is not perceived as a resource if it feels inaccessible to the constituents the organization is meant to serve, respond to, or support. When organizations are located at a distance from people who might otherwise access them or when the language of the organization is not the one most frequently used by potential constituents, or when constituents don't see a person who looks or sounds like them leading the organization, there can be barriers to accessing the support of those organizations for anyone who might need resources. Nathi, a Black transgender man and founder of an organization in South Africa, spoke about the need to build a new organization from the experience of being located in an organization inaccessible to rural people far from the city in which Black people weren't represented and the work tended to be conducted in English:

> And, you know, I felt like, yeah, this is something that, you know, the province that I come from needs, it needs the organization like this. You know, it was so difficult for people to connect and identify with [the organization I was working with] by that time. First of all, it was impossible for them to get to the organization itself physically. It was also difficult ... to relate to the organization because, sometimes most of the work that I was carrying out was done in English, and the issue of language was a barrier. And again, there was an issue of, you know, I wouldn't say it's a power dynamic, but I would say it's more a racial issue. The face of the organization by that time it was led by mostly white—you know, people who were in power within the organization were mostly white and I was almost the only person who was within the organization and Black, and I thought, maybe let me form something that will make people relate more.[60]

There are a range of things that make advocacy and activism more difficult for queer and trans organizers in out-of-the-way places, and those difficulties cannot be reduced to which side of a metronormatively defined pink line (opposed to or supportive of queer and trans rights) they find themselves on. Funders do not simply disburse funds to organizations and individuals without expectations of how the work organizations and individuals do will be structured. The organizational structures encouraged and sometimes required by funders, the language of reporting to funders, the location of organizations, and challenges around mobility for queer and trans populations combine with homo-/trans-antagonisms in organizers' contexts to exacerbate rather than alleviate perceptions of the foreignness of LGBTI rights demands.

Home Is Where Your Politics Are: "In Addition to Loving It, It's Also Just Home"

As the conversations about language above suggest, narratives that emerge from out-of-the-way places beyond the metropole can involve not only relationships with a community of similarly identified lgbtiq people, but also deep commitments to families and communities of origin. Heather, who has interviewed and documented the lives of rural queer people across the United States, speaks matter-of-factly of motivations that are involved in staying put when all the messages queer people might receive make leaving seem like the better option: "I think people have strong reasons for wanting to stay a lot of times, or they just never thought of leaving ... why would you? They're like—this is home. I think people know that there are all sorts of opportunities they could be having in cities that they don't have in the place that they are staying, but maybe they don't want those opportunities, or they don't want them as much as they wanna be in the place they love. You know what I mean?"[61] LGBTIQ people located in out-of-the-way places suggest that their embeddedness in their local communities is inseparable from their liberation. In other words, their queer existence cannot be treated in isolation from their existence as members of their families and their communities. While the subject of LGBT(I) rights discourse is expected to experience persecution or pride, violence or affirmation *as* a lesbian, gay, bisexual, transgender, intersex, or queer person *because* they are a lesbian, gay, bisexual, transgender, intersex, or queer person, the reality is that individuals are rarely so one-dimensional. Sometimes other relationships, connections, or identities within the space of home take precedence. Heather speaks to how this sometimes works for queer people living in rural areas in the United States:

> But like in rural areas, a lot of people I have interviewed are like yeah, I am gay but like I am also, I work at the chemical plant and work at this and I work at that. You know, I am a farmer, I am a whatever, like I am a Presbyterian, I am whatever, I am a Kentuckian. Like just, I think ... there are other things that people want to talk a lot more than their queerness. Everyone I've interviewed, they were like, yeah, I came out, it was fine, whatever, it was hard, like, it is fine, I have a partner, I am fine and look at my horses, you know.

In this way, the requirement that lgbtiq people claim "rights" through one element of their identity—the element often most important to national and international advocacy organizations, state governments, and other institutions identified by Gevisser as arbiters of the pink line—is actually a reduction of who people are, a simplification of their complexity in order to become legible as the universal subject of LGBT(I) rights. Alternatively, an expansion or a full accounting of their complexity would reveal that lives lived as members of families and communities are also inseparable from the histories in which the conditions of their geographies have been shaped. Often, these are histories of exploitation, struggles over land and resources, and state-enforced racial divisions that continue to have a social and political life of their own, long after formalized policies of racial segregation have been legally dismantled.

Jeanne, a white lesbian who lives in a rural area of the U.S. South, spoke to this during an interview in which I asked about the regional organization that Jeanne co-founded with Cynthia (whom we met in chapter 4), one that focuses on intersectional organizing in the U.S. South. The organization itself is firmly rooted in the South, and Jeanne is embedded in the rural community where Jeanne lives: "You know, you can't live in the South without knowing the raging battles that we have had over land and resources and human rights. . . . We have a very rich and impoverished land." Conditions of geographical marginality go beyond the feeling of isolation so often identified as the most pervasive element of queer existence in out-of-the-way places that it has become a taken-for-granted trope of queer knowledge. Instead, queer populations are embedded in the same conditions of marginality that characterize their home for everyone living there.

Questions of access to a range of material needs (such as water, land, economic stability, educational opportunities) can make life precarious, or at least constrained, for everyone inhabiting peripheralized geographies, "regardless of who [they] are," but also, as the following speaker at a regional LGBTQ-focused conference in the U.S. South describes, *specific* to who they are: "Whether you're a white cis male or you're a black trans woman or a black nonbinary person like me, poverty is why we're oppressed. We're poorer than hetero-cis people. And in the South, we're poorer than everybody else. We have to fight economic violence. That's part of our work as LGBTQ people. That's why I felt we needed living wages as one of the things we're fighting for."[62] This conference participant spoke to the need to incorporate two things in advocacy work. The work should address both the specific needs of lgbtiq people *and* issues that emerge from the needs of the context in which its potential constituents are located. Queer work should be embedded in local communities to make a difference in those communities, and some participants identified ways that queer work is already situated in other progressive work. For Jeanne, queer work that happens in rural American spaces, particularly in the U.S. South, is often embedded in other work rather than in formalized LGBT rights organizations: "And I would say that in some ways probably the majority of queer work that is being done in the South is being done by people who are not in queer organizations. Now people might debate that. But we have so many folks and progressive organizations who do queer work in the reproductive justice and domestic violence, you know, across the board. I think you particularly find rural queers . . . doing the work from wherever they stand."[63] The perspective Jeanne articulates here is very similar to Murungi's feelings about allowing African activists to self-identify rather than conform to the globally hegemonic model of identity-based rights work.[64] Situating queer perspectives in a range of "progressive organizations" allows for the cultivation of coalitional possibilities.

In a discussion of coalitional work between immigration rights organizations and LGBT rights organizations, Karma Chavez discusses how fraught coalition work is, especially when there are issues that impact communities differently and the advocacy priorities for different groups attempting to forge coalitions may conflict with one another.[65] Such coalitions, though, foster an indispensable resilience in the face of conservative political interests that have multiple targets for their oppression. Such coalitions, too, require a kind of commitment and a level of communication between constituencies that may not be required in single-issue-focused organizations. This type of intentional collaboration can build a force that is harder for conservative interests to neutralize. Victor, a white gay organizer with ties to university spaces in two southern states, described doing activist work in multiple settings.[66] Victor moved from Alabama, a state with a reputation for extremely conservative politics, to North Carolina, a state with a reputation for more progressive attitudes and legislative terrain (despite the flashpoints of Amendment 1 and the Bathroom Bill). When interviewed, Victor described both the necessity of coalitional work in more politically conservative spaces and the way that coalitional work felt "much tighter" and "more connected" than work where each organization prioritizes its own set of issues:

> When I came to [North Carolina], the biggest change for me was that, oh no, this group does that, and this group does that. In Alabama you called up Equality Alabama or the LGBT groups from the different colleges. Oh yeah, we were working on women discrimination, and trans inclusion and like a host of things because that's what you did. Like if you went in and got the entrance into the president's office or whatever, you went in with a full spectrum approach because you didn't know when it was going to happen again. Because of that I felt like the communities that I came from in Alabama were much tighter, like I felt more connected.

Organizations that form around common concerns within peripheralized contexts can be critical in building what Jeanne describes as a "political home."[67] HIV/AIDS work, expansion of health care, access to employment and other resources in addition to a range of other issues for people in out-of-the-way places, are important not only for queer people but for all of the people who live there. These may be the points of intervention that matter most for people living in out-of-the-way places, but they are not the type of advocacy work that will result in a place registering as on the map of LGBT rights.

Coalitions Collapse or Coalesce

The question of urgency does not only come up in relation to violence. It also arises in relation to political campaigns that attract interest from those beyond the campaigns' immediate context. The campaign against Amendment 1 in North Carolina is an example of a situation where North Carolina advocates and activists felt that their own efforts had been hijacked by outside interests, something that caused division and tension, and it seemed—in 2015, at least—that it would take a significant amount of time to heal. I want to note something here, which I find important to acknowledge in relation to a discussion of urgency. Before Amendment 1, there was no way to access same-sex marriage in the state of North Carolina. Like any other state that did not have a constitutional ban on same-sex marriage but had not codified a way for same-sex couples to marry or register for domestic partner benefits, same-sex marriage was not a legal possibility in the state. In a sense, nothing was going to change. There would be no change in legal status to same-sex relationships in North Carolina as a result of Amendment 1. This might seem like a technicality when a political battle with your rights at the center is unfolding around you, but it also could be an opportunity to pause to consider the stakes. Legally speaking, the stakes were very low, given that not much was going to change. Politically speaking, the stakes were very high in that the rhetoric about which family formations deserved protections was heated. The "Coalition to Protect All North Carolina Families" (hereafter, "the Coalition") argued one way of thinking about families in North Carolina. The passage of Amendment 1 suggested another way of thinking about families in North Carolina. These competing definitions of family set the terms for the political battle that ensued. When outside interests come in with a sense of urgency and a large budget, a precise sense of what the stakes actually are can be lost. Here is how the battle over Amendment 1 unfolded, according to multiple differently situated activists who spoke to me about it.

The Coalition's campaign against Amendment 1 was described by organizers as a campaign run by an "outsider" from the North and identified near universally by organizers with whom I spoke as a disaster that did damage (beyond the adoption of the ban) by using language that the organizers indicated would not resonate in the state they worked in every day. At the same time, what choice did organizers have but to join an effort to stop a piece of legislation like Amendment 1, legislation that would establish a constitutional ban on same-sex marriage in North Carolina? In several spaces I found myself in in this state, the aftermath of this campaign held trauma and fostered distrust between organizations because it was so badly handled.

One of the first groups I visited was in a rural area of North Carolina. When I asked to connect with them, they invited me for a "queer BBQ."[68] Nowhere near the thirty members of the group that sometimes join them for these BBQs was there, but I was greeted at the home that served as the center of this group by people who described themselves as family to one another. The group was multiracial. The contact who had invited me to the meeting to introduce me to the folks who often housed queer youth needing support was a Black gay man. The house where we met seemed to be the only house populated by a white family in an otherwise Black neighborhood. As I drove through the neighborhood to reach the house, I was conscious of my whiteness in a way I rarely feel in West Virginia, but similar to the way I am conscious of it in many contexts in South Africa. I wasn't sure where I was going. I had, in fact, missed the road.

As I drove through the neighborhood, there were many folks milling about in their yards, some of them taking notice of me, some of them not. It struck me that I was in unfamiliar territory, and I felt nervous about how I might be perceived. In the context of the moment, though, just after the death of Michael Brown, I reminded myself of the threat of my own whiteness as I tried to figure out what to do. At one point, I pulled off of the road. I attempted to orient myself. Another car pulled up and asked me if I needed help. I hadn't wanted to pull into someone's driveway, but it must have been very clear that I was lost. I wasn't sure how to ask the person offering help for directions: "I'm looking for the white lesbian couple that lives near here? I'm on my way to a queer BBQ." I somehow told the driver where I was trying to go, and they led the way. I was again struck by how unwelcome a presence I could be where I found myself lost. At the same time, I was being made to feel welcome and cared for in a way that I would not soon forget. I thought of the many Black men and women who have lost their lives simply asking for help like the help I needed now in an all-white neighborhood, or even just from approaching a house where a white person opened the door.

The house itself served as accommodation for queer youth who did not have housing, even though it was shared already by a family consisting of a married white lesbian couple with five children. We talked late into the evening of things that were and were not related to my research. A few members of the group talked about the way that their expansion of kinship consisting of queer people who were "chosen" family confronts the sense of isolation that sometimes characterizes rural queer life. The only discussion of resources was their general scarcity. The vision described by Kathy, a married white lesbian grassroots community organizer who seemed to be very much at the center of this network of queer kinship, was of grant funding that would provide housing to homeless queer youth and a community center for queer people who don't have other spaces to socialize:

> My wife and I have five children and all of our older kids have—I don't know—antennae, if you will, and watch for and look for other gay kids or kids with gay parents so that they can kind of acclimate here in the rural South. Especially—it's been my experience that I felt like I was the only gay person around and we hear that story over and over again with the other youth and young adults that come into our group and into our circle of friends, so they're always scouting and looking and listening to stories and they're very much allies to the LGBT community. So, we started just opening our homes to folks that wanted to kind of be part of, you know, a bigger community to know that they're not the only gay kid or gay man or gay woman in this rural space and that's where we started and we've just gone from there. Our circle probably includes—what—thirty that identify as LGBT and at least thirty more that are allies thereof.[69]

Two organizers present at the queer BBQ I attended, Kathy and Damien, spoke to the dynamics of community trauma that were a result of what the organizer refers to as "scorched earth syndrome" after Amendment 1.[70] Damien is a Black gay pastor whose interest is in the intersection of religion and sexuality. Damien introduced me to the group in the first place and had this to say—being especially critical of the movement against Amendment 1:

> Human Rights Campaign funneled money into the state, developed this whole ... coalition to protect [the state's] families or something. I forget the name now, and I was with [a regional organization], so they got all these partner organizations that that funnel monies or the funders channel the funds into the campaign—not the community, but the campaign. So that when the campaign is over, you know, the money is gone, too. The people are gone, too.
>
> And they've gone to the next state ... what that leaves is what's called the scorched earth syndrome, you know? So, not only—one of the challenges they're having ... now is we don't wanna participate in another campaign because we know the day after the vote, y'all and your money is leaving our community. Y'all don't care about us. You want our votes, and we're sick of being used to accomplish your agendas. You know? That really is the attitude among a lot of the people. I'm directly connected with ... [someone who] is working that county and her challenge now is these people don't wanna move because they've got that scorched earth syndrome going on with them. So, definitely there is that perception. Rural organizing is not just about getting people to the polls as much as it is about building relationship, building family.

Even with the failure of the Coalition's campaign, at least one rural organizer in attendance at the same gathering felt that the fight against a conservative political element that was "meant to destroy us" resulted not only in increased resilience but in connections that challenged the isolation that often characterizes descriptions of queer rural life:

> I actually have a different perspective. Pre-Amendment 1 fight, I understood the distance and the disconnect of rural communities, but during [the] fight, something happened. We connected. You know? And we started getting a sense of a hope that we did not have before that said, I may not be able to get to [this other small town]. ... I may not be able to get to [another small town], but I know they're there. You know what I'm saying? Before I didn't know they were there. One of the groups that I think about ... I mean, organized on the campus of a fundamentalist Baptist college. But they organized around Amendment 1. When I found out they were there, I was like, what? I grew up in [that town]! This close to my people. You know? And never knew. Well, here we are post-Amendment 1 and [that town] just celebrated its first Pride this year. June 2014. OK, it was a big dinner, but it was Pride.[71]

This grassroots community organizer was not the only one who recognized the power among people who were committed to queer and trans survival and well-being in the state of North Carolina. There are ways to tell the story of Amendment 1 where the failure of the Coalition to keep the amendment from passing is not the most important part of the story. However, thinking about the networks of grassroots and organizational support and accounts of a well-funded campaign run by someone who was not a North Carolinian *does* force an acknowledgment of disparities between how different types of work are funded and whose urgency is deemed deserving of a response.

Some advocates were part of the campaign against Amendment 1 in a way that did emphasize relationship-building, even if that was not the best-funded part of the advocacy work confronting the amendment. Another North Carolinian was the featured speaker at the "Bold Not Broken" Louisiana Queer Conference and told the story of the speaker's own role in the campaign to defeat Amendment 1, emphasizing the importance of relationships that were built during the statewide push against the amendment. The speaker chronicles the way that the issue of the same-sex marriage ban became embedded in coalitional work around progressive issues that was already happening in the state:

> When the LGBT movement in North Carolina called Reverend Barber, he came. He was busy, there is a lot of poverty in our state, there is a lot of racial injustice in our state. The NAACP [National Association for the Advancement of Colored People] have a lot of fish to fry in North Carolina. They are a lot of busy people [but] he came, he stood up against the amendment, his church said, . . . "This is not what we asked for," and Reverend Barber came again and again and again. As did many African American pastors, so any myth that existed out in California—the two biggest counties that voted for the amendment were whitey white white, like crayon okay? We killed that, we destroyed it. If I'm proud of anything in North Carolina, we said, . . . "Black people and LGBT people do not hate each other, myth makers, they do not."[72]

The speaker showed a map of how the political landscape of the state shifted as a result of coalitional organizing relationships and one-on-one conversations with the people who live there. Maps detailing the result of the votes contained several narratives that confronted mainstream media and political stories often used to divide marginalized groups. While a narrative persisted in the talk that the "real divide" was "rural vs. urban," the speaker also showed that there was a positive correlation between counties where the grassroots campaign and the coalition of progressive local organizations invested their energy and "no" votes on Amendment 1. Cynthia, co-founder of a regional organization who is based in the same state where the political battle over Amendment 1 unfolded, confirms this correlation when commenting on the way that Black voters are often portrayed in media representations and homo-antagonistic propaganda dealing with issues of LGBT rights in the United States: "What was amazing is that every single predominantly Black electoral district in the state of North Carolina voted against it. That was the win! Huge! Huge! And because the media wanted to—this basic Black vs. gay . . . they couldn't do it because the numbers weren't there."[73]

Because Reverend Barber, a prominent leader within the NAACP who had built a robust coalition around progressive issues in North Carolina decided to support marriage equality by confronting Amendment 1, the NAACP at the national level then also changed its position on marriage equality, resulting in one of the most predominant national racial justice organizations adopting marriage equality as part of their policy platform. More than one participant suggested that this change in the NAACP position gave President Obama the political space to change sides on marriage equality, which the then-president did very soon after the vote that resulted in the anti–same-sex-marriage amendment becoming part of the constitution in North Carolina.

According to many of the participants in this chapter, it was southern organizing that impacted national perspectives, position, and policy in relation to same-sex marriage. Two things happened at once in this scenario. One state—the last of two remaining states in the southern region not to have a constitutional ban on same-sex marriage—adopted a regressive constitutional ban. At the same time, politics at the national level changed as a result of the coalitional organizing efforts on the ground in that state. A failure—interpreted without a doubt as backward movement in the already backward South—at one level shifted dynamics at the national level in a way that would be interpreted as progressive movement forward in a nation that often likes to tell its story as a steady march of progress toward egalitarianism and inclusion.[74] In this way, the South pays a discursive cost for its contribution to the political shift of the entire nation. Amendment 1—the price paid by North Carolina—became law, and President Obama openly embraced a position supportive of same-sex marriage.

Everywhere I have gone in this process of gathering materials to analyze here, I have found that there is always somewhere that is further off the map, and the place that is further away is where things are framed discursively as always worse for queer life. These "further away" places are simultaneously those places most economically disadvantaged and embedded in the most challenging ways within the legacies and contemporary shapes of colonialisms and racisms. Out-of-the-way places seem necessary in constructing the hegemonic narrative about what LGBT(I) rights are. However, participants' reflections in this chapter indicate that local dynamics complicate the hegemonic narrative in unpredictable and myriad ways.

CHAPTER 7

When Whiteness Gets in the Way

In the waters of lived and embodied resistances to political and economic injustice, what are white people up to? What are the overt troubles we cause? How does one begin to unravel those covert, denied, erased and . . . imagined ways of being human which result from racialisation within contemporary whitenesses?
—Jane Bennett, "'Queer/White' in South Africa"

In this final chapter, I would like to turn to the context of my own home as a way of thinking through the implications of whiteness on LGBT rights advocacy work. I do this not because whiteness is more prevalent in West Virginia—though the state is more densely populated with white people than other states in the U.S. South. I do this, instead, to utilize my own context as an example of these dynamics. I have invested the majority of my life noticing, thinking about, theorizing, and advocating around different issues of justice in the place I call home. In order to remain faithful to the argument at the center of this book, I return to my home—West Virginia, specifically, and Appalachia, more broadly, to read much more closely not the interactions/relationships *between* places but the dynamics/interactions *within* a place. Then, after reflecting on two actions to which I was a witness (in both) and a participant (in a more involved capacity in one), I turn to two powerful engagements with home that I witnessed during the course of my research. One of these is a grassroots organization's approach to navigating overt symbols of white supremacy in the U.S. South, and the other is the use of an indigenous language for organizing purposes even when the global regime of LGBT(I) rights work insists upon the use of colonial languages to do the work of advancing LGBT(I) rights. Finally, I reflect on what it might mean to struggle for queer and trans liberation without the burden of neoliberal discourses of rights as an added layer of politics to navigate.

When it comes to queer and trans advocacy, whiteness has a history of getting in the way.[1] As is true of spaces that are not explicitly queer, whiteness in queer spaces is sometimes allowed to dominate the space through its overbearing presence among those who show up. Queerness, or gender and sexual nonconformity, too, when inhabited in conjunction with whiteness, can act as a "passport beyond whiteness."[2] While this is only one approach to thinking about the intersection of queerness and whiteness employed by South African gender and sexualities scholar Jane Bennett, it is the most relevant to our consideration of whiteness in this chapter. And while Bennett is writing very specifically about the South African context, Bennett also observes that this particular strategy is one that has characterized the intersection of queerness and whiteness at a global scale: "I would argue that this notion that self-identification as gay or lesbian warranted access to a political space free of intersectional accountability lies at the roots of what can be termed 'LGBTI rights' discourse, in northern environments, and I would not be alone here."[3]

Given the permission whiteness grants itself to find a refuge from critical examination, in queerness, whiteness can dominate queer spaces and ideas about who is gay even by going unmentioned. To explore the ways that whiteness "goes without saying" in the contexts under discussion here, I examine two scenes from West Virginia, a state at the heart of Appalachia—a region that extends north beyond the cluster of states I have referred to throughout this book as the U.S. South, but a region with significant geographic and cultural overlap with that region—a state I call home.[4] I do this to make an argument that even (or perhaps *especially*) in spaces dominated by whiteness, discussions of how ideas about race and racism shape what queerness and queer activism look like are critical but largely missing from our perception of who white Appalachians are, except when those conversations are forced by Appalachians of color.

West Virginia is the second-least racially diverse state in the United States.[5] As long as numerically dominant whiteness is allowed to dominate the advocacy and activism efforts on behalf of queer people in Appalachia, the hegemony of whiteness will not be dislodged from such efforts. Queer advocacy work being shaped by whiteness, even in a state with numerically dominant whiteness, is to the detriment of a broader vision of justice that could better serve the most marginalized in our communities. In this examination of whiteness, I also want to demarcate the limits of Mary Gray's concept of familiarity which captured my imagination at the beginning of this process of research, but that, like much else, is limited because of the functioning of white supremacy in so many of the contexts where organizing on behalf of queer people occurs.[6]

The plethora of bills that have been introduced and made into law in state legislatures across the United States seeking to limit the accurate teaching of historical events demonstrates the necessity of evaluating the role of whiteness in every process we examine as scholars.[7] Understanding the exclusions and marginalizations that result in the oppression of those who are targets of racism, sexism, homo-/trans-antagonism, xenophobia, and other forms of intersecting intolerance is a central subject for critical race theorists, feminist theorists, and queer theorists among the bodies of literature I have drawn from in this book. Understanding *how* power is maintained by those who exert disproportionate influence, hold disproportionate power, and control a disproportionate number of resources is a necessary step in dismantling the power dynamics that keep marginalized people oppressed.

There are multiple ways through which power is consolidated by dominant groups. Dominant groups have access to resources, knowledge, and opportunities that are shared with other members of their group.[8] "Bonding," according to Maureen Redding, who reflects on the practice in relation to whiteness and heterosexuality, is behavior (conscious or not) through which members of a dominant group identify one another and conduct themselves in a way that relies on and reinforces shared assumptions of the dominant group, while at the same time shoring up the dominance of that group.[9]

If we continue to organize and advocate under the neoliberal principles that a legacy of rights-based advocacy has left us with, we may not be able to return from a point where whiteness sabotages the well-being of the most marginalized. For national campaigns, such as the campaign to end the prohibition of same-sex marriage, it was possible to rely on the funds of affluent white constituencies to achieve policy goals that could potentially benefit entire queer populations. However, at a local level, and for communities facing multiple overlapping and intersecting oppressions, the wealthy white donor will not provide the answer.

In this chapter, I put two of Crystal Good's short, blog-style pieces about white supremacy in white progressive spaces in conversation with my own ethnographic research, which also unfolded in some of those predominantly white progressive (and some conservative!) spaces. Crystal Good, media entrepreneur and fellow West Virginian, is well known for forcing conversations about both white supremacy and the resulting lack of documentation of Black Appalachian experience in West Virginia. Good has done a range of things to amplify the experience of Black West Virginians, the latest of which is a news media publication called *Black by God* with a statewide distribution network. Good's two pieces, "Appalachia's White Inferiority Pushed Out My Trans, Black Daughter" and "Consuming Blackness in 'Progressive' West Virginia" articulate what goes without saying when whiteness is not addressed in politically progressive but predominantly white spaces.[10]

Approaches to advocating for rights and progressive policy agendas in West Virginia (as elsewhere) can be done in multiple ways. The scene I examine from Elkins, West Virginia, during the campaign advocating for a nondiscrimination policy at the municipal level, suggests that building relationships in order to engage with communities on policy questions that have the potential to become contentious is an effective way to advocate. This approach might utilize the familiarity Gray writes about in *Out in the Country*. The other scene I examine is from Buckhannon, West Virginia, where organizers did not engage in a community-wide conversation but instead hoped to pass a municipal nondiscrimination ordinance inclusive of sexual orientation and gender identity quietly. This suggests that the potential for familiarity to shape politics can just as easily result in or occur through

Redding's conceptualization of whitely bonding. While building relationships (as the Elkins example demonstrates) is critical, bonding among groups of white people with presumably shared racial assumptions gets in the way of white Appalachians disrupting white supremacy and forming meaningful interpersonal and advocacy relationships with Appalachians of color.

Defensive Whiteness

When I first read Crystal Good's 2019 essay "Appalachia's White Inferiority Pushed My Trans, Black Daughter Out," my own gut response was a defensive one. There are progressive white people in West Virginia like the ones Good describes, but I am not one of them, I thought. When Good called white queer folks to affirm and validate Good's daughter's value as an Appalachian and to address the hurtful things that had happened to Good's daughter, I thought, "They didn't call me!" After living with the discomfort of that gut-level response for quite a while, I explored the insecurity and uncertainty that was underlying my own response.

White progressives in Appalachia often do not feel legible in the larger progressive communities in the United States because of our "Appalachianness," and we are not legible in our own geographic context because our politics don't always translate well. The race-and-class-based "trashing" of poor white people (often dismissed as "hillbillies" or "rednecks") that designates them as outside of whiteness, or makes them, as Matt Wray has called it, "not quite white," is important in showing us how the construction of race functions, but, at the same time, subordinated whiteness continues to be structured by, and interested in maintaining, the racial dominance of whiteness.[11] When largely white communities of progressives in Appalachia defend our humanity (of which our whiteness is a part), we also defend our whiteness, even if we do it without saying.[12] This is what reading Crystal Good has taught me.

Good, though, writes about the implications of this dynamic for people of color in Appalachia. For Good's daughter, the consequence of racism and trans-antagonism in LGBT spaces was feeling unwelcome enough that Good's daughter could not imagine a safe and comfortable home in West Virginia.[13] For Good, this dynamic has meant feeling chastised from all sides for bringing up critical conversations about racism where white people say there isn't any.[14]

The invocation of the term "Affrilachian" by poet Frank X Walker speaks to the reality that Appalachian identity is coded as white.[15] Though not all Black Appalachians refer to themselves as Affrilachian, it would not have been necessary to generate a term in the first place to indicate the intersection of racial and regional identity if "Appalachian" had not already been coded white. Good acknowledges this, writing that sometimes it is a relief to be from West Virginia and also be Black. Good makes this reflection in relation to traveling outside of West Virginia, where the hillbilly stereotype would be likely to follow if it had not been already coded white. Being Black means Good can forget about being a hillbilly. Good can forget about being a hillbilly because the term is a racialized stereotype: hillbillies are white.[16] The coding of "Appalachian" or "West Virginian" as white is something that goes unmentioned in most progressive indignation about the hillbilly stereotype. The coding of queer or gay as white is also something that frequently goes unmentioned.[17] As Redding suggests, this "invisibility" of whiteness is attributable to a national paradox around whiteness in the United States. Whiteness is, at the same time, everywhere and nowhere. Or, as Redding writes, "the invisibility of whiteness as whiteness" persists in order to mask the social and cultural dominance of whiteness as (neutral) norms that govern everyone.[18]

Like Good, Neema Avashia has also written, in a memoir of growing up the child of Indian immigrants in southern West Virginia, that whiteness serves as the arbiter of normative identity in the state and in the region.[19] For Avashia, growing up in an Indian family in southern West Virginia, so far from everything that had shaped Avashia's parents' sense of the world, did not only affect Avashia's sense of racial identity. The pervasive whiteness of West Virginia also meant that gender norms were constructed around whiteness—standards of beauty and expectations for femininity governed by whiteness limited Avashia's sense of what possibilities existed in terms of the way gender could be expressed. The white standards of beauty that proliferated in American popular culture during Avashia's youth also contradicted the standards of beauty present in Bollywood films and Indian femininity—the other models for gender expression to which Avashia had access. All of these models were heteronormative ones, and none of them felt comfortable. While Avashia would have had to contend with Avashia's mother's version of femininity wherever in the world the family called home, the hypervisibility of the conflation of beauty and whiteness and the invisibility of whiteness as a construct structuring the standards for that beauty added another layer to Avashia's discomfort with gender and sexuality.

Not only did Avashia have to contend with heteronormativity structuring the expectations that governed gender norms, Avashia also had to contend with being outside of the whiteness structuring those norms in southern West Virginia. Even as an adult, working among other Appalachian writers, questions and contradictions complicate Avashia's sense of whether or not to call Appalachia home. Seeing so many Appalachian writers with ancestry dating back centuries in the region, Avashia asks questions about how many generations of family and what kinds of connections to the land are required to be able to lay claim to an Appalachian identity. Displacement and alienation are very much a part of Avashia's queer Appalachian identity, and Avashia, too, demonstrates the way that "hillbilly" is coded as white.

Good writes, and I have seen, how white progressive organizers themselves serve as gatekeepers "guarding" Appalachian identity.[20] We know and expect some white people to play that role. The "Trump Country" narrative predicts that those gatekeepers voted for Donald Trump. However, what white progressives and white conservatives in Appalachia share over and above our indignation at being seen as backward or uneducated is our whiteness. This shared whiteness is rarely discussed by progressive organizers, who, I sense, prefer to be seen as different kinds of white people than the white people who voted for Trump. However, as Aida Hurtado reminds us, "The lack of disclosure by those with power maintains their privilege."[21]

The scenes I put into conversation with Good's critique of white progressive spaces in Appalachia below demonstrate a standoff between white people with different political views, "be they white women who claim a feminist identity, or white gay men, or just poor hard working white people who know the economic struggle; the struggle that is most of West Virginia."[22]

A Tale of Two Towns

Both the towns of Elkins and Buckhannon attempted to adopt policies to prohibit discrimination against people based on sexual orientation and gender identity in their municipalities.[23] The towns are similar in size and situated in adjacent counties. Both currently have adopted resolutions, a less far-reaching municipal policy that applies to hiring and firing by city agencies but not to private businesses in the towns, to prohibit discrimination against people based on sexual orientation.[24]

In negotiations over the meaning of "home," spatial politics shaped the discursive exchanges in the room. Just as in one rural North Carolina county, protesters referenced the city of Asheville as "the gathering of the gays" to express their idea of what their county should not be (see chapter 4), local knowledge of spatial relations were called upon to communicate ideas about who belongs where, especially when the subject of nondiscrimination or marriage or bathrooms came up in municipal proceedings. A former Buckhannon City Council member who was invited to Elkins in 2015 to discuss adopting a nondiscrimination resolution referenced the narrative of spatial politics through which both towns are legible: "The feedback we received is all extremely positive from students at the college, from people in our community or people around the state. Buckhannon isn't always first to things, OK? I would have assumed that a progressive and positive and creative and unified community like Elkins, West Virginia, would have gotten to this before us."[25] The speaker clearly feels that this comparison with another town one county away should say something about how Elkins City Council should proceed with its decision on the nondiscrimination resolution.

The towns pursued a very similar policy agenda, and both experienced the adoption of the same policy, virtually verbatim. The proposed policies, however, generated very different responses from community members, and I suggest here that this is because those who wanted to adopt the policy in one town (Buckhannon) attempted to adopt the policy in secret, hoping no one would notice, and those who wanted to adopt the policy in the other town (Elkins) mobilized a community-wide campaign to appeal to the city council to adopt the policy. I suggest that while the adoption of the policy was the same in both instances, the approaches accomplished something radically different in terms of building relationships. I would argue that the work of making the world safer for queer people happens at the level of these relationships and community-wide struggles over norm-building. After introducing these scenes, I explore the dynamics of whiteness in relation to how those relationships are built. I do this to suggest that building relationships is not enough if those relationships solidify the dominance of whiteness in their attempt to advance LGBT equality.

I do not want to suggest that these outcomes would have been the same under any circumstances. I understand that fluctuating dynamics of political power, political courage, and changes in the weather could have resulted in other outcomes. The outcome in the Elkins example could ultimately have been different had a random passerby not walked into the city council proceedings, been perceived as an ally to the conservative interest in preventing the resolution, been (for that reason!) allowed to speak, and then become the last word on the topic.[26] The outcome in the Elkins example could also have been different had the mayor allowed the council to go into executive session, dismissing the crowd that had gathered to watch the proceedings so that the council would have been able to deliberate in private. The outcome in the Elkins example could also have been different if the mayor had refused to moderate the session or vote in the proceedings.[27] Any change in these factors could have changed the outcome of the policy enacted by the city council. So, my suggestion is not that the policy outcomes are indicative of something that "worked" in one case and did not "work" in the other—both of the policy outcomes were the same. My interest, in this analysis, is not policy outcomes at all.

I suggest, instead, that the dynamics of the relationships established through one organizing strategy were radically different than the dynamics of the relationships established through the other strategy. I want to suggest that these relationships are valued by people living in their communities but have been overlooked by national and (often) state organizations. It is that dynamic—the relationships within a community and whether or not those relationships matter to a campaign—that I argue *do matter* in thinking about home as the place where we invest our political energy. I want to explore what it would mean to build those relationships not through the bonding of white people as people with whiteness in common but in a way that would subvert the establishment of whiteness as a nearly homogenous dynamic of Appalachia by conservative and progressive white people alike.[28]

Buckhannon

In 2019, the town of Buckhannon, where I am employed as a college professor, tried to quietly pass a nondiscrimination ordinance that was inclusive of sexual orientation and gender identity. In American states where these protections did not exist at the state level, it has been legal to deny employment to lgbtiq people because of their sexual orientation and/or gender identity. That changed with a Supreme Court decision in 2020 dictating that Title VII employment nondiscrimination protections extend to lgbtiq citizens.[29] In 2013, Buckhannon had become the fifth West Virginia city to pass a nondiscrimination resolution inclusive of sexual orientation. However, in 2019 the mayor was interested in upgrading that resolution to an ordinance. The initial 2013 resolution was passed quietly and without much fuss. In 2013, "no one spoke out in opposition to the resolution."[30]

The former Buckhannon City Council member quoted above describes the passage of the nondiscrimination resolution through the council in 2013:

> Now we bring a lot of things to city council and about everything we brought the city council was divisive, including but not limited to urban deer hunting—still tabled to this day—engine break annoyance ordinances, changing our red lights to four-way stops signs—that's my fault—I'm still apologizing for that to this day. But these are the type of things that we brought and everyone would have an opinion. Everyone would take a very strong opinion on . . . how we took this issue up. When we brought this [resolution], it named the city [as] a place they would not have discrimination based on sexual orientation and then encouraging other businesses to do the same. There was no debate. There was no debate, it was unlike anything we brought to Buckhannon City Council because almost anything people were forming their opinions about was delayed for meetings and meetings. There were a couple of questions initially like, "Are you talking about marriage or something?" and we would go, "No, this is just someone's basic right to work and live somewhere and to have the same inalienable rights that every other human being deserves." We would go, OK. The state's already weighed in on marriage, so if anybody's not sure. As we progressed through it, we went through a first reading and a second reading and the ordinance passed unanimously among our council. Not much ever passes unanimously among the Buckhannon City Council; it is a smaller council than this is. So, there is a little less room for those differences of opinion. After that [resolution] passed, save for a couple of the anonymous posters, . . . we didn't get any feedback in the meetings that was negative—in fact, quite the opposite.

In 2019, however, it was not the case that there was no debate. In Buckhannon, the strategy for adopting the ordinance was to put it on the agenda and quietly pass it without much involvement from residents of the city. This did not go well. In 2019, different individuals were on the council. A different mayor was presiding. Same-sex marriage, the subject of the council's only reservation in 2013, was legal in all parts of the United States, including Buckhannon. Donald Trump had been elected president with overwhelming support from West Virginia and overwhelming support from Upshur County, where Buckhannon is located. A fourteen-year-old Caiden Cowger had created public furor over his very public anti-gay remarks.[31] Cowger had subsequently launched his own media platform as a conservative commentator with ties to conservative religious communities in Buckhannon.

Email correspondence from the statewide LGBT advocacy organization Fairness WV sent on January 2, 2019, announced an important decision being taken by Buckhannon City Council on January 3. The gist of the email was that the mayor was "firmly on our side"; the organization expected "the vote to be close" and "our opponents to turn out" and use "discredited fear-mongering tactics." Recipients of the form email were encouraged to show up to tell the city council how important it was for Buckhannon to become the "12th city in West Virginia to protect its LGBTQ citizens from discrimination in housing, employment, and public accommodations." We were instructed to counter the "false narrative" of our neighbors and co-workers, and we were instructed to "do so respectfully."

In January 2019, that city council meeting lasted several hours and involved commentary from several religious figures and organizations, including Caiden Cowger, who claimed not to hate queer people but demanded that their "freedom" to have differences of opinions be legally protected in the right to discriminate, should they wish to. Whereas some other towns have been able to claim that most of the opposition to their LGBT nondiscrimination ordinance was brought in from outside of town, Buckhannon had raised its own anti-queer lightning rod of a conservative personality, who was present with cameras in tow throughout the duration of the meeting. It was Cowger's people who were organized at the Buckhannon City Council meeting. Supporters of the ordinance were scattered and disorganized, without a clear appeal.

In the meeting it was clear that council members had difficulty understanding how sexual orientation worked as a part of identity. Members were uncomfortable with the conflation of race and sexual orientation as categories that deserved equal protection under the law. Several times, members spoke to their uncertainty that sexual orientation should have the same protection from discrimination that racial identity has according to federal nondiscrimination law. (It was possible to hear the wheels turning as council members wondered, without receiving clarity on this issue: "Are you saying that being gay is like being Black?" The suggestion that Black people do not experience discrimination in Buckhannon is an incredibly debatable one, but that was not the issue up for discussion that January evening.)

Very few openly queer people spoke at the meeting, though several allied straight people pled their case in front of the council. For the most part, cisgender straight people spoke about the hardship of being queer in a place like Buckhannon. In order for us to be worthy of protection, it seemed we had to have a painful, unenviable existence—the kind of existence no one would *choose*. Council members themselves, who spoke at great length about their "no" votes, also seemed confused about the necessity of the ordinance. Same-sex marriage had been won—what else were lgbtiq people demanding and wanting? Anyone who knew anything about queer history could hear the echo of the "special interest" and "special rights" argument generated to discredit queer claims to humanity and assertions of dignity in the 1980s. The fulfilment of nationally projected dreams of the "gay agenda" had come in the form of a Supreme Court judgment in 2015, and straight cisgender people like the ones on Buckhannon City Council had been able to do nothing about it, even if they had wanted to. I got the sense that some of them had wanted to. Cisgender straight people framed themselves as persecuted in this environment. Cisgender straight allies framed themselves as persecuted because of their allyship with us—their queer neighbors, co-workers, and friends.

The city council meeting was not the only controversy related to sexual orientation in Buckhannon in 2019. Later that year, the Upshur County Public Library generated controversy over a children's book in its collection featuring two princes who fall in love with each other. After objections over the book, the library wasn't sure whether the book should be removed from circulation or placed in the adult section. The suggestion to put the story in the adult section was also a suggestion that some children's books—those with lgbtiq characters—are less appropriate for children than others. The city council meeting, however, had set a precedent for what confrontations over sexual orientation and freedom of religion would look like in Buckhannon. The exchanges became uglier and uglier.

Elkins

In 2015, Elkins City Council had a nondiscrimination resolution inclusive of sexual orientation and gender identity on their agenda. One particular council member was vehemently opposed to the original proposal of a nondiscrimination ordinance and, over the course of several months, used the council position to stall proceedings in the interest of removing it from the council's consideration altogether. That council member was ultimately successful in modifying the demand for an ordinance to a resolution on the council's agenda. However, the member was unable to derail the resolution from reaching a public discussion and subsequent vote.

What began as a proposed ordinance had become a more limited resolution by the time it reached the agenda, which meant that if advocates of an ordinance wanted to pursue it, they would have to present it to the council twice, just like what had happened in Buckhannon. On March 4, Fairness WV again sent a blast email to its supporters in the state to let people know that "opposition is building in Elkins" in preparation for the March 5 meeting of the city council to vote on the anti-discrimination resolution. That particular meeting was postponed to March 19 because of heavy snow.

The March 19 meeting followed months and months of community organizing by a grassroots group (which I was a member of) that eventually called themselves "Fairness Elkins." The group was organized by a young college student who kept meticulous track of communication and strategy, and served as a point person for liaising with the city council and the group as a whole, but the effort was collective. Because the young person was not out to their family at that time, others in the group served as representatives of the organization to the media and/or other outside entities interested in what Fairness Elkins was doing. Individuals in the group offered up spaces in their businesses and churches where the group could meet. Others prepared testimonies that they would offer to the city council during the meeting. The statewide advocacy organization, Fairness WV, was also involved in amplifying our efforts.

Personal relationships resulted in the nondiscrimination resolution reaching a vote at Elkins City Council on March 19. In addition to the council members who were hostile to any discussion of nondiscrimination policies inclusive of sexual orientation and gender identity, a few council members were actively supportive of the measure. Some other council members were supportive of the spirit of the resolution but were concerned about the legal ramifications for a small city with a small budget, should businesses or individuals sue the city over a policy that did not exist at the state level or the federal level. These council members were the ones we had in mind as we mobilized the city to support the policy. The nonexistence of these policies at the state and federal level was, after all, the point of asking municipalities to make these changes on their own. As many activists shared with me during my fieldwork collecting research for this book, it is often easier in the U.S. South to accomplish things at the level of individual schools, cities, or counties because while state governments in the region tend to lean heavily conservative, the professional, political, and social networks that exist in smaller communities are more receptive to progressive policy change. Asking municipalities to embrace nondiscrimination in relation to sexual orientation and gender identity was meant to be a strategy that would demonstrate to state and federal lawmakers that this was something the populations they governed endorsed.

After the delay in placing the prospective ordinance on the council's agenda, we received correspondence from our contacts at Fairness WV suggesting that we should send a message to the city council that we expected to see the ordinance on the agenda. They sent us a list of several action items they thought we should take in order to get the council's attention and force their hand. We counted our votes. If we could not get the ordinance on the agenda, we agreed that it would make sense to "send a message" to the city council at a future meeting. However, we did not feel we were at that point. After we communicated that we had a few avenues we wanted to exhaust before taking a confrontational approach, we did not receive further assistance with strategy from Fairness WV, though we wrote to them to try to strategize, since they were a better-resourced statewide organization more experienced with advocacy. They did, however, send an email blast to their followers the day before the Elkins City Council meeting, prompting people to show up to a meeting Fairness Elkins had been preparing for months.

Rather than do what had happened in Buckhannon once our policy vote was delayed—keeping quiet, hoping for the best, allowing only our opposition the opportunity to mobilize—we developed a strategy. We would continue coordinating with the supportive members of the council, but at the same time, we would collect municipality-wide support for the resolution. We followed every contact we had in order to collect signed statements of support and letters indicating the same. We approached business owners (because of the specific nature of the policy), religious leaders (because we anticipated our most robust opposition coming from them), and other people known community-wide and asked them to sign statements supporting the adoption of the resolution by the city. We asked members of the group to write their own letters about what the nondiscrimination resolution would mean to them. The young person coordinating the campaign presented a collection of all of these statements and letters to each council member, who had ample time to peruse what their constituents in the city of Elkins and residents in some of the surrounding areas of Randolph County had to say, if they chose to look at the materials we gave them.

Given the wide-ranging support from business owners that we received in Elkins in the form of a collection of over seventy signed statements of support, I felt that the policy would ultimately be primarily symbolic. Many businesses in the town signed declarations of support and put the "Fairness Elkins" sticker (a sign of visible support) in their windows; some businesses still had that sticker in their window more than five years later. By "symbolic," I do not mean to suggest that discrimination does not happen in Elkins. Rather, if businesses were not opposed to this measure, who *could* be opposed, since the measure would affect the hiring/firing policies of the municipality and businesses only? We know that even the legally outlawed kinds of discrimination continue to happen, but it was heartening to see business owner after business owner nonchalantly and matter-of-factly endorse a policy that they seemed to tacitly agree to abide by.[32] We began to read these as pledges against discrimination, and given the limitations of the law in addressing things like employment discrimination, perhaps pledges against discrimination on the part of business owners themselves might be more valuable in attempting to shape community norms and values than policies banning discrimination that would have to be actively pursued for redress *after* a person experienced discrimination.[33]

The qualitative difference between what happened in Elkins in 2015 and what happened in Buckhannon in 2019 is that in Elkins we asked, "What kind of community is this?" and we received documentation in the form of pledges of support that affirmed our presence in our community. If Buckhannon City Council had asked what kind of community Buckhannon was on the evening of their vote, it would have seemed that the answer was a community devoid of a vocal queer population where cisgender straight people were more concerned with protecting their ability to discriminate, should they want to do that, than embracing the queer and transgender people who live and work there.

The Limits of Familiarity

Most of the conversations in these examples were conversations between white people. The same is not true throughout this book. Demographically, Cape Town and Elkins are very different. The same is true of many of the southern states and cities I visited. The reason I reflect on this dynamic in Elkins and Buckhannon is because these are two of the places where I spend more time than any other place in the world. I do not suggest that the same strategies that may or may not work in Elkins will work in Atlanta. I do not suggest that the same strategies that work in Atlanta will work in Cape Town. Yet, something about the way I feel closer to home in the township of Khayelitsha than I do in New York City tells me that there *are* resonances between peripheralized spaces, as there are often resonances between metropolitan spaces. Additionally, the point about whiteness I make here is one that is relevant to other power structures and understanding *how* bonding works in a way that consolidates power dynamics within and among dominant groups. The critique of the limits of familiarity I offer below is transferrable, but it is specific attention to context that will demonstrate how that critique transfers.

The conversations that tended to happen between white people in Buckhannon and Elkins were sometimes conversations between people who knew one another because Buckhannon and Elkins are relatively small towns with relatively small populations. The networking that happened in these examples happened between people who were politically connected to one another. The networking that happened in these small towns, then, happened between people who shared a geographic space, who understood themselves as residents in the same town, and who were overwhelmingly part of the same racial categorization. What does it mean to let the whiteness of these spaces—not the spaces of Buckhannon or of Elkins or of West Virginia, but the spaces of the city council meetings—go unremarked?

In a study of the lives of queer youth in Kentucky, *Out in the Country*, Mary Gray employs the concept of familiarity to discuss the way that queer youth navigate their surroundings. Part of what Gray's study does is to interpret rural queer life ethnographically. Gray's work begins to dismantle the metronormative assumptions underpinning narratives about what it means to be queer. Part of this dismantling has to do with the way Gray understands familiarity as a mechanism. While the imaginary of the metropole projects rural spaces as suffocating and inhospitable to queer life because they lack the signature anonymity that is supposed to make the city the queerest of destinations, Gray demonstrates how the knowledge that residents of rural areas and small towns have of their contexts allows them to navigate those contexts.

The importance of familiarity would be difficult to overemphasize in my research as well, especially at the community level. What I want to explore in thinking about the dynamics of whiteness, however, is the *limits* of familiarity. The context examined by Gray is a context that is racially divided and where a disproportionate number of residents *and* those who are making political decisions for communities are white. Everyone, however, is not white—just like everyone, in those contexts is not straight or cisgender. Gray seems to accept that there are fewer people of color in the context and leave it at that. What, however, is the effect of this near-homogeneity on people of color *who are there*, regardless of whether they make up 3 percent of the population or 30 percent? What do we miss when we accept near-homogeneity *as* homogeneity?

Familiarity, for instance, could be understood differently through the lens offered by Redding's conceptualization of bonding as a mechanism through which white supremacy and heteronormativity are maintained and reproduced. When thinking from Appalachia, I'm interested in thinking through the interplay between what Gray calls familiarity and what Redding calls bonding. In March 2021,

Crystal Good wrote about the intersecting marginalizations that shape the experiences of communities of color in West Virginia, *especially* among progressive white West Virginians. Good was writing about white women who dominate social justice–oriented nonprofit organizations in West Virginia. Good's work is an indictment of the white-dominated nonprofit industrial complex in West Virginia—a state we both call home. What is true of the organizations critiqued by Good is true of organizations whose purpose is to defend the rights of lgbtiq West Virginians. At the heart of what Good argues is that the bonding that occurs between the white people who lead social justice organizations in West Virginia—whether that happens at a gala featuring sushi served from a human body (as in the case Good writes about) or at a gala where attendees pay for an expensive ticket to drink champagne in celebration of marriage equality (which I have attended)—excludes some of the West Virginians who would see the issues facing the state without the cataracts of whiteness that obscure the vision of white-led organizations. These events—expensive, exclusive, culturally specific, designed with donors as their audience—make it clear who should be communicating on behalf of the organizations and who is there on a donated ticket. These events are spectacles of white bonding, even when they feature people of color as presenters or award winners.[34]

In order to do better work at the intersection of racial, gender, queer, and spatial justice, it is necessary for those of us who are white or straight or belong to some other dominant category to be willing to leverage our familiarity with the decision makers who hold our rights hostage *in the interest of* what is best for those who are most marginalized in our communities. This has long been the interest of thinking intersectionally. However, there are major barriers between acknowledging whiteness as a *way things are* and *leveraging* familiarity in the interest of those who are marginalized *by* whiteness.

What does it look like for a state like West Virginia, where the racial demographics of the state are 92.8 percent white, according to 2022 population estimates provided by U.S. Census data, to put racial justice at the center of its measures for well-being in the state?[35] This is a question that Crystal Good presses us to answer by reminding us that "where there's a health disparity or a social problem in West Virginia, [Black West Virginians] are likely to be caught in the crosshairs."[36]

Another Way

I want to preface my call for another way of thinking and working on the spatial politics of sexuality with the recognition that organizations like the STAY (Stay Together Appalachian Youth) Project are *already* bringing other ways of organizing and being into existence. There are organizations focused on mutual aid, prison abolition, racial justice, and economic justice through an intersectional lens throughout Appalachia. Such organizations privilege the perspective that white supremacy and capitalism are the primary forces of destruction with which we, as

Appalachians (and Americans), need to reckon. With that said, we are beyond the place where reflecting on our own whiteness in progressive spaces dominated by white people will do much good beyond recentering our own identities and experiences. Patricia Hill Collins writes about the limits of consciousness-raising and asks whether or not "the personal is still political." My interpretation of what Collins concludes when answering that question is that white people sitting in a room discussing our/their own experiences rather than leveraging our/their connections and relationships politically speaking risks becoming a kind of self-indulgence.

It is clear that a mainstream advocacy approach not only has limited effects; it also speaks for a limited constituency. By not mentioning the whiteness of the people in the room, what happened in Buckhannon happens on a larger scale. White lawmakers and other leaders who influence the political landscape on which our lives unfold *see* white people advocating for queer inclusion, *hear* white people advocating for queer inclusion, and conflate queer with white. There is a problem with mainstream media representation of queer as white historically that has reinforced the perception of queerness as white, queerness as affluence, queerness as demanding "special" rights and privileges that "not quite white" Appalachians are likely to not have themselves. Whiteness does not need to be spoken to influence a room.[37] When whiteness is what is left unsaid, queer people of color are even more vulnerable to harassment in geographic spaces dominated (numerically or financially) by whiteness because they live at the intersection of homo-/trans-antagonism and racism. This makes it even more imperative for folks who are working toward queer futures to work against the unsaid assumptions about queerness, whiteness, and location.

What I watched unfold in Elkins over the course of several months was incredible. A community of people took ownership of the narrative in their/our town, and while the city's policies did not radically shift as a result, the narrative about queer people in that town, who we are and how we live; the consistency of our hopes and dreams; and our integration into the fabric of the town and the county are on the public record. The presence of queer people in the town of Elkins expressed itself through the intentional building of relationships around a piece of policy that was the initial goal of the establishment of Fairness Elkins. Though there were people who spoke in favor of an ordinance shielding queer people from discrimination in Buckhannon, there was not a visible community of people who had coordinated themselves to support this issue. Individuals, most of whom were cisgender and straight, spoke at the meeting as individuals. There was no narrative at the Buckhannon meeting about Buckhannon being a home to queer people, a place where queer people longed to belong, a place where queer people desired relationships with those around them. This was, to me, the primary difference between what happened at the city council meeting in Elkins in 2015 and the city council meeting in Buckhannon in 2019.

What I am arguing at this book's conclusion requires a synchrony between self-determination and self-reflection. When we engage with lawmakers or community leaders or any other audience, we need to be sure that the relationships we build do not come at the expense of racial justice or multiply marginalized queer people. We need to build relationships that will work toward sustaining the least resourced queer and trans folks instead of reinforcing the hegemony of the most resourced. Building relationships needs to be done intentionally. Who we are in relationship with shapes how we do advocacy and activism. Relationships shape advocacy and activism in ways that are not always or even usually accounted for in considering what demands are generated and how those demands are pursued. Just like Fairness Elkins maintained our autonomy from Fairness WV when the latter suggested different next steps than the steps we ourselves wanted to take, community autonomy is crucial to navigating relationships and implementing strategy, and it is crucial to pursuing demands at the community level (and beyond). However, reflecting on the shape that autonomy takes and who benefits from it is equally important. The following gestures toward accountable autonomy come from the U.S. South and South Africa, and are, I believe, fitting examples with which to end this book. Each example points toward possibilities for insisting on a relationship with the space in which queer and trans people live. Symbols of identity linked to place (like the Confederate flag in the South) and language (like isiXhosa in South Africa) provide challenges when translating one's local reality into the global story of rights. They also provide opportunities, however. Engaging the challenges and opportunities posed by elements that are distinctly local is one way to reject the alienation of metronormativity and do work that values home as a space for the living of queer life. My final reflection in the book, following these examples, is one that applies the framework of self-determination and self-accountability to my own experience, as the person who was drawn to questions about the spatial politics of sexuality. I think about difficult discourses, how to live with them, and what I take away from the work I have done that has become this book.

Context as Ontology

While there are many examples from the time I spent with organizers in so many different contexts that gesture toward possibilities beyond what hegemonic discourses of rights condition us to imagine, I want to offer one example from each context that, to me, demonstrates how deeply embedded the work of expanding possibilities is in the context of the locations in which it is rooted. In the U.S. South context, the dominance of whiteness in the geographic context and in the structure of hegemonic discourses is a barrier that activists must negotiate. In the South African context, a language outside of the hegemonic discourses of rights provides an opportunity or resource for doing community work, even as it means that funders are without a mechanism for translation in understanding the work. On the one hand, the work resists colonization. On the other hand, it remains largely unfunded.

These examples demonstrate the work that it takes to dismantle the hegemonic whiteness structuring LGBT(I) advocacy work. Donna Haraway's framework of "staying with the trouble" requires engagement with contexts and relationships that are uncomfortable, messy, necessary, and transformative. Staying with the trouble may be one of the only ways to confront whiteness and to ward off colonization of the work. Below is a reflection about two organizations' work of staying with the trouble in two different ways. I observed a grassroots trans-focused organization in the U.S. South putting in the work that it takes to address issues with intentional and consistent interventions. Similarly, I spent a lot of time with Free Gender, and I reflect here on how they use language in their work in Khayelitsha, a township in Cape Town. The gestures I sketch here are based on my own ethnographic observations drawn from time spent with each organization.

The organization in the U.S. South began as a few people meeting socially and wanting to create the space for other transgender and gender-nonconforming people to do the same. The group very quickly grew into a membership of several hundred people, participating in a hybrid model of online and in-person community. This group considers themselves a family, and they work very hard to create the kind of support that is not always available to transgender people in their families of origin. This is the kind of support that can serve as a lifeline for members in the group. In developing a leadership structure, the founders and members deeply invested in the group's existence grappled over and over again with what it means for an organization to evolve on its own, in the political context of the rural South.

On the one hand, the capacity of white people in the South to wear, display, and otherwise affiliate with the Confederate flag is an enormous barrier to inculcating values of racial justice in a space that is not led, facilitated, or majority-populated by people of color. On the other hand, the potential for the flag to be an issue marks a visible point of intervention that is not always available in northern spaces where defensive whiteness can claim that its defensiveness is not racially motivated. The flag, its attendant politics, and the likelihood of at least one white person showing up with it on an article of clothing manifests itself as a potential point of intervention for white-led organizations who value incorporating racial justice work in their organizing and advocacy.

The reality of the leadership of this organization wanting to have a very clear commitment to racial justice at the same time that their members would sometimes show up with confederate flag accessories speaks to the shape that any group can take, if it is dominated by white members, forms organically, and the trouble of whiteness is not engaged meaningfully. The tensions here were enough to collapse the group or cause it to coalesce around the idea that the flag can stay in the space but "personal politics" around the flag and around state violence against people of color should stay home. Such an idea would have enormous potential to alienate potential members of color. A shared experience of queerness, transgender identity, or gender nonconformity is not enough to create an ethic of organizing that does not succumb to exclusionary and normative whiteness. Without a consciousness around these issues, the group could become an exclusively white organization without ever intending to be. It takes intentional leadership to struggle a meaningful engagement with racial justice into place when both the structure of the United States and the structure of LGBT(I) rights discourses have been dominated by whiteness. It was a struggle that bewildered the organization early on in the context of heated debates between members on social media about police violence, about the meaning of the Confederate flag, and about a desire to be accountable to racial justice while being a white-led organization. However, it was a struggle I watched them embrace and wrestle with through growth, commitment, and time. Rather than acquiescing to the defensiveness or obviousness of whiteness described by Bérubé about groups that "just happen" to be white, this organization struggled an ethic of racial justice into being in their organization.[38] While racial justice is not at the center of the group's work, they refused to let LGBTIQ "stay white" through the "not saying" that Allan Bérubé says characterizes many mainstream, white-dominated LGBT rights advocacy attempts.[39] They embraced the risk of alienating white members of the group by addressing the flag's presence on a T-shirt here and a belt buckle there rather than risking alienating potential members of color by refusing to address the presence of the flag or ignoring the potential pain that the presence of its image could create.

While the inertia of whiteness can work against the organic formation of organizations with an intersectional focus, sometimes the structures that organizations commit to in their formation are transformative in and of themselves. When Free Gender operates in Khayelitsha, they operate in isiXhosa.[40] This has several functions, and it has meant several things for me in my work with them. I rarely fully understand what is going on, which is important in foregrounding the situated nature of knowledge and knowledge-production, especially in reminding me of the edge of the limitations of what I can know myself, let alone what my research can claim.[41] More importantly, this allows Free Gender to interact with the communities in which it is located in a way that indigenizes queer issues for those communities. The primary objection to same-sex sexuality on the African continent is that it is "unAfrican." Scholarly and historical work on persistent histories of same-sex sexuality has not been able to unseat the accusation of "unAfrican-ness" launched at same-sex sexuality and gender nonconformity. As I've argued in this book, the result of work that is done "in town" and takes place in English is that it further entrenches the conflation of whiteness and foreignness with same-sex sexuality.

Unapologetic work that happens in an African language, a language that community members experience all facets of their lives thinking, feeling, and speaking, fosters familiarity between that experience of language and deep conversations around same-sex sexuality and gender nonconformity. The importance of this cannot be underestimated. This use of isiXhosa to organize in Khayelitsha is a way of staying with the trouble that resists the colonization of Free Gender's work by the metronormative structure of global LGBT(I) advocacy work. In the excerpt below, I chronicle a little of the evolution of my thinking about the issue of language in Free Gender's work before engaging in a discussion of how their use of isiXhosa and their refusal to seek formalized funding resist colonization of their work.

> Going to Khayelitsha on a daily basis has shown me the politics of language more clearly than I could ever understand by asking questions about language. isiXhosa is the language that Free Gender speaks. It wouldn't make sense to use any other language. There was never any question of operating in English because isiXhosa is the language spoken in Khayelitsha. When [an organization located "in town"] goes into [a township space], the language they use to run a discussion is English. When we go to a meeting in town, the language that is used is English. This is often done for practical purposes. There is usually (though not always) a mixed group, meaning that English is the *most* common language among them. However, this does not erase the power dynamics in the space. And it also locks in the reality that while everyone speaks English and many speak Afrikaans, few speak isiXhosa and almost no white people speak isiXhosa. The people who have access to the resources speak English and English is spoken in the spaces where resources are decided upon.

The more obvious way that Free Gender resists colonization of their work is through their rejection of most formal relationships with funders. The importance of this has been articulated clearly to me over and over again. If your organization is supported by a funder, you "do the work of the funder." This is a resistance that is difficult to sustain, however, especially in communities where conditions of poverty, lack of access to safe and reliable transportation, and barriers to a range of services make organizing without a salary untenable, which is one of the reasons a shift away from hegemonic whiteness and gender normativity in LGBT(I) advocacy work will require a redistribution of resources and power. However, the link between resources and language is not so easily disrupted. Funding bodies require extensive reporting that must be done in English; work that is funded is often carried out in European languages; and work that is accessible to funders is work that funders can easily understand. Because of the location of funders and the hegemonies of global funding structures, work that is valued (and funded) is very rarely work that happens in indigenous African languages.

Free Gender is actively courted by many funding bodies. They have refused most of those offers of funding. This strategy protects the organization's autonomy and integrity and positions it well to resist colonization by funders. At the same time, this is a posture that puts enormous strain on the sustainability of the organization. Refusing formal relationships with funders means that the work members do for the organization is in addition to work that they do to ensure their own survival. I have seen the hours and hours of labor that go into sustaining an organization and trying to forge a movement for social justice for lgbtiq people in this funder-driven world. There is no way that this work should remain unremunerated in out-of-the-way places. The dominant strategies relied upon in order to pursue funding and the professionalization of movement spaces have had serious consequences for the direction in which LGBT(I) rights work has been able to develop.

Conclusion: On Discourse and Rage, Defensiveness, and Letting Go

Queer people in places as far apart and demographically different as Khayelitsha and Elkins make a way for themselves by navigating the multilayered politics that shape space and sexuality, telling them who and how they should be. This book began with a consideration of colonization as alienation from land, and universal rights norms as discourse that alienates marginalized peoples from their contexts. The research question that brought me to these considerations was driven by rage about the discursive positioning of some places as ideal for queer life and flourishing and other places as antagonistic to queer life and existence.

As I write, trying to put into words the feeling that motivated my exploration of the spatial politics of sexuality, rage seems like an extreme response to discourse. Discourse is a double-edged sword. As Jim Thomas argues, "Ideas possess a dual-edged capacity to both control and liberate."[42] During the course of my research, I learned something very specific about how discourse operates while considering my own rage in relation to the rage I heard expressed from very different, but sometimes similarly located, sources. In the spring and summer of 2015, enormous public controversy erupted in the United States over the meaning of the Confederate flag. This contestation over the flag simmers beneath the surface of public political discourse in the United States, "as familiar as grits and sweet tea" in the South.[43]

On June 17, 2015, there was a mass shooting at a historically Black church in Charleston, South Carolina. A young white man who had become radicalized as a white supremacist sat with the church community during their Bible study and then opened fire on the group of nine who were there, killing them all. In the chilling photos of the shooter that circulated widely after the arrest, the Confederate flag figured as prominently as an accomplice.[44] The flag is a clear symbol of white supremacy and yet it was flying on the grounds of many southern institutions at the time of this debate. It is claimed as a symbol of regional "heritage" by some southerners. Debates erupted around the display of the flag, especially on public grounds. Some state houses removed the flag from their buildings.[45] Barbara Kingsolver, a clear voice in southern fiction writing, demanded that it was (past) time to find another expression for what it means to be southern.[46] This debate continued into the following years about Confederate statues and most recently morphed into widespread debates-turned-legislative-proposals about the teaching of critical race theory in schools.

In the debate about the flag that erupted after this incident, I was forced to rethink, or at the very least grow uncomfortable with, my rage. I had been angry that entire regions of the United States were discounted as terrifying or impossible as locations for queer people to exist and thrive. I had been angry that conversations about the queer and the rural already took place within the purviews of this assumption of hostility as an organizing frame. I had been angry that resources and infrastructure were/are withheld from us and our organizing needs, causing the narrative about the impossibility of queer rural life to become a self-fulfilling prophecy. I had been angry that the story of queer migration is a complicated one but had been collapsed into a story about how impossible queer life is in rural America, meaning that if you are queer, getting to a city is the only thing that could make your life worth living. I had been angry as I observed the coercive use of something described as LGBT rights within our foreign policy discourses directed at other countries, primarily ones on the African continent and in the Middle East. I had been angry because our own history around how we treat queer people in America was used as a gold standard as it was exported as part of a foreign policy agenda around tolerance and liberalism that also shores up American imperialism. I had been angry that symbolic and (even) legal rights were prioritized above the redistribution of wealth or other gestures that, according to Dean Spade, would improve the "life chances" of the most vulnerable of queer populations among us.[47]

I had been thinking of the metronormative U.S. North (New York City always makes a good repository for such frustrations, partly because of its cultural and financial dominance, partly because of its metropolitan status) and national LGBT rights organizations, such as the Human Rights Campaign, as colonizing forces. I still think this, of course, but there was a moment when people who were aligned in very different ways from me, politically, were saying the things that I'd been saying: framing the North as colonizing, telling northerners to stop telling them what to do, telling "elitist" northerners that they didn't understand the southern context. These voices were angry, full of rage—rage that sounded very similar to mine. I am opposed to flying the Confederate flag. However, I realized that between my framing the metronormative North as colonizing and Confederate enthusiasts framing the North as colonizing, there is a line as thin as a razor's edge between the political purpose for which such discourses are put to work. We were saying the same things, but we did not mean the same things.

In thinking through the uses and misuses of intersectionality, Black feminist thinker Jennifer Nash advocates "letting go" of the kind of defensive posture that keeps Black feminists preoccupied with the ownership and citational integrity of intersectionality. Nash's plea to let go of defensiveness and ownership is applicable to spatial politics. At times, we can become so embroiled in defending our territory from the metronormative gaze (extractive, exploitative, and patronizing though it may be) of outsiders looking in on us that we forget the complexity of the very space on behalf of which we advocate. In getting caught up in a position of victimization based on our exploitation, we forget how we are imbricated in not only the extractive economies that ravage our region, but also the dynamics of domination that continue to shape racisms, sexisms, and homo-/trans-antagonisms in our region as well.

Nash's encouragement to let something go prompts me to ask myself: What can *I* let go? Letting go of a defensiveness in relation to Appalachia and the South allows me to better see how our own context fits into the larger context of white supremacy and heteronormativity of global capitalism. Not being on constant guard defending the region against its bad reputation in the rest of the country and the rest of the world (I found the U.S. South in South Africa when participants there casually referenced the terror-invoking Bible Belt) means being able to be honest about the huge obstacles we face in relation to the political terrain that constrains us at the same time that we are able to also practice letting go of the despair that drives many of us from our homes. The political struggles that we face are not pretty. Yet, the very clear constraints we face at every political level give us a practical knowledge about the compromised operation of democracy that people located in more progressive areas have difficulty comprehending. The shock that metronormatively located Americans felt about the election of Donald Trump was not a surprise to those of us who are surrounded by the aggrieved entitlement of white people whose whiteness has not produced the benefits promised by narratives about white privilege.

When the protestors in chapter 4 describe Asheville as "the gathering of the gays," a thing they did not want their small town to become, they were gripped by a defensiveness over their home. They had a clear idea of what they did not want that home to become. And yet, when they were caught on video expressing their disgust and fear of what their community would become if it became like Asheville, they were aware that they risked "looking really bad" to an audience outside of their home—an audience that might have the power to condemn and mock them beyond the contest that was playing out locally with other community members in their midst. The proponents of a universal gay subject of rights might suggest that the fear of "looking really bad" to outside audiences is a productive fear to instill because it might keep the worst of homo-/trans-antagonistic behavior in check. This is certainly the logic that was used to promote sanctions against African countries where politicians promoted anti-gay legislation. However, what might it look like to navigate the space of home without the pressure of outside discourses, both for those who are queer and trans within the space and for those who are afraid of "the gathering of the gays"? The answer to this question is best generated by those doing the everyday work of sustaining queer community and insisting on queer habitability in the very specific contexts in which they/we live.

Appendix

TABLE 1

U.S. SOUTH (INTERVIEWS)

Pseudonym of participant	Date of interview	Location of interview	Organization type	Organization focus	Participant position in organization
Damien and Kathy	08/13/2014	North Carolina	Community-based, grassroots organization	Rural organizers	Rural organizers
Florence	08/14/2014	North Carolina	State equality organization	LGBT equality	Director
Jack	08/14/2014	North Carolina	National organization	LGBT equality	Regional coordinator
Jeanne	10/07/2014	Phone (spoke to me from Tennessee)	Regional organization (U.S. South)	Intersectional queer liberation	Co-founder
Max	12/15/2014	South Carolina	Grassroots organization	Transgender advocacy	Co-founder
Cynthia	12/19/2014	Phone (spoke to me from North Carolina)	Regional organization (U.S. South)	Intersectional queer liberation	Co-founder
Hal	12/29/2014	Phone (spoke to me from Georgia)	National organization with regional focus (U.S. South)	Building power for Black gay men	Founder

(continued)

TABLE 1
U.S. SOUTH (INTERVIEWS) *(continued)*

Pseudonym of participant	Date of interview	Location of interview	Organization type	Organization focus	Participant position in organization
Victor	01/23/2015	North Carolina	University	Safe spaces for queer youth	Archivist and organizer
Stacey	01/30/2015	Phone (spoke to me from North Carolina)	Regional organization (U.S. South)	LGBT equality	Founder
George	01/30/2015	Georgia	State equality organization	LGBT equality	Director
Jerome	02/13/2015	Phone (spoke to me from Georgia)	National organization (southern U.S. regional offices)	LGBT equality	Outreach
Meredith	03/14/2015	Louisiana	State equality organization	LGBT equality	Media coordination
Heather	03/07/2015	West Virginia	Story collection and archiving	Documenting rural queer life	Founder
Leslie	05/13/2015	Phone (spoke to me from Washington, DC)	Government department	Focus on cultivating relationships with LGBTQ farmers	Program coordinator
Cameron	06/14/2015	Interviewed while driving from Georgia to Virginia	Regional organization (Appalachian region)	Focus on rural queer youth	Steering committee
Manuel	06/17/2015	Phone (spoke to me from North Carolina)	Regional organization (U.S. South)	LGBT equality	Outreach
Frank	06/24/2015	Skype (spoke to me from West Virginia)	Film festival	Queer film festival	Co-founder
Ethel	06//27/2015	North Carolina	Community-based organization	Rural community building	Co-founder

TABLE 2

SOUTH AFRICA (INTERVIEWS)

Pseudonym of participant	Date of interview	Location of interview	Organization type	Organization focus	Participant position in organization
David	02/09/2016	Johannesburg	Global funder (regional offices)	LGBT equality	Regional director
Garth	02/09/2016	Johannesburg	National organization	Transgender advocacy	Founder
Nathi	02/10/2016	Johannesburg	National organization	Transgender advocacy	Founder
Asa	01/29/2016	Eastern Cape	National organization	Transgender advocacy focused on transgender women	Founder
Andile	02/01/2016	Eastern Cape	National organization	LGBTI equality	Outreach coordinator
Brenda	02/03/2016	Eastern Cape	National organization	Transgender advocacy focused on transgender women	Outreach coordinator
Liza	/03/28/2016	Cape Town	National organization	Transgender advocacy	Founder
Pete	03/31/2016	Cape Town	National organization	LGBTI advocacy	Founder
Janet	04/16/2016	Cape Town	National organization	LGBTI advocacy	Outreach
Kayla	04/16/2016	Cape Town	Grassroots organization	Black lesbian advocacy	Founder
Xolani	04/16/2016	Cape Town	National organization	LGBTI advocacy	Outreach
Kian	04/26/2016	Cape Town	National organization	LGBTI advocacy with focus on Islam	Founder
Alice	05/30/2016	Cape Town	Funder	Social issues	Program director (LGBTI focus)

TABLE 3
U.S. SOUTH (EVENTS)

Event	Date of event	Location of event	Organization
The Campaign: Film screening	06/27/2014	Morgantown, West Virginia	Appalachian Queer Film Festival
Queer BBQ: Social gathering	08/13/2014	Liberty, North Carolina	Rural organizers
Charlotte Pride	08/17/2014	Charlotte, North Carolina	Multiple organizations
Transgender Information and Empowerment Summit	10/04/2014	Richmond, Virginia	Virginia Equality
Carolina Conference on Queer Youth	10/17/2014	Charlotte, North Carolina	Multiple organizations
Appalachian Queer Film Festival	10/23–26/2014	Lewisburg, West Virginia	Appalachian Queer Film Festival
Bring It Home Conference: Executive Director Update	11/15/2014	Charleston, West Virginia	Fairness WV
Bring It Home Conference: Keynote	11/15/2014	Charleston, West Virginia	Fairness WV
"LGBT People and the New Cold War over Human Rights": West Virginia Wesleyan College Honors Athenaeum Campus talk	11/18/2014	Buckhannon, West Virginia	Buzzfeed International LGBT correspondent
The Blueprint Dialogue: Celebrating Ourselves and Building Community: Panel discussion of Black gay men	11/19/2014	Atlanta, Georgia	Counter Narrative Project
Transgender Day of Remembrance: Commemoration of the loss of transgender lives	11/20/2014	Atlanta, Georgia	Georgia Equality
Chant Down the Walls: Not 1 More campaign action	11/21/2014	Atlanta, Georgia	Southerners on New Ground
Transgender Day of Resilience: Celebration of transgender resilience	11/21/2014	Atlanta, Georgia	Lambda Legal
Gala dinner: Annual fundraising dinner	11/22/2014	Greensboro, North Carolina	North Carolina Equality
Gender Benders meeting	12/14/2014	Greenville, South Carolina	Gender Benders

(continued)

TABLE 3
U.S. SOUTH (EVENTS) *(continued)*

Event	Date of event	Location of event	Organization
West Virginia Gay & Lesbian Community Center (WVGLCC) meeting	12/16/2014	Beckley, West Virginia	WVGLCC
New Thanksmas: Holiday celebration	01/03/2015	Greenville, South Carolina	Gender Benders
We Are One community dinner to express solidarity in the face of an incident of racism	01/12/2015	Hillsboro, West Virginia	Country Queers
WVGLCC meeting	01/13/2015	Beckley, West Virginia	WVGLCC
Martin Luther King Jr. Day lobby activities	01/19/2015	Charleston, West Virginia	Fairness WV
Citizen advocacy training	01/24/2015	Atlanta, Georgia	Georgia Equality
Southerners on New Ground General Meeting	01/29/2015	Atlanta, Georgia	Southerners on New Ground
Bold Not Broken: Queer Resilience in the South: Louisiana Queer Conference	03/14/2015	Baton Rouge, Louisiana	Louisiana LGBTQ organizations
City council meeting	03/19/2015	Elkins, West Virginia	Fairness Elkins
Commemorative march to mark the 50th anniversary of the march from Selma to Montgomery	03/21/2015	Selma, Alabama	Gender Benders
LGBT in the South Conference	04/18/2015	Asheville, North Carolina	Campaign for Southern Equality
Trans Lives Matter	05/21/2015	Birmingham, Alabama	Community organizations
Say Her Name: Performance (play)	05/22/2015	New Orleans, Louisiana	BreakOUT!
USDA LGBT Summit	05/26/2015	Atlanta, Georgia	U.S. Department of Agriculture, local LGBT organizations
Mobile Marriage Town Hall: Panel discussion about marriage equality	05/27/2015	Mobile, Alabama	Campaign for Southern Equality

(continued)

TABLE 3
U.S. SOUTH (EVENTS) *(continued)*

Event	Date of event	Location of event	Organization
Decision Day Rally: Rally to celebrate the Supreme Court's marriage equality decision	06/26/2015	Asheville, North Carolina	Campaign for Southern Equality
Southern Fried Queer Pride	06/27/2015	Atlanta, Georgia	Southern Fried Queer Pride
Pride: Film screening	06/27/2015	Bakersville, North Carolina	Mitchell County Gay Straight Alliance
Gaycation: Annual camp	06/11–14/2015	Savannah, Georgia	Southerners on New Ground
Chant Down the Walls: Protest against Etowah County Detention Center	06/20/2015	Gadsden, Alabama	Southerners on New Ground

TABLE 4
SOUTH AFRICA (EVENTS)

Event	Date of event	Location of event	Organization
Alternative and Inclusive Pride (AIP) planning meeting	01/21/2016	Cape Town	AIP members
Global Sexuality Summer School session	01/25–27/2016	Cape Town	Journalist covering LGBTI rights
Free Gender planning meeting for Pride event	01/29/2016	Khayelitsha, Western Cape	Free Gender
Queer City Tour	01/30/2016	Cape Town	AIP members
Troubling the Civil Union Act: Community meeting to discuss the campaign to remove Section VI from the Civil Union Act	02/02/2016	Khayelitsha, Western Cape	Free Gender
Troubling the Civil Union Act campaign strategy meeting with coalition members	02/05/2016	Cape Town	Free Gender, Commission on Gender Equality (CGE), Access Chapter 2, Legal Resources Center
AIP final planning meeting	02/18/2016	Cape Town	AIP members
God Hates Uganda: Film screening	02/19/2016	Cape Town	Triangle Project
Media training	02/20/2016	Khayelitsha, Western Cape	Free Gender
"What Are the Most Important Issues Facing LGBTIQ People Today?": AIP panel discussion	02/22/2016	Bellville, Western Cape	Gender Equality Unit (University of the Western Cape)
"The Churches and Same-Sex Relationships: Will They Ever Come Around?": AIP panel discussion	02/23/2016	Cape Town	AIP
"Kinky Politics, *EXIT Newspaper* and a *Moffie* Called Simon: Re-Reading African Queer Visibility through Representations of Simon Nkoli": AIP Seminar	02/25/2016	Institute for Humanities in Africa, University of Cape Town	AIP
Trans Collective meeting: AIP event	02/26/2016	University of Cape Town	AIP
Cape Town Pride disruption	02/27/2016	Cape Town	AIP

(*continued*)

TABLE 4
SOUTH AFRICA (EVENTS) *(continued)*

Event	Date of event	Location of event	Organization
Lovedale College HIV testing	03/02/2016	Eastern Cape	Social, Health and Empowerment Feminist Collective of Transgender Women (SHE)
Support group meeting	03/03/2016	Mdantsane, Eastern Cape	SHE
Centering Human Rights: A Queer Discourse: Panel discussion	03/18/2016	Stellenbosch, Western Cape	Free Gender
Annual general meeting	03/30/2016	Cape Town	Hate Crimes Working Group
Mass same-sex wedding	04/29/2016	Knysna, Western Cape	Pink Loerie Mardi Gras and Arts Festival
Call Me Kuchu Film screening	05/12/2016	Elsie's River, Western Cape	Triangle Project
Khumbulani Pride launch	05/14/2016	Langa, Western Cape	Free Gender
International Day Against Homophobia, Transphobia and Biphobia (IDAHOT) dialogue with political parties: Khumbulani Pride event	05/17/2016	Langa, Western Cape	Free Gender Legal Resources Centre
Traditional Healers Forum: Khumbulani Pride event	05/20/2016	Langa, Western Cape	Traditional Healers
Khumbulani Pride March	05/21/2016	Langa, Western Cape	Free Gender

Acknowledgments

Teaching at a small liberal arts college often means working in a kind of intellectual isolation. It is not uncommon to be the only member of one's discipline in a very small department. That has been the case for me as long as I have taught at West Virginia Wesleyan College. I appreciate the fruitful discussions of pedagogy I have with colleagues on a regular basis at the college, but when it comes to discussing ideas that are central to my particular intellectual interests, the most rewarding and thought-provoking conversations I have are with students. Many students—too many to name here individually—have encouraged me, supported me, cheered me on, showed me grace, and, most importantly, helped me formulate the many transitions that have characterized my thinking about this text and every other intellectual challenge I embrace.

Dr. Boyd Creasman, in his then role of vice president of academic affairs at West Virginia Wesleyan College, offered me very important support while I was engaged in collecting the data that ultimately became this book. Dr. Creasman allowed me a leave of absence to spend a semester in South Africa, and supported my tenure (literally) and development as a scholar at a teaching-focused institution, allowing me to imagine ways of writing and teaching in a setting that is not designed to accommodate that combination of activities. Dr. Creasman also invited me to deliver a campus-wide lecture on the research that became this book. That opportunity was the first of many to begin moving what had been dissertation research into the shape of a book.

I am so appreciative to Kimberly Guinta for believing in this book through the different rounds of reviews, drafts, and revisions. Those rounds of revisions transported me from the book I had written to the book I wanted to write. That is the book you now have before you.

This book would not have been possible without the mentorship and friendship of Dr. Jane Bennett and Funeka Soldaat. Both of these individuals, with whom I hope to have deep and abiding lifelong friendships, have shaped my understanding of South African, global, and queer politics in ways that are impossible to recount in the conventions of academic publication. The influence of both of these individuals is a literal presence in the lens through which I view the world, so profoundly have they affected my ability to process and understand discourse. Conversations with Dr. Zethu Matebeni, none of which are documented as any part of the "data" present in this book, were also crucial to shaping my understanding of South African queer politics. I am not aware of anyone who has done more ethnographic research of Black lesbian existence in South Africa than Dr. Matebeni. To understand queer politics in South Africa, it is crucial to take seriously the lives, perspectives, and experiences of Black lesbians. Dr. Matebeni also encouraged me to participate in a seminar on queer politics in Cape Town where I was able to write, talk, and think with South African scholars—a very different experience from working primarily with American academics while doing research that focused partially on the South African context. Liesl Theron traveled with me, talked politics with me, shared meals with me, and made introductions for me to many of the activists whose words are documented as part of this text. Many of the experiences I recount in the South African examples in this book are experiences that Liesl and I shared. As an American, it would have been possible for me to write *a* book, but without open and dynamic dialogue with the South Africans I have named here, it would not have been possible for me to write *this* book. This book is meant to honor those relationships and conversations, and I hope I have done justice to them here.

This book would not have been possible without Dr. Melody Meadows in a very different way. As the person I share my life most closely with, Melody made sure that our animals were fed and our commitments to family and friends were honored, even if I dropped the ball because I was attempting to complete this book or looking for distractions to put off the completion of this book. Like so many folks in the rest of the world, the past several years that have been marked most dramatically by the COVID-19 pandemic, and we have experienced a not-insignificant amount of loss. Melody has been a constant comfort, companion, and partner throughout the writing of this book and throughout our shared life. Melody has not read any prepublication version of this text (though she did offer to listen, should I wish to read the text in its entirety aloud to her). I know that when it is a book she can hold in her hands, she will read it, and I hope she likes it.

The book was read on several occasions by my most trusted intellectual confidantes, Jane Bennett and Evid Miller. Writing a book that attempts to speak to two different contexts, each of which is not immediately knowable to the people in the other of those contexts, is a challenge. The two people I asked to read this text in various forms are familiar with both contexts. In an early draft of this text, I sent a chapter to Evid and Jane. Evid's response to what I had written about the U.S. context was a suggestion to include newer literature on a particular issue. Jane's response to what I had written about the South African context was to include older literature on a particular issue. I took their advice when formulating the next draft. Every suggestion made by each of these most treasured readers—my only readers outside of the external reviews solicited by the editorial staff—made this manuscript stronger. Obviously, though, for any weaknesses in the text, I am solely responsible.

Around the world there are individuals who dedicate their entire working lives to struggling toward LGBTIQ liberation in many different forms. This book is meant to elucidate one particular dynamic of that work—the relationship between queer/trans activism and spatial politics. I hope that I have honored the work done by so many organizations in the U.S. South, in Appalachia, and in South Africa by writing this book. I am incredibly indebted to the organizations that allowed me to see what it means to live and work in the space of organizing and advocacy for queer and trans existence, rights, and liberation where those things are under constant contestation. Without those organizations, there would be no book. More importantly, though, without those organizations, the ideas I have written about here would just be ideas. The work of these organizations has brought those ideas to life. I am especially grateful to Free Gender in Khayelitsha, South Africa, and the Gender Benders in Greenville, South Carolina. Both of these organizations welcomed me, gave me a new name, and treated me as a beloved friend, allowing me to love them and making me feel loved in return. Every single person I interviewed while writing this book is doing incredible work. They are the ones who insist on queer and trans existence in all the places they call home in the world every day of their lives. We are all better for the work that they do.

Notes

CHAPTER 1 — INTRODUCTION

1. Richard Socarides, "Why Bill Clinton Signed the Defense of Marriage Act," *New Yorker*, March 8, 2013, https://www.newyorker.com/news/news-desk/why-bill-clinton-signed-the-defense-of-marriage-act.

2. Legal Information Institute, "Defense of Marriage Act (DOMA)," Cornell Law School, accessed March 2, 2023, https://www.law.cornell.edu/wex/defense_of_marriage_act_(doma).

3. Pew Research Center, "Same-Sex Marriage, State by State," June 26, 2015, https://www.pewresearch.org/religion/2015/06/26/same-sex-marriage-state-by-state-1/.

4. Karen McVeigh, "North Carolina Passes Amendment 1 Banning Same-Sex Unions," *Guardian*, May 9, 2012, https://www.theguardian.com/world/2012/may/09/north-carolina-passes-amendment-1.

5. This book is not about marriage. The examples I have included here to open the book deal with marriage because marriage was something that came up regularly in conversations, at meetings, and in interviews. The last is partly because I introduced marriage as a subject through questions that I asked during interviews. When I was traveling the U.S. South talking to people about LGBTIQ activism and existence in 2015, marriage was a subject of legal advocacy, public presentations, and other discussions. At the end of that year, same-sex marriage became a legal reality in the United States. When I was observing events and conducting interviews, same-sex marriage was on the way, and we all knew that. It was 2016 when I was traveling in South Africa, and beyond my own introduction of the subject of marriage into interview questions, that year marked ten years since same-sex marriage became a legal possibility in South Africa. South Africa had adopted the Civil Union Act of 2006, making 2016 an important anniversary year for the legislation. Impending marriage (in the United States) and a marriage anniversary (South Africa) aside, the issue of marriage itself has been influential in shaping LGBT rights advocacy over the past several decades. I have written elsewhere about how marriage has been used as a metric for measuring the availability of rights for LGBTIQ people in the world. When conservative legislation has been introduced in different countries around the world—the recriminalization of same-sex sexuality in countries like Uganda, Nigeria, and Kenya, for instance—the claim of government representatives in those places is that such recriminalization is to preclude the possibility of same-sex marriage. It is also my personal belief from

watching campaigns about marriage unfold in the United States and having many, many conversations about marriage in South Africa (during research I did as a master's student there) that marriage is fundamentally a conservative issue. This leaves us in a strange situation when thinking about queerness, trans identities, and marriage as an indicator of rights or climate in any given place. In the United States in 2024, same-sex marriage is a legal right, but many states are criminalizing any other element of queer and trans identity that they can.

6. I will use several terms referring to queer populations and the work of advocacy claiming to represent them in specific ways in this book. I want to be clear about how I am doing that. Most generally, institutionalized advocacy organizations in the United States use the acronym LGBT, though there are sometimes variations, such as LGBTQ or LGBTQ+. In South Africa, as is true across the continent, the dominant acronym used to describe the work of advocacy is LGBTI, which is "more inclusive" than the dominant acronym employed in the U.S. context because of its inclusion of intersexuality. Intersex individuals face a distinct set of challenges related to gender norms that are not encompassed in the acronym LGBT. For American organizations to use the acronym LGBT, it seems that either they consider these distinct issues—which are nevertheless directly related to how gender acts coercively on bodies through institutions such as hospitals and medical research—to exist outside of LGBT issues, or they have not "heard of intersex people and their rights in this struggle," as Sokari Ekine notes ("Contesting Narratives of Queer Africa," in *Queer African Reader*, ed. Sokari Ekine and Hakima Abbas [Nairobi: Pambazuka, 2013], 88).

To keep this distinction in mind in an attempt to be mindful of context, even as qualitative materials from both contexts are considered together, I refer to institutionalized advocacy efforts in the U.S. South and in an international context launched from the Global North with the acronym LGBT. I refer to institutionalized advocacy efforts in South Africa and on the African continent with the acronym LGBTI. When referring to institutionalized advocacy efforts in the two contexts together, I modify the acronym to LGBT(I), so that the South African context is not subsumed within the hegemony of the less inclusive acronym LGBT, erasing the very real ways in which the acronym in use by African movements around gender and sexual diversity has normalized a more expansive constellation of queer existence than the U.S. acronym, whether or not there is substantive work happening in relation to intersex issues at all organizations that claim to work on LGBTI rights or not. It can and should be argued that the "T," the "I," and the "B" occupy a more liminal space in terms of the priorities set by organizations claiming to work as "LGBT(I)" organizations in both the United States and South Africa.

I employ the term "queer" in two ways. Queer will either indicate a subversive political position—a "politics"—or it will serve as a descriptive term that does not seek to distinguish between the "L," "G," "B," "T," or "I," but at the same time acknowledge the existence of people who claim an identity that is subversive in relation to dominant norms of gender and sexuality or people who are generally treated by law and policy as outside of the boundaries of heteronormativity. The legacy of colonial laws does not distinguish between what is understood as a subversion of gender and what is seen as a subversion of sexuality. Instead, these laws can be invoked to punish same-sex sexuality or gender nonconformity without distinction, even as it is always imperative to recognize the subtleties of how people claim their identities and live their existences. In terms of discussing lgbtiq people, I use the acronym in the lower case, inclusive of the i and the q. I do this to signal the distinction between lgbtiq lives and institutionalized efforts claiming to represent those lives. I use all of the letters in the lower case to signal the variety—both diversity of experiences and contradictions in perspectives—within queer and trans lives as they are aligned with the acronym.

There is another element of this language that I would like to confront throughout this book. The language of LGBT rights as originating in the United States is English. In English, pronouns are binary. Because of the influence of gender nonconforming, genderqueer, and nonbinary individuals, the use of the singular "they" pronoun and select other genderless or gender neutral "neo-pronouns" or titles (Mx., ze/hir, etc.) has been gaining enough traction to become a source of contention. Some people welcome more inclusive developments in language. Some resist it in the way they resist dismantling other binary gender norms.

In isiXhosa, the language spoken by the people I spent the majority of my time with in South Africa during the six months I was there conducting interviews for this book, there is no gendered pronoun. You might refer to someone in a gendered way, as *usisi* or *ubhuti* ("sister" or "brother"), as a term of endearment or a way to reference a person, but the one pronoun always used to refer to anyone in the third person is "u." The pronouns she/her or he/him literally do not translate into isiXhosa, except into a universal "u" pronoun.

Some people I have spoken to have transitioned since we conducted the interviews. Academics and scholars also transition between publications. While our practice in addressing people in everyday life is that we should use the pronouns that people use for themselves, I do not want to lock participants or authors into a set of pronouns that may one day be inaccurate for them. My impulse in writing this text was to universally refer to scholars and participants alike with the singular they. I find they/them to be the most flexible linguistic formation for acknowledging that gender is changeable, developing over time, and could refer to anyone. Instead of using they/them for scholars who publicly (on their websites or elsewhere) refer to themselves by a set of binary pronouns, I have attempted to erase all usage of pronouns from this book. I will refer to authors and participants by name only, except when quoting individuals who themselves use a gendered pronoun to refer to someone else. My attempt to work with language in a way that seeks to de-emphasize binary gender conventions is an attempt to honor the work of participants whose work confronts a binary gender system as one source of the violence they face.

7. Louisiana Queer Conference: "Bold Not Broken: Queer Resilience in the South" (hosted by Louisiana LGBT advocacy organizations in Baton Rouge, Louisiana), attended by the author, March 2015. "North Cakalacky" is a nickname for Noth Carolina.

8. John Raby, "GOP Increases Supermajority in West Virginia House, Senate," *Associated Press*, November 9, 2022, https://apnews.com/article/general-elections-west-virginia-wheeling-government-and-politics-20003d4aece817fe37cdea0b5d341635; Ballotpedia, "Party Control of West Virginia State Government," accessed March 2, 2023, https://ballotpedia.org/Party_control_of_West_Virginia_state_government.

9. Roberto Igual, "Marking Ten Years of Same-Sex Marriage in South Africa," *Mamba Online*, November 30, 2016, https://www.mambaonline.com/2016/11/30/marking-ten-years-sex-marriage-south-africa/.

10. Roberto Igual, "I Do × 15! History Made at Africa's First Mass Gay Wedding," *Mamba Online*, April 29, 2016, https://www.mambaonline.com/2016/04/29/x-15-history-made-africas-first-mass-gay-wedding/.

11. Pink Loerie Mass Same-Sex Wedding (Pride Festival event, Western Cape), attended by the author, April 2016.

12. When I first encountered the term "metronormative," it was in Jack Halberstam's *A Queer Time and Place: Transgender Bodies, Subcultural Lives* (New York: New York University Press, 2005). The term and its attendant meanings resonated very strongly with me. I am indebted to Halberstam not only for the use of the term, but for an application of this

term to contexts that are both internal (rural) and external (Global South) to the United States because that is the trajectory my thinking followed any time I invoked the term.

13. Mark Gevisser, *The Pink Line: Journeys across the World's Queer Frontiers* (New York: Farrah, Straus and Giroux, 2020), 21.

14. Gevisser, *The Pink Line*.

15. Zethu Matebeni, *Black Lesbian Sexualities and Identities in South Africa: An Ethnography of Black Lesbian Urban Life* (Saarbrucken, Germany: Lambert Academic Publishing, 2012).

16. B Camminga, *Transgender Refugees and the Imagined South Africa: Bodies over Borders and Borders over Bodies* (London: Palgrave Macmillan, 2019).

17. Camminga, *Transgender Refugees and the Imagined South Africa*, 11.

18. Mumbi Machera, "Opening a Can of Worms: A Debate on Female Sexuality in the Lecture Theatre," in *Re-Thinking Sexualities in Africa*, ed. Signe Arnfred (Uppsala, Sweden: Nordic Africa Institute, 2004), 157–172.

19. Machera, "Opening a Can of Worms," 163.

20. Camminga, *Transgender Refugees and the Imagined South Africa*, 13.

21. Mary Gray, *Out in the Country: Youth, Media, and Queer Visibility in Rural America* (New York: New York University Press, 2009).

22. Gray, *Out in the Country*, 22.

23. Carlos Dews and Carolyn Law, *Out in the South* (Philadelphia: Temple University Press, 2001); Gray, *Out in the Country*; Colin Johnson, *Just Queer Folks: Gender and Sexuality in Rural America* (Philadelphia: Temple University Press, 2013); Karen Osborne and William Spurlin, *Reclaiming the Heartland: Gay and Lesbian Voices from the Midwest* (Minneapolis: University of Minnesota Press, 1996). I take the term "out-of-the-way places" from Anna Tsing, whose work has been so central to my own thinking about space.

24. Marcus Anthony Hunter and Zandria Robinson, *Chocolate Cities: The Black Map of American Life* (Oakland: University of California Press, 2016), 43.

25. Irene Fubara-Manuel, "At Home but Homeless: Queer African Migrants Critically Reflect on 'Home,'" in *Boldly Queer: African Perspectives on Same-Sex Sexuality and Gender Diversity*, ed. Theo Sandfort, Fabienne Simenel, Kevin Mwachiro, and Vasu Reddy (Nairobi: Hivos, 2015), 25–32.

26. Dean Spade, *Normal Life: Administrative Violence, Critical Trans Politics, and the Limits of Law* (Brooklyn: South End Press, 2011).

27. Kevin Mwachiro, "The Lost Chapter Found: An Interview with Binyavanga Wainaina," in Sandfort et al., *Boldly Queer*, 97–102.

28. Binyavanga Wainaina, "I Am a Homosexual, Mum," *Guardian*, January 21, 2014, https://www.theguardian.com/commentisfree/2014/jan/21/i-am-a-homosexual-mum-binyavanga-wainaina-memoir; Binyavanga Wainaina, "Since Everything Was Suddening into a Hurricane," *Granta*, February 13, 2017, https://granta.com/since-everything-suddening-hurricane/; TEDx Talks, "Conversations with Baba | Binyavanga Wainaina," YouTube video, January 16, 2015, https://www.youtube.com/watch?v=z5uAoBu9Epg.

29. Mark Gevisser, "Love in Exile: One Woman's Journey from Malawi to South Africa," *Guardian*, November 27, 2014, https://www.theguardian.com/news/2014/nov/27/-sp-transgender-relationship-jail-exile-tiwonge-chimbalanga.

30. Gevisser, "Love in Exile"; Barry Bearak, "Gay Couple Convicted in Malawi," *New York Times*, May 18, 2010, https://www.nytimes.com/2010/05/19/world/africa/19malawi.html.

31. Ekine and Abbas, *Queer African Reader*, 1.

32. Ekine and Abbas, *Queer African Reader*, 1.

33. Ekine and Abbas, *Queer African Reader*, 2.

34. Ryan Thoreson, *Transnational LGBT Activism: Working for Sexual Rights Worldwide* (Minneapolis: University of Minnesota Press, 2014).

35. Anna Tsing, *In the Realm of the Diamond Queen: Marginality in an Out-of-the-Way Place* (Princeton, NJ: Princeton University Press, 1993).
36. This is a question discussed in more detail in Chapter 3.
37. Thoreson, *Transnational LGBT Activism*.
38. Thoreson, *Transnational LGBT Activism*.
39. Joseph Massad, "Re-Orienting Desire: The Gay International and the Arab World," *Public Culture* 14, no. 2 (2002): 361–385.
40. Carly Thomsen, *Visibility Interrupted: Rural Queer Life and the Politics of Unbecoming* (Minneapolis: University of Minnesota Press, 2021).
41. Ekine and Abbas, *Queer African Reader*.
42. William Spurlin, *Imperialism within the Margins: Queer Representations and the Politics of Culture in Southern Africa* (New York: Palgrave Macmillan, 2006).
43. Ryan Lee Cartwright, *Peculiar Places: A Queer Crip History of Rural White Nonconformity* (Chicago: University of Chicago Press, 2021), 168.
44. Alexandra Chasin, *Selling Out: The Gay and Lesbian Movement Goes to Market* (New York: St. Martin's Press, 2000).
45. The term "life chances" is one used by Spade in *Normal Life*.
46. Julia Carrie Wong, "LGBT People of Color Alienated by San Francisco Pride's Plan for More Police," *Guardian*, June 22, 2016, https://www.theguardian.com/world/2016/jun/22/san-francisco-pride-police-presence-orlando-shooting-lgbt.
47. Thomsen, *Visibility Interrupted*, 13.
48. Ashley Currier, *Out in Africa: LGBT Organizing in Namibia and South Africa* (Minneapolis: University of Minnesota Press, 2012), 55.
49. Ekine and Abbas, *Queer African Reader*.
50. This is a riff on an idea about the "durability" of crises; see Laura Ann Stoler, *Duress: Imperial Durabilities in Our Time* (Durham, NC: Duke University Press, 2016).
51. This happens on both the African continent, where presidents and other leaders can claim to fight neocolonialism by rejecting human rights directives from the colonizing Global North and in places in the United States often characterized as "Trump Country."
52. Gray, *Out in the Country*; Halberstam, *In a Queer Time and Place*; Scott Herring, *Another Country: Critical Queer Rusticity* (New York: New York University Press, 2010); Johnson, *Just Queer Folks*; Massad, *Desiring Arabs* (Chicago: University of Chicago Press, 2007).
53. Ekine and Abbas, *Queer African Reader*; Gray, *Out in the Country*; Halberstam, *In a Queer Time and Place*; Robert Lorway, *Namibia's Rainbow Project: Gay Rights in an African Nation* (Bloomington: Indiana University Press, 2015); Massad, *Desiring Arabs*; Graeme Reid, *How to Be a Real Gay: Gay Identities in Small-Town South Africa* (Scottsville: University of KwaZulu Natal Press, 2013).
54. Myrl Beam, *Gay, Inc.: The Nonprofitization of Queer Politics* (Minneapolis: University of Minnesota Press, 2018); Alan Bérubé, "How Gay Stays White and What Kind of White It Stays," in *Privilege: A Reader*, ed. Michael Kimmel and Abby Ferber (Boulder, CO: Westview Press, 2010), 272–328; Chasin, *Selling Out*; Spade, *Normal Life*; Urvashi Vaid, *Virtual Equality: The Mainstreaming of Gay and Lesbian Liberation* (New York: Anchor Books, 1996).
55. Jessica Scott, "Disruption and Withdrawal: Responses to 21st Century Prides from the South," in *Beyond the Mountain: Queer Life in "Africa's Gay Capital,"* ed. Zethu Matebeni and B Camminga (Pretoria: UNISA Press, 2021), 171–185.
56. For a discussion of the 2016 Cape Town Pride theme, see Scott, "Disruption and Withdrawal," 175–178.
57. Gray, *Out in the Country*; Lorway, *Namibia's Rainbow Project*; Reid, *How to Be a Real Gay*.

CHAPTER 2 — POSITIONALITY AND METHOD

1. Donna Haraway, *Simians, Cyborgs, and Women: The Reinvention of Nature* (London: Free Association Books, 1991); Donna Haraway, *Staying with the Trouble: Making Kin in the Chthulucene* (Durham, NC: Duke University Press, 2016); Amina Mama, "Is It Ethical to Study Africa? Preliminary Thoughts on Scholarship and Freedom," *African Studies Review* 50, no. 1 (2007): 1–26; Tsing, *In the Realm of the Diamond Queen*.

2. Haraway, *Simians, Cyborgs, and Women*, 187.

3. Mama, "Is It Ethical to Study Africa?"; Chandra Mohanty, *Feminism without Borders* (Durham, NC: Duke University Press, 2003); Amanda Swarr and Richa Nagar, *Critical Transnational Feminist Praxis* (Albany: State University of New York, 2010).

4. Haraway, *Staying with the Trouble*, 82.

5. Haraway, *Simians, Cyborgs, and Women*.

6. Jim Thomas, *Doing Critical Ethnography* (Newbury Park, CA: Sage, 1993), 2–3.

7. Thomsen, *Visibility Interrupted*, 120.

8. Thomas, *Doing Critical Ethnography*, 7.

9. Thomas, *Doing Critical Ethnography*, 8.

10. Gray's *Out in the Country* is situated entirely within the state of Kentucky; Tsing's *In the Realm of the Diamond Queen* was developed in deep relationship with the Meratus Dayak people of Indonesia; Anna Tsing, *The Mushroom at the End of the World: On the Possibility of Life in Capitalist Ruins* (Princeton, NJ: Princeton University Press, 2015).

11. Mama, "Is It Ethical to Study Africa?," 9.

12. Mama, "Is It Ethical to Study Africa?"

13. Sara Ahmed, *Complaint!* (Durham, NC: Duke University Press, 2021), 14.

14. I'm thinking here of the following pair of studies: Currier, *Out in Africa* and Thoreson, *Transnational LGBT Rights*.

15. Currier, *Out in Africa*.

16. Thoreson, *Transnational LGBT Activism*.

17. George Marcus, "Ethnography of/in the World System: The Emergence of Multi-Sited Ethnography," *Annual Review of Anthropology* 24 (1995): 97.

18. Thomas, *Doing Critical Ethnography*, 62.

19. Michael Foucault, *The Archaeology of Knowledge* (1972, Reprint, New York: Vintage, 2010).

20. U.S. Census Bureau, "Quick Facts Randolph County," accessed July 18, 2022, https://www.census.gov/quickfacts/randolphcountywestvirginia.

21. Lynsey Bourke, Sian Butcher, Nixon Chisonga, Jumani Clarke, Frances Davies, and Jessica Thorn, "Fieldwork Stories: Negotiating Positionality, Power, and Purpose," *Feminist Africa* 13 (2009): 95–105.

22. Alice Walker, *In Love and Trouble*. (New York: Harcourt Brace Jovanovich, 1973).

23. Oyeronke Oyewumi, *The Invention of Women: Making an African Sense of Western Gender Discourses* (Minneapolis: University of Minnesota Press, 1997), 3.

24. Haraway, *Simians, Cyborgs, and Women*.

CHAPTER 3 — SITES OF STRUGGLE

1. National Center for Lesbian Rights, " NCLR and USDA Announce National LGBTQ Rural Pride Campaign," May 7, 2014, https://www.nclrights.org/about-us/press-release/usda-and-nclr-launch-lgbt-rural-pride-campaign/.

2. Leslie (pseudonym, government department, program coordinator, based in Washington, DC), in discussion with the author, May 2015.

3. Title VII of the Civil Rights Act of 1964 prohibits employment discrimination for certain protected classes. At the time of my conversation with Leslie, those classes included: "race, color, religion, sex and national origin" (U.S. EEOC). Sexual orientation and gender identity are not enumerated in that list. However, multiple legal challenges over the "scope" of sex have expanded that definition to include sexual orientation (U.S. EEOC). The most decisive of these challenges was *Bostock v. Clayton County*, in which the U.S. Supreme Court ruled: "an employer who fires an individual merely for being gay or transgender violates Title VII" (Gruber, 2020). Leslie is discussing the approach of the Obama administration to interpreting "sex" in Title VII in a way that includes sexual orientation and gender identity as protected classes.

4. Leslie, in discussion with the author, May 2015.

5. Cartwright, *Peculiar Places*, 8.

6. Dan Nosowitz, "Rush Limbaugh Terrified of Lesbian Farmers for Some Reason," *Modern Farmer*, August 26, 2016, https://modernfarmer.com/2016/08/rush-limbaugh-lesbian-farmers/.

7. Elizabeth Harrington, "Feds Holding Summits for Lesbian Farmers," *Washington Free Beacon*, August 16, 2016, https://freebeacon.com/issues/feds-holding-summits-lesbian-farmers/.

8. Nosowitz, "Rush Limbaugh Terrified of Lesbian Farmers for Some Reason."

9. Nosowitz, "Rush Limbaugh Terrified of Lesbian Farmers for Some Reason."

10. Julie Moreau, "Why Is Rush Limbaugh so Afraid of Lesbian Farmers?" NBC, August 27, 2016, https://www.nbcnews.com/feature/nbc-out/why-rush-limbaugh-so-afraid-lesbian-farmers-n638736; Joseph Erbentraut, "These Lesbian Farmers Aren't Here to Take Over America. They Want to Grow It," *Huffington Post*, September 4, 2016, https://www.huffpost.com/entry/lesbian-farmers-rush-limbaugh_n_57c879d6e4b0e60d31ddf5c0; Nick Duffy, "Rush Limbaugh Is Terrified that Obama Is Helping Lesbian Farmers Take Over the South," *Pink News*, August 24, 2016, https://www.thepinknews.com/2016/08/24/rush-limbaugh-is-terrified-that-obama-is-helping-lesbian-farmers-take-over-the-south/; Cody Permenter, "Lesbian Farmers Are Taking Over the Country, If You Believe Rush Limbaugh," *Grist*, August 24, 2016, https://grist.org/food/lesbian-farmers-are-taking-over-the-country-if-you-believe-rush-limbaugh/; Tressa Glass, "Look Out, Limbaugh: A 'Lesbian Farmer' Shirt Now Exists," *Des Moines Register*, August 25, 2016, https://www.desmoinesregister.com/story/entertainment/2016/08/25/lesbian-farmers-shirt-now-exists/89351722/; J. B. Trepagnier, *Attack of the Lesbian Farmers* (Amazon, 2016).

11. The review containing this quote can be found on the Amazon site with the novel's product details: https://www.amazon.com/Attack-Lesbian-Farmers-JB-Trepagnier-ebook/dp/B01MPWC4OF/ref=cm_cr_arp_d_pl_foot_top?ie=UTF8. The review was posted by Jeff and titled "Clever and Humane Fantasy with a Ring of Truth."

12. Catherine Venable Moore, Introduction to *The Book of the Dead* by Muriel Rukeyser (Morgantown: West Virginia University Press, 2018), 4.

13. This term is Patricia Hill Collins's; see Patricia Hill Collins, *Another Kind of Public Education: Race, Schools, the Media, and Democratic Possibilities* (Boston: Beacon Press, 2009).

14. Matt Wray, *Not Quite White: White Trash and the Boundaries of Whiteness* (Durham, NC: Duke University Press, 2006); Elizabeth Catte, *What You Are Getting Wrong about Appalachia* (Cleveland: Belt Publishing, 2016).

15. Jessica Scott, "Hillbilly Horror and the New Racism: Rural and Racial Politics in *Orange Is the New Black*," *Journal of Appalachian Studies* 23, no. 2 (2017): 221–238.

16. Kim TallBear, *Native American DNA: Tribal Belonging and the False Promise of Genetic Science* (Minneapolis: University of Minnesota Press, 2013).

17. Scott, "Hillbilly Horror and the New Racism."

18. Mary Gray, Brian Gilley, and Colin Johnson, eds., *Queering the Countryside: New Frontiers in Rural Queer Studies* (New York: New York University Press, 2016); Halberstam, *In a Queer Time and Place*; Herring, *Another Country*; Johnson, *Just Queer Folks*.

19. Silvia Federici, *Caliban and the Witch: Women, the Body, and Primitive Accumulation* (Brooklyn: Autonomedia, 2004).

20. Vine Deloria Jr., *Custer Died for Your Sins: An Indian Manifesto* (Norman: University of Oklahoma Press, 1969).

21. Deloria, *Custer Died for Your Sins*, 34.

22. Federici, *Caliban and the Witch*, 68–75.

23. Deloria, *Custer Died for Your Sins*, 42.

24. Federici, *Caliban and the Witch*, 68.

25. Federici, *Caliban and the Witch*.

26. John Pape, "Black and White: The 'Perils of Sex' in Colonial Zimbabwe," *Journal of Southern African Studies* 16, no. 4 (1990): 699–720.

27. Sol Plaatje, *Native Life in South Africa* (1916, Reprint, Athens: Ohio University Press, 1991); Tembeka Ngcukaitobi, *The Land Is Ours: South Africa's First Black Lawyers and the Birth of Constitutionalism* (Cape Town: Penguin, 2018).

28. Ngcukaitobi, *The Land Is Ours*, 76–77.

29. Plaatje, *Native Life in South Africa*, 21.

30. Bessie Head, Foreword to Plaatje, *Native Life in South Africa*, ix.

31. Head, Foreword, ix.

32. Michelle Alexander, *The New Jim Crow: Mass Incarceration in the Age of Colorblindness* (New York: New Press, 2010).

33. "Coloured" is an apartheid-era racial designation for those with a "mixed" racial background, though this term really means "not" white and "not" Black. "Coloured" is still used in South Africa, both as an identity term and as a demographic term, though its use is not uncontested. Christiaan Beyers, "Identity and Forced Displacement: Community and Colouredness in District Six," in *Burdened by Race: Coloured Identities in Southern Africa*, ed. Mohamed Adhikari (Cape Town: UCT Press, 2009), 79–103; Henry Trotter, "Trauma and Memory: The Impact of Apartheid-Era Forced Removals on Coloured Identity in Cape Town," in Adhikari, *Burdened by Race*, 51.

34. Beyers, "Identity and Forced Displacement," 79.

35. Trotter, "Trauma and Memory," 51.

36. Trotter, "Trauma and Memory," 50.

37. Mark Gevisser and Edwin Cameron, *Defiant Desire: Gay and Lesbian Lives in South Africa* (New York: Routledge, 1995), 5.

38. I discuss the assumptions underpinning Tucker's work and the lens employed to view "visibility" in Cape Town much further in chapter 5, but the study I'm referencing here is Andrew Tucker, *Queer Visibilities: Space, Identity, and Interaction in Cape Town* (Malden, MA: Wiley-Blackwell, 2009).

39. Deloria, *Custer Died for Your Sins*, 47, 29, 43, 41.

40. Deloria, *Custer Died for Your Sins*, 29.

41. Ta-Nehisi Coates, "The Case for Reparations," *Atlantic*, June 15, 2014, https://www.theatlantic.com/magazine/archive/2014/06/the-case-for-reparations/361631/.

42. Todd Lewan and Dolores Barclay, "When They Steal Your Land, They Steal Your Future," *Los Angeles Times*, December 2, 2001, https://www.latimes.com/archives/la-xpm-2001-dec-02-mn-10514-story.html.

43. Vann R. Newkirk II, "The Great Land Robbery: The Shameful Story of How 1 Million Black Families Have Been Ripped from Their Farms," *Atlantic*, September 15, 2019, https://www.theatlantic.com/magazine/archive/2019/09/this-land-was-our-land/594742/.

44. Newkirk, "The Great Land Robbery."

45. Newkirk, "The Great Land Robbery."

46. Newkirk, "The Great Land Robbery."

47. Hunter and Robinson, *Chocolate Cities*, 72.

48. Cynthia Griggs Fleming, *In the Shadow of Selma: The Continuing Struggle for Civil Rights in the Rural South* (Lanham, MD: Rowman Littlefield, 2004), 72.

49. Fleming, *In the Shadow of Selma*, 15.

50. Fleming, *In the Shadow of Selma*, 120.

51. Farrow et al., *Complicity*, 2.

52. Farrow et al., *Complicity*, 14.

53. Anne Farrow, Jennifer Lang, and Joel Frank, *Complicity: How the North Promoted, Prolonged, and Profited from Slavery* (New York: Penguin Random House, 2005).

54. Hunter and Robinson, *Chocolate Cities*.

55. Hunter and Robinson, *Chocolate Cities*, 43.

56. Hunter and Robinson, *Chocolate Cities*, 43.

57. Zethu Matebeni, "*Ihlazo*: Pride and the Politics of Race and Space in Johannesburg and Cape Town," *Critical African Studies* 10, no. 3 (2018): 319.

58. Imani Perry, *Vexy Thing: On Gender and Liberation* (Durham, NC: Duke University Press, 2018).

59. Perry, *Vexy Thing*, 52–56.

60. Alexander, *The New Jim Crow*.

61. Alexander, *The New Jim Crow*, 28.

62. Catherine Coleman Flowers, *Waste: One Woman's Fight against America's Dirty Secret* (New York: New Press, 2020), 109–113.

63. Gevisser and Cameron, *Defiant Desire*.

64. Camminga, *Transgender Refugees*.

65. Gevisser and Cameron, *Defiant Desire*.

66. Gevisser and Cameron, *Defiant Desire*, x.

67. Ngcukaitobi, *The Land Is Ours*.

68. Gevisser and Cameron, *Defiant Desire*, 3.

69. Nonhlanhla Mkhize, Jane Bennett, Vasu Reddy, and Relebohile Moletsane, *The Country We Want to Live In: Hate Crimes and Homophobia in the Lives of Black Lesbian South Africans* (Cape Town: HSRC, 2010), 7.

70. This trajectory is chronicled well from multiple perspectives in Melanie Judge, Anthony Manion, and Shaun de Waal, *To Have and To Hold: The Making of Same-Sex Marriage in South Africa* (Johannesburg: Jacana Media, 2008).

71. Mkhize et al., *The Country We Want to Live In*, 8.

72. Mkhize et al., *The Country We Want to Live In*, 8.

73. Matebeni, *Black Lesbian Sexualities and Identities in South Africa*, 9.

74. Perry, *Vexy Thing*.

75. Michael Gross, "Gay Is the New Black: The Last Great Civil Rights Struggle," *The Advocate*, November 16, 2008, https://www.advocate.com/news/2008/11/16/gay-new-black.

76. Adam Liptak, "Supreme Court Invalidates Key Part of Voting Rights Act," *New York Times*, June 25, 2013, https://www.nytimes.com/2013/06/26/us/supreme-court-ruling.html.

77. Michelle Kelsey Kearl, "'Is Gay the New Black?': An Intersectional Perspective on Social Movement Rhetoric in California's Proposition 8 Debate," *Communication and Critical/Cultural Studies* 12, no. 1 (2015): 64.

78. Cartwright, *Peculiar Places*, 9.

79. Cartwright, *Pecluliar Places*, 10.

80. John D'Emilio, "Capitalism and Gay Identity," in *The Gay and Lesbian Studies Reader*, ed. Henry Abelove, Michele Aina Barale, and David Halperin (New York: Routledge, 1993), 467–478.

81. D'Emilio, "Capitalism and Gay Identity," 470.

82. Eli Clare, *Exile and Pride: Disability, Queerness, and Liberation* (Cambridge, MA: South End Press, 2009), 41.

83. Clare, *Exile and Pride*, 47.

84. Clare, *Exile and Pride*, 40.

85. Gray, *Out in the Country*, 3.

86. Gray, *Out in the Country*, 4.

87. Mutua, *Human Rights*, 142.

88. Ngcukaitobi, *The Land Is Ours*, 1.

89. Ngcukaitobi, *The Land Is Ours*, 1.

90. Mutua, *Human Rights*.

91. Mutua, *Human Rights*, 142.

92. Mutua, *Human Rights*, 142.

93. Mutua, *Human Rights*, 142; Government of South Africa, "Land Reform," accessed July 25, 2022, https://www.gov.za/issues/land-reform.

94. Mutua, *Human Rights*, 137.

95. Mutua, *Human Rights*, 137.

96. Mutua, *Human Rights*, 129.

97. Azad Essa, "Unpacking South Africa's Fraught and Complex Land Debate," *Al Jazeera*, August 30, 2018, https://www.aljazeera.com/news/2018/8/30/unpacking-south-africas-fraught-and-complex-land-debate.

98. Essa, "Unpacking South Africa's Fraught and Complex Land Debate."

99. S'thembile Cele, "ANC and EFF Differ on which Land Should Be Expropriated," *Times Live*, March 5, 2020, https://www.timeslive.co.za/politics/2020-03-05-anc-and-eff-differ-on-which-land-should-be-expropriated-without-compensation/.

100. Essa, "Unpacking South Africa's Fraught and Complex Land Debate."

101. Essa, "Unpacking South Africa's Fraught and Complex Land Debate."

102. Mutua, *Human Rights*, 129.

103. International Day Against Homophobia, Transphobia and Biphobia (IDAHOT) Dialogue with Political Parties (hosted by Free Gender, Khumbulani Pride event based in Langa, Western Cape), attended by the author, May 2016.

104. Ngcukaitobi, *The Land Is Ours*, 271.

105. Ngcukaitobi, *The Land Is Ours*.

106. Sindiwe Magana, *Living, Loving, and Lying Awake at Night* (Cape Town: David Philip, 1991), 109.

107. T. Dunbar Moodie, Vivienne Ntadshe, and British Mbuye, "Migrancy and Male Sexuality on the South African Gold Mines," *Journal of Southern African Studies* 14, no. 2 (1988): 228–256.

108. The same is not true for couples where a partner transitions gender. Because there is a separate law for legislating same-sex marriages in South Africa, if a couple is married

NOTES TO PAGES 62–70   173

under the Marriage Act and one partner subsequently transitions, the couple is forced to divorce and remarry under the Civil Union Act.

CHAPTER 4 — WELCOME TO MODERNITY

1. Ethel (pseudonym, rural community-based advocacy organization, co-founder, based in North Carolina), in discussion with the author, June 2015.
2. Manuel (pseudonym, regional LGBT equality organization, outreach coordinator, based in North Carolina), in discussion with the author, June 2015.
3. Gevisser, *The Pink Line*.
4. Global Sexuality Summer School Session (University of Cape Town), attended by the author, January 2016 (hereafter, "Global Sexuality Summer School Session").
5. Global Sexuality Summer School Session.
6. Doug van Gundy, email to Campus Community of West Virginia Wesleyan College, November 14, 2014.
7. Massad, *Desiring Arabs*.
8. Global Sexuality Summer School Session.
9. Global Sexuality Summer School Session.
10. Pete (national LGBTI advocacy organization, founder, based in Gauteng), in discussion with the author, March 2016.
11. David (pseudonym, global funder, regional office, based in Gauteng), in discussion with the author, February 2016.
12. Andile (pseudonym, national LGBTI advocacy organization, based in the Eastern Cape), in discussion with the author, February 2016.
13. Xolani (pseudonym, national LGBTI advocacy organization, outreach officer, Western Cape), in discussion with the author, April 2016.
14. David, in discussion with the author, February 2016.
15. Alternative Inclusive Pride panel discussion: "What Are the Most Important Issues Facing LGBTIQ People Today?" (Western Cape), attended by the author, February 2016.
16. Kian (pseudonym, LGBTIQ advocacy organization focused on religious communities, founder), in discussion with the author, April 2016.
17. Gevisser, *The Pink Line*.
18. Pete, in discussion with the author, March 2016.
19. Asa (pseudonym, advocacy organization focused on queer and trans women, Eastern Cape) in discussion with the author, January 2016.
20. The term "regional" in South Africa, when regional advocacy was a condition for funding, meant a group of countries outside of South Africa. For instance, if a South African organization wanted to host strategy sessions or meetings to incubate new organizations for other African countries in South Africa, where the legal terrain was friendlier for LGBTIQ rights work, their proposal might look more appealing or establish eligibility for funding in some cases. In those same applications, organizations might not be eligible for funding if they were working on issues of access or education or safety from violence for South Africans within South Africa. In the U.S. South, the term "regional" referred to the South as a region—a collection of states *within* the United States. While regional organizations do exist in the U.S. South and in some other regions of the United States, applying for funding within a collection of states did not come up as something that would make grant applications more successful.
21. George (pseudonym, LGBTQ advocacy, statewide organization, director, based in Georgia), in discussion with the author, January 2015.
22. Nick Estes, *Our History Is the Future: Standing Rock versus the Dakota Access Pipeline and the Long Tradition of Indigenous Resistance* (Brooklyn: Verso, 2019).

23. Perry, *Vexy Thing*.
24. Hanne Blank, *Straight: The Surprisingly Short History of Heterosexuality* (Boston: Beacon Press, 2012).
25. Mutua, *Human Rights*.
26. Camminga, *Transgender Refugees*.
27. Federici, *Caliban and the Witch*; Sarah Franklin, *Dolly Mixtures: Remaking the Meaning of Genealogy* (Durham, NC: Duke University Press, 2007); Johnson, *Just Queer Folks*.
28. Franklin, *Dolly Mixtures*, 111.
29. Franklin, *Dolly Mixtures*, 111.
30. Catte, *What You Are Getting Wrong about Appalachia*.
31. Franklin, *Dolly Mixtures*, 111.
32. Franklin, *Dolly Mixtures*, 110.
33. Johnson, *Just Queer Folks*, 66.
34. Johnson, *Just Queer Folks*, 39, 52, 53.
35. Johnson, *Just Queer Folks*, 68.
36. E. Cram, "(Dis)locating Queer Citizenship: Imagining Rurality in Matthew Shepard's Memory," in Gray et al., *Queering the Countryside*, 297.
37. F. Hollis Griffith, *Feeling Normal: Sexuality and Media Criticism in the Digital Age* (Bloomington: Indiana University Press, 2016), 23.
38. Beam, *Gay, Inc.*
39. Jessica Scott, "The Distance between Death and Marriage: Citizenship, Violence, and Same-Sex Marriage in South Africa," *International Feminist Journal of Politics* 23, no. 4 (2013): 534–552.
40. Beam, *Gay, Inc.*
41. Beam, *Gay, Inc.*; Clare, *Exile and Pride*; Spade, *Normal Life*.
42. Gray, *Out in the Country*.
43. Cram, "(Dis)locating Queer Citizenship," 297.
44. Clare Sears, *Arresting Dress: Cross-Dressing, Law, and Fascination in Nineteenth Century San Francisco* (Durham, NC: Duke University Press, 2014).
45. Sears, *Arresting Dress*, 3.
46. Sears, *Arresting Dress*, 3.
47. Sears, *Arresting Dress*; Robin Henry, "Queering the American Frontier: Finding Queerness and Sexual Difference in Late Nineteenth-Century and Early Twentieth-Century Colorado," in Gray et al., *Queering the Countryside*, 304–323.
48. Henry, "Queering the American Frontier," 317.
49. Sears, *Arresting Dress*, 11.
50. George, in discussion with the author, January 2015.
51. Jack (pseudonym, national LGBT equality organization, regional coordinator, based in North Carolina), in discussion with the author, August 2014.
52. Elena Schneider, "The Bathroom Bill That Ate North Carolina," *Politico*, March 23, 2017, https://www.politico.com/magazine/story/2017/03/the-bathroom-bill-that-ate-north-carolina-214944/.
53. Tim Carpenter, "Kansas Cities Push Back against House Bill Nullifying Local Anti-Discrimination Ordinances," *Kansas Reflector*, February 15, 2023, https://kansasreflector.com/2023/02/15/kansas-cities-push-back-against-house-bill-nullifying-local-anti-discrimination-ordinances/.
54. Cynthia (pseudonym, southern regional queer liberation organization, co-founder, based in North Carolina), in discussion with the author, December 2014.
55. George, in discussion with the author, January 2015.

56. Stacey (pseudonym, southern regional LGBTQ advocacy organization, director, based in North Carolina), in discussion with the author, January 2015.
57. Cynthia, in discussion with the author, December 2014.
58. Garth (pseudonym, national transgender advocacy organization, founder, based in Gauteng), in discussion with the author, February 2016.
59. Asa, in discussion with the author, January 2016.
60. Matebeni, *Black Lesbian Sexualities and Identity in South Africa*, 9.
61. Matebeni, *Black Lesbian Sexualities and Identity in South Africa*, 9.
62. Matebeni, *Black Lesbian Sexualities and Identity in South Africa*, 9.

CHAPTER 5 — METRONORMATIVITY AS ALIENATION

1. The first time that Cape Town Pride was disrupted by Alternative Inclusive Pride is written about here: Lwando Scott, "The Politics of Pride—Cape Town," *Queer Consciousness* (blog), March 17, 2015, https://queerconsciousness.com/the-politics-of-pride-cape-town/.
2. Roberto Igual, "Cape Town Pride to Change Controversial 2016 Theme," *Mamba Online*, December 3, 2015, https://www.mambaonline.com/2015/12/03/cape-town-pride-change-controversial-2016-theme/.
3. "We The Brave: The Brave Float," Ads of the World, accessed March 7, 2023, https://www.adsoftheworld.com/campaigns/the-brave-float.
4. We The Brave (@WeTheBraveSA), "Our #BraveEnough Float Is Tweet-Active! Tweet @ Us to Make Our #Cockfloat Blow It's Load With Glitter! #gay #lgbti," Twitter, February 27, 2016, https://twitter.com/WeTheBraveSA/status/703522066381860864.
5. We The Brave (@WeTheBraveSA), "Having Made an Appearance in Cape Town, Our Giant Dick Float Will Be at #Durbanpride This Year!," Twitter, July 16, 2016, https://mobile.twitter.com/wethebravesa/status/754329842145832960.
6. Ivan Toms Centre for Health, "Campaign Bolsters Bravery amongst Men Who Have Sex with Men," accessed November 13, 2023, https://ivantomscentre.africa/2015/06/26/campaign-bolsters-bravery-amongst-men-who-have-sex-with-men/.
7. Odette Herbert, "The Alternative Inclusive Pride Network 2016 Cape Town," YouTube video March 6, 2016, https://www.youtube.com/watch?v=nRcI3LG6cmY.
8. Blank, *Straight*.
9. Oyeronke Oyewumi, *The Invention of Women: Making an African Sense of Western Gender Discourses* (Minneapolis: University of Minnesota Press, 1997).
10. Massad, *Desiring Arabs*.
11. Tsing, *In the Realm of the Diamond Queen*, xi.
12. Melissa Steyn and Micki van Zyl, *The Prize and the Price: Shaping Sexualities in South Africa* (Cape Town: HRSC Press, 2009).
13. Spade, *Normal Life*.
14. Reid, *How to Be a Real Gay*, 37.
15. Lorway, *Namibia's Rainbow Project*, 4.
16. Currier, *Out in Africa*.
17. Currier, *Out in Africa*, 6.
18. Gray, *Out in the Country*, 9.
19. Thomsen, *Visibility Interrupted*.
20. Sokari Ekine, "Contesting Narratives of Queer Africa," in Ekine and Abbas, *Queer African Reader*, 78–91; Kagendo Murungi, "Small Axe at the Crossroads: A Reflection on African Sexualities and Human Rights," in Ekine and Abbas, *Queer African Reader*, 229–243.
21. Thomsen, *Visibility Interrupted*.
22. Johnson, *Just Queer Folks*, 7.
23. Thoreson, *Transnational LGBT Activism*.

24. Thoreson, *Transnational LGBT Activism*, 90.
25. Thoreson, *Transnational LGBT Activism*, 90.
26. Thoreson, *Transnational LGBT Activism*, 78.
27. Thoreson, *Transnational LGBT Rights*, 90.
28. Ekine and Abbas, *Queer African Reader*.
29. Thoreson, *Transnational LGBT Rights*, 78, 90.
30. Thoreson, *Transnational LGBT Rights*, 55.
31. Thoreson, *Transnational LGBT Rights*, 211.
32. Massad, *Desiring Arabs*.
33. Thoreson, *Transnational LGBT Rights*, 6; Massad, "Re-Orienting Desire," 384.
34. Massad, "Re-Orienting Desire," 384.
35. Natalie Oswin, "Researching 'Gay Cape Town': Finding Value-Added Queerness," *Social and Cultural Geography* 6, no. 4 (2005): 578.
36. Matebeni and Camminga, *Beyond the Mountain*.
37. Tsing, *In the Realm of the Diamond Queen*, xi.
38. Oswin, "Researching 'Gay Cape Town,'" 579.
39. Oswin, "Researching 'Gay Cape Town,'" 580.
40. Reid, *How to Be a Real Gay*, 1.
41. Reid, *How to Be a Real Gay*, 111.
42. Reid, *How to Be a Real Gay*, 27.
43. Malika Zouhali-Worrall and Katherine Wright, "They Will Say We Are Not Here," *New York Times*, January 26, 2012, https://www.nytimes.com/video/opinion/100000001307281/they-will-say-we-are-not-here.html.
44. Zethu Matebeni, "*Ihlazo*," 317.
45. Funeka Soldaat, "Black Lesbian Politics and Organising Spaces," in Matebeni and Camminga, *Beyond the Mountain*, 137–146.
46. Matebeni, "*Ihlazo*," 320.
47. Matebeni, "*Ihlazo*," 320.
48. Apartheid-era racial designation for those with a "mixed" racial background. This term is still used in South Africa, both as an identity term and as a demographic term for the purposes of census data, though its use is not uncontested.
49. Nigel Patel's excellent piece "Violent Cisterns" examines the intersections of race, class, and gender in a discussion of bathroom experiences for transgender people in Cape Town. Because of the widespread controversy in the United States about gendered bathroom laws, this is an incredible piece to use to think about how access to bathrooms and other gender and racially segregated spaces has been shaped historically and plays out for people who do not have reliable and safe access to clean water and sanitation within their own homes, placing them in closer proximity to the danger of gender-based violence. Nigel Patel, "Violent Cisterns: Trans Experiences of Bathroom Space," *Agenda* 31, no. 1 (2017): 51–63.
50. Liza (pseudonym, transgender advocacy organization, founder, Western Cape), in discussion with author, March 2016.
51. Kian (pseudonym, religious LGBTIQ advocacy organization, founder, Western Cape), in discussion with the author, April 2016.
52. Asa (pseudonym, queer and transgender women advocacy organization, founder, Eastern Cape), in discussion with the author, January 2016.
53. Kayla (pseudonym, grassroots Black lesbian advocacy organization, founder, Western Cape), in discussion with the author, April 2016.
54. Xolani (pseudonym, LGBTIQ advocacy, outreach officer, Western Cape), in discussion with the author, April 2016.

55. Kayla, in discussion with the author, April 2016.

56. Scott, "Disruption and Withdrawal," 171–185.

57. Ryan Cochran, "Grab Your Boo and #LoveNOLA," *Go NOLA*, August 28, 2015, https://gonola.com/lgbt-new-orleans/lovenola-movement-lgbt-community.

58. Nico Lang, "The 5 Worst States for LGBT People," *Rolling Stone*, November 24, 2014 https://www.rollingstone.com/politics/politics-news/the-5-worst-states-for-lgbt-people-198931/.

59. Hristina Byrnes, John Harrington, and Grant Suneson, "Supreme Court Decision Aside, Some States Are Better—and Some Are Worse—for LGBT Community," *USA Today*, June 19, 2020, https://www.usatoday.com/story/money/2020/06/19/the-best-and-worst-states-for-lgbtq-people/111968524/.

60. The South is so closely associated with political conservatism that a *Forbes* contributor suggested that there are three political parties in the United States, one of which is a distinct genre of conservatism that is distinctly southern. See Chris Ladd, "Southern Conservatives Are America's Third Party," *Forbes*, March 16, 2017, https://www.forbes.com/sites/chrisladd/2017/03/16/southern-conservatives-are-americas-third-party/?sh=e825c55406b8.

61. Southern Fried Queer Pride (SFQP)'s website has been updated and no longer includes this original description, but it has been preserved, with a graphic from one of the early SFQP festivals on the Atlanta Trans Teens Tumblr in a post dated June 1, 2015; see https://atlantatransteens.tumblr.com/.

62. This language is from excerpts from an interview with an organizer affiliated with SFQP. Those excerpts can be found here in Adron McCann and Jim Burress, "The Annual Southern Fried Queer Pride Offers an Inclusive, Diverse Lineup," *WABE*, June 22, 2022, https://www.wabe.org/the-annual-southern-fried-queer-pride-festival-offers-an-inclusive-diverse-line-up/.

63. McCann and Jim Burress, "The Annual Southern Fried Queer Pride Offers an Inclusive Diverse Lineup."

64. Hal (pseudonym, national organization with a regional focus, founder, based in Georgia), in discussion with the author, December 2014.

65. Jerome (pseudonym, national organization, southern regional office, based in Georgia, outreach), in discussion with the author, February 2015.

66. George (pseudonym, statewide organization, director, based in Georgia) in discussion, with the author, January 2015.

67. Hal, in discussion with the author, December 2014.

68. Leon Stafford, "Despite Progress HIV/AIDS in Georgia Remains Disproportionately Black in Georgia," *Atlanta-Journal Constitution*, February 24, 2022, https://www.ajc.com/life/despite-progress-hiv-remains-disproportionately-black-in-georgia/MOUFBE4GUZFS5GJTOEKAOG2SMU/.

69. George, in discussion with the author, January 2015.

70. Hal, in discussion with the author, December 2014.

71. Jerome, in discussion with the author, February 2015.

72. Tucker, *Queer Visibility*.

CHAPTER 6 — QUEER ORGANIZING IN OUT-OF-THE-WAY PLACES

1. Massad, *Desiring Arabs*.

2. Garth (pseudonym, national transgender advocacy organization, founder, Johannesburg), in discussion with the author, February 2016.

3. Garth (pseudonym, national transgender advocacy organization, founder, Johannesburg), in discussion with the author, February 2016.

4. Haraway, *Staying with the Trouble*.
5. Mutua, *Human Rights*.
6. Stoler, *Duress*.
7. Massad, *Desiring Arabs*.
8. Currier, *Out in Africa*.
9. Janet (pseudonym, national LGBTIQ rights organization, outreach officer, based in Cape Town), in discussion with the author, April 2016.
10. Kayla (pseudonym, Black lesbian grassroots advocacy organization, founder, Western Cape), in discussion with the author, April 2016.
11. Andile (pseudonym, national LGBT advocacy organization, outreach coordinator, Eastern Cape), in discussion with the author, January 2016.
12. Thoreson, *Transnational LGBT Activism*.
13. David (pseudonym, international organization, South African office), in discussion with the author, February 2016.
14. Massad, *Desiring Arabs*.
15. Nkunzi Nkabinde, *Black Bull, Ancestors and Me: My Life as a Lesbian Sangoma* (Johannesburg: Fanele, 2009).
16. Andile, in discussion with the author, January 2016.
17. Sibongile Ndashe, "The Single Story of 'African Homophobia' Is Dangerous for LGBTI Activism," in Ekine and Abbas, *Queer African Reader*, 155.
18. Ndashe, "The Single Story of 'African Homophobia,'" 155.
19. Ndashe, "The Single Story of 'African Homophobia,'" 156.
20. Ndashe, "The Single Story of 'African Homophobia,'" 90.
21. Judith Butler, *Frames of War: When Is Life Grievable?* (New York: Verso, 2009); Jasbir Puar, *Terrorist Assemblages: Homonationalism in Queer Times* (Durham, NC: Duke University Press, 2007).
22. Reid, *How to Be a Real Gay*.
23. Reid, *How to Be a Real Gay*, 41.
24. Reid, *How to Be a Real Gay*, 43.
25. Reid, *How to Be a Real Gay*, 41.
26. Reid, *How to Be a Real Gay*, 42.
27. Reid, *How to Be a Real Gay*.
28. Jane Bennett, "'Solemnis(ing) Beginnings': Theories of Same-Sex Marriage in the USA and South Africa," *Culture, Health & Sexuality* 17, suppl. 1 (2015): 56.
29. Bennett, "Solemnis(ing) Beginnings," 54–55.
30. Gevisser and Cameron, *Defiant Desire*.
31. A Supreme Court decision in the summer of 2020 finally resulted in the protection of lesbian, gay, and transgender people from employment discrimination under Title VII for the first time nationwide. See Adam Liptack, "Civil Rights Law Protects Gay and Transgender Workers, Supreme Court Rules," *New York Times*, June 25, 2020, https://www.nytimes.com/2020/06/15/us/gay-transgender-workers-supreme-court.html.
32. See Bill Chappell, "Supreme Court Declares Same-Sex Marriage Legal in All 50 States," *NPR*, June 26, 2015, https://www.npr.org/sections/thetwo-way/2015/06/26/417717613/supreme-court-rules-all-states-must-allow-same-sex-marriages.
33. Bennett, "Solemnis(ing) Beginnings."
34. John D'Emilio, "The Marriage Fight Is Setting Us Back," in *Against Equality: Queer Critiques of Gay Marriage*, ed. Ryan Conrad (Lewiston, ME: Against Equality Press, 2010), 37–42.
35. D'Emilio, "The Marriage Fight Is Holding Us Back," 37.

36. Nancy Polikoff, *Beyond (Straight and Gay) Marriage: Valuing All Families under the Law* (Boston: Beacon Press, 2008).
37. Lorway, *Namibia's Rainbow Project*, 76.
38. Lorway, *Namibia's Rainbow Project*, 92, 4.
39. Lorway, *Namibia's Rainbow Project*, 92.
40. Lorway, *Namibia's Rainbow Project*, 13.
41. Lorway, *Namibia's Rainbow Project*, 77.
42. Lorway, *Namibia's Rainbow Project*, 47.
43. Massad, "Re-Orienting Desire," 385.
44. Lorway, *Namibia's Rainbow Project*, 81.
45. Lorway, *Namibia's Rainbow Project*, 82.
46. Kaitlin Dearham, "NGOs and Queer Women's Activism in Nairobi," in Ekine and Abbas, *Queer African Reader*, 193.
47. Dearham, "NGOs and Queer Women's Activism in Nairobi," 193.
48. Dearham, "NGOs and Queer Women's Activism in Nairobi," 195.
49. Dearham, NGOs and Queer Women's Activism in Nairobi," 194.
50. Mkhize et al., *The Country We Want to Live In*, 15.
51. Lorway, *Namibia's Rainbow Project*, 8.
52. Murungi, "Small Axe at the Crossroads," 239.
53. Murungi, "Small Axe at the Crossroads," 240.
54. Foucault, *The Archaeology of Knowledge*.
55. Spurlin, *Imperialism within the Margins*.
56. Gray (*Out in the Country*) and Lorway (*Namibia's Rainbow Project*) have demonstrated this in both the U.S. South and southern African contexts, respectively.
57. Reid, *How to Be a Real Gay*, 69.
58. Murungi, "Small Axe at the Crossroads," 239.
59. Heather (pseudonym, oral history project documenting queer life, founder, West Virginia), in discussion with the author, July 2015.
60. Nathi (pseudonym, organization focused on access to transgender affirming care for rural individuals, founder, Guateng), in discussion with the author, February 2016.
61. Heather, in discussion with the author, July 2015.
62. Panel discussion (LGBT in the South Conference, Campaign for Southern Equality, Asheville, NC), attended by the author, April 2015.
63. Jeanne (pseudonym, regional intersectional queer liberation organization, cofounder, based in Tennessee), in discussion with the author, October 2014.
64. Murungi, "Small-Axe at the Crossroads"
65. Karma Chavez, *Queer Immigration Politics: Activist Rhetoric and Coalitional Possibilities* (Champaign: University of Illinois Press, 2013).
66. Victor (pseudonym, safe spaces for queer youth, university archivist and organizer, North Carolina), in discussion with the author, January 2015.
67. Jeanne, in discussion with the author, October 2014.
68. A BBQ is a social event organized around food. Barbecued meats are often served at BBQ gatherings. This grassroots organisation often came together over BBQs for their meetings, which they called "queer BBQs" when they invited me.
69. Kathy (pseudonym, community-based grassroots organization, co-founder, North Carolina), in discussion with the author, August 2014.
70. Damien (pseudonym, community-based grassroots organization, gathering attendee, North Carolina), in discussion with the author, August 2014.
71. Kathy, in discussion with the author, August 2014.

72. Keynote address given at the Louisiana Queer Conference: "Bold Not Broken: Queer Resilience in the South" (hosted by Louisiana LGBT advocacy organizations in Baton Rouge, Louisiana), attended by the author, March 2015.

73. Cynthia (pseudonym, regional intersectional queer liberation organization, cofounder, based in North Carolina), in discussion with the author, December 2014.

74. Johnson, *Just Queer Folks*.

CHAPTER 7 — WHEN WHITENESS GETS IN THE WAY

1. Bérubé, "How Gay Stays White and What Kind of White It Stays"; Chasin, *Selling Out*; Vaid, *Virtual Equality*.

2. Jane Bennett, "'Queer/White' in South Africa: A Troubling Oxymoron?," in *Queer in Africa: LGBTQI Identities, Citizenship, and Activism*, ed. Zethu Matebeni, Surya Monro, and Vasu Reddy (London: Routledge, 2018), 111.

3. Bennett, "'Queer/White' in South Africa," 108.

4. Bérubé, "How Gay Stays White and What Kind of White It Stays."

5. WBOY reported that Maine is the least diverse state in the United States and West Virginia is the second-least diverse state, based on data from the 2020 census. See Shayla Klein, "What the Latest Census Data Says about West Virginia," *WBOY*, August 12, 2021, https://www.wboy.com/top-stories/what-the-latest-census-data-says-about-west-virginia/.

6. Gray, *Out in the Country*.

7. Sarah Schwartz, "Map: Where Critical Race Theory Is Under Attack," *Education Week*, July 15, 2022, https://www.edweek.org/policy-politics/map-where-critical-race-theory-is-under-attack/2021/06.

8. Aida Hurtado, *The Color of Privilege: Three Blasphemies on Race and Feminism* (Ann Arbor: University of Michigan Press, 1997).

9. Maureen Redding, "Invisibility/Hyperinvisibility of Normative Whiteness: The Paradox of Normative Whiteness," in Kimmel and Ferber, *Privilege: A Reader*, 155–168.

10. Bérubé, "Why Gay Stays White and What Kind of White It Stays."

11. For a "cultural history" of the representation of the hillbilly, see Anthony Harkins, *Hillbilly: A Cultural History of an American Icon* (New York: Oxford University Press, 2003). See also Wray, *Not Quite White*; and bell hooks, *Where We Stand: Class Matters* (New York: Routledge, 2000).

12. Bérubé, "How Gay Stays White and What Kind of White It Stays."

13. Crystal Good, "Appalachia's White Inferiority Pushed My Trans, Black Daughter Out," *100 Days of Appalachia*, February 19, 2019, https://www.100daysinappalachia.com/2019/02/appalachias-white-inferiority-pushed-my-trans-black-daughter-out/.

14. Crystal Good, "Consuming Blackness in 'Progressive' White Appalachia," *Scalawag*, March 5, 2021, https://scalawagmagazine.org/2021/03/wv-ywca-racism/.

15. Kim Kobersmith, "Frank X Walker's 'New Word Order.'" *The Bitter Southerner*, August 5, 2021, https://bittersoutherner.com/southern-perspectives/2021/frank-x-walkers-new-word-order.

16. Crystal Good, "Behind the Scenes in Black Appalachia," *Scalawag*, December 23, 2020, https://scalawagmagazine.org/2020/12/hillbilly-movie-black-appalachia/.

17. Bérubé, "How Gay Stays White and What Kind of White It Stays."

18. Redding, "Invisibility/Hypervisibility," 155.

19. Neema Avashia, *Another Appalachia: Coming Up Queer and Indian in a Mountain Place* (Morgantown: West Virginia University Press, 2022).

20. Good, "Consuming Blackness in 'Progressive' White Appalachia."

21. Hurtado, *The Color of Privilege*, 128.

22. Good, "Appalachia's White Inferiority Pushed My Trans, Black Daughter Out."

23. Katie Kuba, "Buckhannon Votes Down Non-Discrimination Ordinance," *My Buckhannon*, January 4, 2019, https://www.mybuckhannon.com/buckhannon-votes-down-non-discrimination-ordinance/; "Elkins to Consider Resolution," *Intermountain*, March 18, 2015, https://www.theintermountain.com/news/local-news/2015/03/elkins-to-consider-resolution/.

24. As of 2019, Elkins, West Virginia, had an estimated population of 6,990, and Buckhannon, West Virginia, had an estimated population of 5,394. Additionally, the population of Elkins is estimated at 92 percent white; the population of Buckhannon is estimated at 89.8 percent white. See U.S. Census Bureau, "Quick Facts: Elkins City, West Virginia," https://www.census.gov/quickfacts/fact/table/elkinscitywestvirginia/PST045219; U.S. Census Bureau, "Quick Facts: Buckhannon City, West Virginia," https://www.census.gov/quickfacts/buckhannoncitywestvirginia; and Travis Crum, "Buckhannon 5th W.Va. City to Pass LGBT Protections," *Charleston Gazette-Mail*, May 3, 2013, https://www.wvgazettemail.com/news/politics/buckhannon-5th-w-va-city-to-pass-lgbt-protections/article_235f9696-8c4f-5a9d-9fea-8119c3b775ea.html. There is no explicit language in either town's policies that would protect gender identity from discrimination, but it is important to note that there is now federal legal precedent for the protection against the discrimination of gender identity based on "sex," a class that is already legally protected in Title VII and Title IX. See Katie Rogers, "Title IX Protections Extend to Transgender Students, Education Dept. Says," *New York Times*, June 16, 2021, https://www.nytimes.com/2021/06/16/us/politics/title-ix-transgender-students.html; and Nina Totenberg, "Supreme Court Delivers Major Victory to LGBTQ Employees," *NPR*, June 15, 2020, https://www.npr.org/2020/06/15/863498848/supreme-court-delivers-major-victory-to-lgbtq-employees.

25. Elkins City Council meeting, attended by the author, March 2015.

26. After the public comment section had concluded, a man who claimed to be at the meeting for an entirely different purpose (something related to parking and his small business) stood up and asked to be allowed to speak. The man was gruff, confident, legibly local, and self-identified as an ex-marine. With the approval of the council members most opposed to the resolution, the man was permitted to speak. These remarks changed the tenor of the proceedings because speakers supporting the resolution had spoken first while those who opposed the resolution had spoken last. The last remarks about the resolution had been from speakers who spoke about the evils of same-sex sexuality, casting a grim atmosphere over the entire proceedings. As everyone waited to hear what this man would say, the man began to express confusion over why we were even discussing discrimination. The man expressed dismay that discrimination against gay, lesbian, bisexual, and transgender people was still legal. The man twice embraced the position of a hypothetical bisexual, asking, "Are you saying that if I say I am bisexual, you will not hire me? Are you saying that?" Many of us who were there advocating for the resolution believe that this man altered the outcome that evening. After these comments, the city council seemed unsure what to do, but when more individuals demanded an opportunity to speak, they closed public comments. Despite all of our efforts to build community support for the resolution, there is no way of knowing whether or not the adoption of the resolution would have been successful had this man's unprompted and unexpected comments not taken everyone off guard. We had all been prepared for the remarks of the speakers who had signed up to comment publicly, but none of us had been prepared for random passersby to insert themselves into the proceedings the way this man did.

27. "Elkins Passes Non-Discrimination Measure," *Intermountain*, March 20, 2015, https://www.theintermountain.com/news/local-news/2015/03/elkins-passes-nondiscrimination-measure/.

28. All of the information in the following scenes derives from my personal observations while in attendance at the events. I recorded and transcribed the proceedings at the Elkins City Council meeting as part of the larger project of this book. I attended the Buckhannon City Council meeting after the completion of that fieldwork and so did not record the event. When I quote verbatim, I am relying on the recordings or on accounts in the news media (which are identified by citations). The correspondence from Fairness WV that I draw on is from emails to Fairness WV's list of supporters and, in one case, personal correspondence with contacts at the organization. My familiarity with Fairness WV goes beyond being on their list of email contacts. I was a member of its board of directors from 2011 to 2014. Information drawn from other sources is indicated by citations.

29. Liptack, "Civil Rights Law Protects Gay and Transgender Workers."

30. Crum, "Buckhannon 5th W.Va. City to Pass LGBT Protections."

31. Marcus Constantino, "Teen Defends Show after Anti-Gay Comments," *Charleston Gazette-Mail*, June 11, 2012, https://www.wvgazettemail.com/news/teen-defends-show-after-anti-gay-comments/article_dd6a0f8f-b0ad-5934-92df-2ae95423b128.html.

32. Spade, *Normal Life*.

33. Spade, *Normal Life*.

34. Good, "Consuming Blackness in 'Progressive' West Virginia."

35. U.S. Census Bureau, "Quick Facts: West Virginia," accessed December 19, 2023, https://www.census.gov/quickfacts/fact/table/WV/PST045222.

36. Good, "Consuming Blackness in 'Progressive' West Virginia."

37. Berube, "Why Gay Stays White and What Kind of White It Stays."

38. Bérubé, "How Gay Stays White and What Kind of White It Stays."

39. Bérubé, "How Gay Stays White and What Kind of White It Stays."

40. The founder of Free Gender explicitly asked that I use her real name and the name of the organization in the text rather than a pseudonym.

41. Haraway, *Simians, Cyborgs, and Women*.

42. Thomas, *Doing Critical Ethnography*, 20.

43. Nia-Malika Henderson, "Inside the Battle over the Confederate Flag," *CNN*, June 24, 2015, https://www.cnn.com/2015/06/21/politics/south-carolina-confederate-flag-debate/index.html.

44. Frances Robles, "Dylan Roof Photos and a Manifesto Are Posted Online," *New York Times*, June 20, 2015, https://www.nytimes.com/2015/06/21/us/dylann-storm-roof-photos-website-charleston-church-shooting.html.

45. Libby Nelson, "Confederate Flags Are Coming Down: Here's the Latest State by State," *Vox*, June 24, 2015, https://www.vox.com/2015/6/24/8840207/confederate-flag-ban-history-latest-mississippi-south-carolina.

46. Barbara Kingsolver, "A View from the South: Let the Confederate Flag Go," *Guardian*, July 3, 2015, https://www.theguardian.com/commentisfree/2015/jul/03/south-flag-confederate-pride-hatred-racists.

47. Spade, *Normal Life*.

Bibliography

Adam, Barry. "The Defense of Marriage Act and American Exceptionalism: The 'Gay Marriage' Panic in the United States." *Journal of the History of Sexuality* 12, no. 2 (2003): 259–276.
Ahmed, Sara. *Complaint!* Durham, NC: Duke University Press, 2021.
Alexander, Michelle. *The New Jim Crow: Mass Incarceration in the Age of Colorblindness.* New York: New Press, 2010.
Allison, Dorothy. *Two or Three Things I Know for Sure.* New York: Plume, 1995.
American Civil Liberties Union. *Cracks in the System: 20 Years of the Unjust Federal Crack Cocaine Law.* October 26, 2006. https://www.aclu.org/other/cracks-system-20-years-unjust-federal-crack-cocaine-law.
Avashia, Neema. *Another Appalachia: Coming up Queer and Indian in a Mountain Place.* Morgantown: West Virginia University Press, 2022.
Ballotpedia. "Party Control of West Virginia State Government." Accessed March 2, 2023. https://ballotpedia.org/Party_control_of_West_Virginia_state_government.
Beam, Myrl. *Gay, Inc.: The Nonprofitization of Queer Politics.* Minneapolis: University of Minnesota Press, 2018.
Bearak, Barry. "Gay Couple Convicted in Malawi." *New York Times*, May 18, 2010. https://www.nytimes.com/2010/05/19/world/africa/19malawi.html.
Bell, Shannon. *Fighting King Coal: The Challenges to Micromobilization in Central Appalachia.* Cambridge, MA: MIT Press, 2016.
Bennett, Jane. "Queer/White in South Africa: A Troubling Oxymoron?" In *Queer in Africa: LGBTQI Identities, Citizenship, and Activism,* edited by Zethu Matebeni, Surya Monro, and Vasu Reddy, 99–113. New York: Routledge, 2018.
———. "'Solemnis(ing) Beginnings': Theories of Same-Sex Marriage in the USA and South Africa." *Culture, Health & Sexuality* 17, suppl. 1 (2015): 47–60.
Bennett, Jane, and Charmaine Pereira. *Jacketed Women: Qualitative Research Methodologies on Sexualities and Gender in Africa.* Cape Town: University of Cape Town Press, 2013.
Bérubé, Alan. "How Gay Stays White and What Kind of White It Stays." In *Privilege: A Reader,* edited by Michael Kimmel and Abby Ferber, 272–328. Boulder, CO: Westview Press, 2010. Originally published in *The Making and Unmaking of Whiteness,* edited by Brigit Rassmussen, Eric Klinenberg, Irene Nexica, and Matt Wray, 234–265. Durham, NC: Duke University Press, 2001.

Beyers, Christiaan. "Identity and Forced Displacement: Community and Colouredness in District Six." In *Burdened by Race: Coloured Identities in Southern Africa*, edited by Mohamed Adhikari, 79–103. Cape Town: University of Cape Town Press, 2009.

Blank, Hanne. *Straight: The Surprisingly Short History of Heterosexuality*. Boston: Beacon, 2012.

Bourke, Lynsey, Sian Butcher, Nixon Chisonga, Jumani Clarke, Frances Davies, and Jessica Thorn. "Fieldwork Stories: Negotiating Positionality, Power and Purpose." *Feminist Africa* 13 (2009): 95–105.

Butler, Judith. *Frames of War: When Is Life Grievable?* New York: Verso, 2009.

———. *Undoing Gender*. New York: Routledge, 2004.

Butler, Judith, and Gayatri Spivak. *Who Sings the Nation-State? Language, Politics, Belonging*. New York: Seagull Books, 2007.

Byrnes, Hristina, John Harrington, and Grant Suneson. "Supreme Court Decision Aside, Some States Are Better—and Some Are Worse—for LGBT Community." *USA Today*, June 19, 2020. https://www.usatoday.com/story/money/2020/06/19/the-best-and-worst-states-for lgbtq-people/111968524/.

Camminga, B. *Transgender Refugees and the Imagined South Africa: Bodies over Borders and Borders over Bodies*. London: Palgrave Macmillan, 2019.

Carpenter, Tim. "Kansas Cities Push Back against House Bill Nullifying Local Anti-Discrimination Ordinances." *Kansas Reflector*, February 15, 2023. https://kansasreflector.com/2023/02/15/kansas-cities-push-back-against-house-bill-nullifying-local-anti-discrimination-ordinances/.

Cartwright, Ryan Lee. *Peculiar Places: A Queer Crip History of White Rural Nonconformity*. Chicago: University of Chicago Press, 2021.

Catte, Elizabeth. "Passive, Poor, and White? What People Keep Getting Wrong about Appalachia." *Guardian*, February 6, 2018. https://www.theguardian.com/us-news/2018/feb/06/what-youre-getting-wrong-about-appalachia.

———. *What You Are Getting Wrong about Appalachia*. Cleveland: Belt Publishing, 2016.

Cele, S'thembile. "ANC and EFF Differ on Which Land Should Be Expropriated without Compensation." *Times Live*, March 5, 2020. https://www.timeslive.co.za/politics/2020-03-05-anc-and-eff-differ-on-which-land-should-be-expropriated-without-compensation/.

Chappell, Bill. "Supreme Court Declares Same-Sex Marriage Legal in All 50 States." *NPR*, June 26, 2015. https://www.npr.org/sections/thetwo-way/2015/06/26/417717613/supreme-court-rules-all-states-must-allow-same-sex-marriages.

Chasin, Alexandra. *Selling Out: The Gay and Lesbian Movement Goes to Market*. New York: St. Martin's Press, 2000.

Chavez, Karma. *Queer Migration Politics: Activist Rhetoric and Coalitional Possibilities*. Champaign: University of Illinois Press, 2013.

Chomsky, Noam. *Who Rules the World?* New York: Metropolitan Books, 2016.

Clare, Eli. *Exile and Pride: Disability, Queerness and Liberation*. 1999. Reprint, Cambridge, MA: South End Press, 2009.

Coates, Ta-Nehisi. "The Case for Reparations." *Atlantic*, June 15, 2014. https://www.theatlantic.com/magazine/archive/2014/06/the-case-for-reparations/361631/.

Cochran, Ryan. "Grab Your Boo and #LoveNOLA." *Go NOLA*, August 28, 2015. https://gonola.com/lgbt-new-orleans/lovenola-movement-lgbt-community.

Collins, Patricia Hill. *Another Kind of Public Education: Race, Schools, the Media, and Democratic Possibilities*. Boston: Beacon Press, 2009.

Constantino, Marcus. "Teen Defends Show after Anti-Gay Comments." *Charleston Gazette-Mail*, June 11, 2012. https://www.wvgazettemail.com/news/teen-defends-show-after-anti-gay-comments/article_dd6a0f8f-b0ad-5934-92df-2ae95423b128.html.

Cram, E. "(Dis)locating Queer Citizenship: Imagining Rurality in Matthew Shepard's Memory." In *Queering the Countryside: New Frontiers in Rural Queer Studies*, edited by Mary L Gray, Colin R. Johnson, and Brian J. Gilley, 282–303. New York: New York University Press, 2016.

"Critical Race Theory Is Being Weaponised. What's the Fuss About?" *Economist*, July 14, 2022. https://www.economist.com/interactive/united-states/2022/07/14/critical-race-theory-is-being-weaponised-whats-the-fuss-about.

Crum, Travis. "Buckhannon 5th W.Va. City to Pass LGBT Protections." *Charleston Gazette-Mail*, May 3, 2013. https://www.wvgazettemail.com/news/politics/buckhannon-5th-w-va-city-to-pass-lgbt-protections/article_235f9696-8c4f-5a9d-9fea-8119c3b775ea.html.

Currier, Ashley. *Out in Africa: LGBT Organizing in Namibia and South Africa*. Minneapolis: University of Minnesota Press, 2012.

Dearham, Kaitlin. "NGOS and Queer Women's Activism in Nairobi." In *Queer African Reader*, edited by Sokari Ekine and Hakima Abbas, 186–202. Nairobi: Pambazuka, 2013.

Deloria, Vine, Jr. *Custer Died for Your Sins: An Indian Manifesto*. Norman: University of Oklahoma Press, 1969.

D'Emilio, John. "Capitalism and Gay Identity." In *The Lesbian and Gay Studies Reader*, edited by Henry Abelove, Michele Aina Barale, and David Halperin, 467–478. New York: Routledge, 1993.

———. "The Marriage Fight Is Setting Us Back." In *Against Equality: Queer Critiques of Gay Marriage*, edited by Ryan Conrad, 37–42. Lewiston, ME: Against Equality Publishing Collective, 2010.

Dews, Carlos, and Carolyn Law. *Out in the South*. Philadelphia: Temple University Press, 2001.

Duberman, Martin. *Has the Gay Movement Failed?* Oakland: University of California Press, 2020.

Duffy, Nick. "Rush Limbaugh Is Terrified that Obama Is Helping Lesbian Farmers Take Over the South." *Pink News*, August 24, 2016. https://www.thepinknews.com/2016/08/24/rush-limbaugh-is-terrified-that-obama-is-helping-lesbian-farmers-take-over-the-south/.

Duggan, Lisa. *The Twilight of Equality: Neoliberalism, Cultural Politics, and the Attack on Democracy*. Boston: Beacon Press, 2004.

Ekine, Sokari. "Contesting Narratives of Queer Africa." In *Queer African Reader*, edited by Sokari Ekine and Hakima Abbas, 78–91. Nairobi: Pambazuka, 2013.

Ekine, Sokari, and Hakima Abbas, eds. *Queer African Reader*. Nairobi: Pambazuka, 2013.

"Elkins Passes Nondiscrimination Measure." *Intermountain*, March 20, 2015. https://www.theintermountain.com/news/local-news/2015/03/elkins-passes-nondiscrimination-measure/.

"Elkins to Consider Resolution." *Intermountain*, March 18, 2015. https://www.theintermountain.com/news/local-news/2015/03/elkins-to-consider-resolution/.

Erbentraut, Joseph. "These Lesbian Farmers Aren't Here to Take Over America: They're Here to Grow It." *Huffington Post*, September 4, 2016. https://www.huffpost.com/entry/lesbian-farmers-rush-limbaugh_n_57c879d6e4b0e60d31ddf5c0.

Essa, Azad. "Unpacking South Africa's Fraught and Complex Land Debate." *Al Jazeera*, August 30, 2018. https://www.aljazeera.com/news/2018/08/unpacking-south-africa-fraught-complex-land-debate-180830141333926.html.

Estes, Nick. *Our History Is the Future: Standing Rock versus the Dakota Access Pipeline and the Long Tradition of Indigenous Resistance*. Brooklyn: Verso, 2019.

Farrow, Anne, Jennifer Lang, and Joel Frank. *Complicity: How the North Promoted, Prolonged, and Profited from Slavery*. New York: Penguin Random House, 2005.

Federici, Silvia. *Caliban and the Witch: Women, the Body, and Primitive Accumulation.* Brooklyn: Autonomedia, 2004.

Fleming, Cynthia Griggs. *In the Shadow of Selma: The Continuing Struggle for Civil Rights in the Rural South.* New York: Rowman and Littlefield, 2004.

Flowers, Catherine Coleman. *Waste: One Woman's Fight against America's Dirty Secret.* New York: New Press, 2020.

Foucault, Michel. *The Archaeology of Knowledge.* 1972. Reprint, New York: Vintage, 2010.

Franklin, Sarah. *Dolly Mixtures: The Remaking of Genealogy.* Durham, NC: Duke University Press, 2007.

Fubara-Manuel, Irene. "At Home but Homeless: Queer African Migrants Critically Reflect on 'Home.'" In *Boldly Queer: African Perspectives on Same-Sex Sexuality and Gender Diversity,* edited by Theo Sandfort, Fabienne Simenel, Kevin Mwachiro, and Vasu Reddy, 25–32. Nairobi: Hivos, 2015. https://hivos.org/document/boldly-queer-african-perspectives-on-same-sex-sexuality-and-gender-diversity/.

Gevisser, Mark. "Love in Exile: One Woman's Journey from Malawi to South Africa." *Guardian,* November 27, 2014. https://www.theguardian.com/news/2014/nov/27/-sp-transgender-relationship-jail-exile-tiwonge-chimbalanga.

———. *The Pink Line: Journeys across the World's Queer Frontiers.* New York: Farrar, Straus and Giroux, 2020.

Gevisser, Mark, and Edwin Cameron. *Defiant Desire: Gay and Lesbian Lives in South Africa.* New York: Routledge, 1995.

Glass, Tressa. "Look out, Limbaugh: A 'Lesbian Farmer' Shirt now Exists." *Des Moines Register,* August 25, 2016. https://www.desmoinesregister.com/story/entertainment/2016/08/25/lesbian-farmers-shirt-now-exists/89351722/.

Good, Crystal. "Appalachia's White Inferiority Pushed My Trans, Black Daughter Out." *100 Days in Appalachia,* February 19, 2019. https://www.100daysinappalachia.com/2019/02/appalachias-white-inferiority-pushed-my-trans-black-daughter-out/.

———. "Behind the Scenes in Black Appalachia." *Scalawag,* December 23, 2020. https://scalawagmagazine.org/2020/12/hillbilly-movie-black-appalachia/.

———. "Consuming Blackness in 'Progressive' West Virginia." *Scalawag,* March 5, 2021. https://scalawagmagazine.org/2021/03/wv-ywca-racism/.

Government of South Africa. "Land Reform." Accessed July 25, 2022. https://www.gov.za/issues/land-reform.

Gray, Mary. *Out in the Country: Youth, Media, and Queer Visibility in Rural America.* New York: New York University Press, 2009.

Gray, Mary, Brian Gilley, and Colin Johnson, eds. *Queering the Countryside: New Frontiers in Rural Queer Studies.* New York: New York University Press, 2016.

Griffin, F. Hollis. *Feeling Normal: Sexuality and Media Criticism in the Digital Age.* Bloomington: Indiana University Press, 2016.

Gross, Michael Joseph. "Gay Is the New Black: The Last Great Civil Rights Struggle." *The Advocate,* November 16, 2008. https://www.advocate.com/news/2008/11/16/gay-new-black.

Gruber, Sharita. "Beyond *Bostock*: The Future of LGBTQ Civil Rights." Center for American Progress, August 26, 2020. https://www.americanprogress.org/article/beyond-bostock-future-lgbtq-civil-rights/.

Halberstam, J. *In a Queer Time and Place: Transgender Bodies, Subcultural Lives.* New York: New York University Press, 2005.

———. *The Queer Art of Failure.* Durham, NC: Duke University Press, 2011.

Haraway, Donna. *Simians, Cyborgs, and Women: The Reinvention of Nature.* London: Free Association Books, 1991.

———. *Staying with the Trouble: Making Kin in the Chthulucene.* Durham, NC: Duke University Press, 2016.

Harkins, Anthony. *Hillbilly: A Cultural History of an American Icon.* New York: Oxford University Press, 2003.

Harrington, Elizabeth. "Feds Holding Summits for Lesbian Farmers." *Washington Free Beacon*, August 16, 2016. https://freebeacon.com/issues/feds-holding-summits-lesbian-farmers/.

Henderson, Nia-Malika. "Inside the Battle over the Confederate Flag." *CNN*, June 24, 2015. https://www.cnn.com/2015/06/21/politics/south-carolina-confederate-flag-debate/index.html.

Henry, Robin. "Queering the American Frontier: Finding Queerness and Sexual Difference in Late Nineteenth Century and Early Twentieth Century Colorado." In *Queering the Countryside: New Frontiers in Rural Queer Studies*, edited by Mary Gray, Colin Johnson, and Brian Gilley, 304–323. New York: New York University Press, 2016.

Herbert, Odette. "The Alternative Inclusive Pride Network 2016 Cape Town." YouTube video. March 6, 2016. https://www.youtube.com/watch?v=nRcI3LG6cmY.

Herring, Scott. *Another Country: Queer Anti-Urbanism.* New York: New York University Press, 2010.

hooks, bell. *Where We Stand: Class Matters.* New York: Routledge, 2000.

Hunter, Marcus Anthony, and Zandria Robinson. *Chocolate Cities: The Black Map of American Life.* Oakland: University of California Press, 2016.

Hurtado, Aida. *The Color of Privilege: Three Blasphemies on Race and Feminism.* Ann Arbor: University of Michigan Press, 1997.

Igual, Roberto. "Cape Town Pride Parade Goes Ahead despite Protests." *Mamba Online*, March 2, 2015. https://www.mambaonline.com/2015/03/02/cape-town-pride-parade-goes-ahead-despite-protests/.

———. "Cape Town Pride to Change Controversial 2016 Theme." *Mamba Online*, December 3, 2015. https://www.mambaonline.com/2015/12/03/cape-town-pride-changecontroversial-2016-theme/.

———. "I Do × 15! History Made at Africa's First Mass Gay Wedding." *Mamba Online*, April 29, 2016. https://www.mambaonline.com/2016/04/29/x-15-history-made-africas-first-mass-gay-wedding/.

———. "Marking Ten Years of Same-Sex Marriage in South Africa." *Mamba Online*, November 30, 2016. https://www.mambaonline.com/2016/11/30/marking-ten-years-sex-marriage-south-africa/.

Ivan Toms Centre for Health. "Campaign Bolsters Bravery amongst Men Who Have Sex with Men." Accessed November 13, 2023. https://ivantomscentre.africa/2015/06/26/campaign-bolsters-bravery-amongst-men-who-have-sex-with-men/.

Johnson, Colin. *Just Queer Folks: Gender and Sexuality in Rural America.* Philadelphia: Temple University Press, 2013.

Jones, Dustin, and Franklin Johnson. "Not Just Florida: More Than a Dozen States Propose 'Don't Say Gay Bills.'" *NPR*, April 10, 2022. https://www.npr.org/2022/04/10/1091543359/15-states-dont-say-gay-anti-transgender-bills.

Judge, Melanie, Anthony Manion, and Shaun de Waal. *To Have and to Hold: The Making of Same-Sex Marriage in South Africa.* Johannesburg: Jacana Media, 2008.

Kearl, Michelle Kelsey. "'Is Gay the New Black?': An Intersectional Perspective on Social Movement Rhetoric in California's Proposition 8 Debate." *Communication and Critical/Cultural Studies* 12, no. 1 (2015): 63–82.

Kingsolver, Barbara. "A View from the South: Let the Confederate Flag Go." *Guardian*, July 3, 2015. https://www.theguardian.com/commentisfree/2015/jul/03/south-flag-confederate-pride-hatred-racists.

Klein, Naomi. *This Changes Everything: Capitalism vs the Climate*. New York: Simon and Schuster, 2014.

Klein, Shayla. "What the 2020 Census Data Says about West Virginia." *WBOY*, August 12, 2021. https://www.wboy.com/top-stories/what-the-latest-census-data-says-about-west-virginia/.

Kobersmith, Kim. "Frank X Walker's 'New Word Order.'" *The Bitter Southerner*, August 5, 2021. https://bittersoutherner.com/southern-perspectives/2021/frank-x-walkers-new-word-order.

Kuba, Katie. "Buckhannon Votes Down Non-Discrimination Ordinance." *My Buckhannon*, January 4, 2019. https://www.mybuckhannon.com/buckhannon-votes-down-non-discrimination-ordinance/.

Ladd, Chris. "Southern Conservatives Are America's Third Party." *Forbes*, March 16, 2017. https://www.forbes.com/sites/chrisladd/2017/03/16/southern-conservatives-are-americas-third-party/?sh=e825c55406b8.

Lang, Nico. "The 5 Worst States for LGBT People." *Rolling Stone*, November 24, 2014. https://www.rollingstone.com/politics/politics-news/the-5-worst-states-for-lgbt-people-198931/.

Legal Information Institute. "Defense of Marriage Act (DOMA)." Cornell Law School. Accessed March 2, 2023. https://www.law.cornell.edu/wex/defense_of_marriage_act_(doma).

Liptak, Adam. "Civil Rights Law Protects Gay and Transgender Workers, Supreme Court Rules." *New York Times*, June 15, 2020. https://www.nytimes.com/2020/06/15/us/gay-transgender-workers-supreme-court.html.

———. "Supreme Court Invalidates Key Part of Voting Rights Act." *New York Times*, June 25, 2013. https://www.nytimes.com/2013/06/26/us/supreme-court-ruling.html.

Lopez, A., ed. 2005. *Postcolonial Whiteness: A Critical Reader on Race and Empire*. Albany: State University of New York Press.

Lorway, Robert. *Namibia's Rainbow Project: Gay Rights in an African Nation*. Bloomington: Indiana University Press, 2015.

Machera, Mumbi. "Opening a Can of Worms: A Debate on Female Sexuality in the Lecture Theatre." In *Re-Thinking African Sexualities*, edited by Signe Arnfred, 157–172. Uppsala, Sweden: Nordic Africa Institute, 2004.

Magona, Sindiwe. *Living, Loving, Lying Awake at Night*. Cape Town: David Philips, 1991.

Mama, Amina. "Is It Ethical to Study Africa? Preliminary Thoughts on Scholarship and Freedom." *African Studies Review* 50, no. 1 (2007): 1–26.

Marcus, George. "Ethnography of/in the World System: The Emergence of Multi-Sited Ethnography." *Annual Review of Anthropology* 24 (1995): 95–117.

Massad, Joseph. *Desiring Arabs*. Chicago: University of Chicago Press, 2007.

———. "Re-Orienting Desire: The Gay International and the Arab World." *Public Culture* 14, no. 2 (2002): 361–385.

Matebeni, Zethu. *Black Lesbian Sexualities and Identity in South Africa: An Ethnography of Black Lesbian Urban Life*. Saarbrucken, Germany: Lambert Academic Publishing, 2012.

———. "*Ihlazo*: Pride and the Politics of Race and Space in Johannesburg and Cape Town." *Critical African Studies* 10, no. 3 (2018): 315–328.

———. *Queer in Africa III: Queering Cape Town*. Cape Town: Heinrich Boll Stiftung, 2016.

Matbeni, Zethu, and B Camminga, eds. *Beyond the Mountain: Queer Life in "Africa's Gay Capital.*" Pretoria: UNISA Press, 2020.

McCann, Adron, and Jim Burress. "The Annual Southern Fried Queer Pride Offers an Inclusive, Diverse Lineup." *WABE*, June 22, 2022. https://www.wabe.org/the-annual-southern-fried-queer-pride-festival-offers-an-inclusive-diverse-line-up/.

Mkhize, Nonhlanhla, Jane Bennett, Vasu Reddy, and Relebohile Moletsane. *The Country We Want to Live In: Hate Crimes and Homophobia in the Lives of Black Lesbian South Africans*. Cape Town: HSRC Press, 2010.

Mohanty, Chandra. *Feminism without Borders: Decolonizing Theory, Practicing Solidarity*. Durham, NC: Duke University Press, 2003.

Moodie, T. Dunbar, Vivienne Ntadshe, and British Mbuye. "Migrancy and Male Sexuality on the South African Gold Mines." *Journal of Southern African Studies* 14, no. 2 (1988): 228–256.

Moore, Catherine Venable. Introduction to *Book of the Dead* by Muriel Rukeyser. Morgantown: West Virginia University Press, 2018.

Moreau, Julie. "Why Is Rush Limbaugh So Afraid of Lesbian Farmers?" NBC, August 27, 2016. https://www.nbcnews.com/feature/nbc-out/why-rush-limbaugh-so-afraid-lesbian-farmers-n638736.

Murungi, Kagendo. "Small Axe at the Crossroads: A Reflection on African Sexualities and Human Rights—Life Story." In *Queer African Reader*, edited by Sokari Ekine and Hakima Abbas, 229–243. Nairobi: Pambazuka, 2013.

Mutua, Makau. *Human Rights: A Political and Cultural Critique*. Philadelphia: University of Pennsylvania Press, 2002.

Mwachiro, Kevin. "A Lost Chapter Found: Interview with Binyavanga Wainaina." In *Boldly Queer: African Perspectives on Same-Sex Sexuality and Gender Diversity*, edited by Theo Sandfort, Fabienne Simenel, Kevin Mwachiro, and Vasu Reddy, 97–102. Nairobi: Hivos, 2015. https://hivos.org/document/boldly-queer-african-perspectives-on-same-sex-sexuality-and-gender-diversity/.

National Center for Lesbian Rights. "NCLR and USDA Announce LGBTQ Rural Pride Campaign," May 7, 2014. http://www.nclrights.org/about-us/press-release/usda-and-nclr-launch-lgbt-rural-pride-campaign/.

Ndashe, Sibongile. "The Single Story of 'African Homophobia' Is Dangerous for LGBTI Activism." In *Queer African Reader*, edited by Sokari Ekine and Hakima Abbas, 155–164. Nairobi: Pambazuka, 2013.

Nelson, Libby. "Confederate Flags Are Coming Down: Here's the Latest State by State." *Vox*, June 24, 2015. https://www.vox.com/2015/6/24/8840207/confederate-flag-ban-history-latest-mississippi-south-carolina.

Newkirk II, Vann R. "The Great Land Robbery: The Shameful Story of How 1 Million Black Families Have Been Ripped from Their Farms." *Atlantic*, September 15, 2019. https://www.theatlantic.com/magazine/archive/2019/09/this-land-was-our-land/594742/.

Ngcukaitobi, Tembeka. *The Land Is Ours: South Africa's First Black Lawyers and the Birth of Constitutionalism*. Cape Town: Penguin, 2018.

Nkabinde, Nkunzi. *Black Bull, Ancestors, and Me: My Life as a Lesbian Sangoma*. Johannesburg: Fanele, 2009.

Nosowitz, Dan. "Rush Limbaugh Terrified of Lesbian Farmers for Some Reason." *Modern Farmer*, August 26, 2016. https://modernfarmer.com/2016/08/rush-limbaugh-lesbian-farmers/.

Osborne, Karen, and William Spurlin. *Reclaiming the Heartland: Lesbian and Gay Voices from the Midwest*. Minneapolis: University of Minnesota Press, 1996.

Oswin, Natalie. "Researching 'Gay Cape Town', Finding Value-Added Queerness." *Social & Cultural Geography* 6, no. 4 (2005): 567–588.

Oyewumi, Oyeronke. *The Invention of Women: Making an African Sense of Western Gender Discourses*. Minneapolis: University of Minnesota Press, 1997.

Pape, John. "Black and White: The 'Perils of Sex' in Colonial Zimbabwe." *Journal of Southern African Studies* 16, no. 4 (1990): 699–720.

Patel, Nigel. "Violent Cisterns: Trans Experiences of Bathroom Space," *Agenda* 31, no. 1 (2017): 51–63.

Permenter, Cody. "Lesbian Farmers Are Taking Over the Country, If You Believe Rush Limbaugh." *Grist*, August 24, 2016. https://grist.org/food/lesbian-farmers-are-taking-over-the-country-if-you-believe-rush-limbaugh/.

Perry, Imani. *Vexy Thing: On Gender and Liberation*. Durham, NC: Duke University Press, 2018.

Pew Research Center. "Same-Sex Marriage, State by State," June 26, 2015. https://www.pewresearch.org/religion/2015/06/26/same-sex-marriage-state-by-state-1/.

Phelps, Wesley. "The Fall of Roe Forecasts Trouble Ahead for LGBT Rights." *Washington Post*, July 15, 2022. https://www.washingtonpost.com/made-by-history/2022/07/15/fall-roe-forecasts-trouble-ahead-key-lgbtq-rights/.

Phillips, Richard, David Watt, and Diane Shuttleton. *De-Centering Sexualities: Politics and Representations beyond the Metropolis*. New York: Routledge, 2000.

Plaatje, Sol. *Native Life in South Africa*. 1916. Reprint, Athens: Ohio University Press, 1991.

Polikoff, Nancy. *Beyond (Straight and Gay) Marriage: Valuing All Families under the Law*. Boston: Beacon Press, 2008.

Pruitt, Lisa. "What *Hillbilly Elegy* Reveals about Race in Twenty-First Century America." In *Appalachian Reckoning: A Region Responds to* Hillbilly Elegy, ed. Anthony Harkins and Meredith McCarroll, 105–135. Morgantown: West Virginia University Press, 2019.

Puar, Jasbir. *Terrorist Assemblages: Homonationalism in Queer Times*. Durham, NC: Duke University Press, 2007.

Raby, John. "GOP Increases Supermajority in West Virginia House, Senate." *Associated Press*, November 9, 2022. https://apnews.com/article/general-elections-west-virginia-wheeling-government-and-politics-20003d4aece817fe37cdea0b5d341635.

Redding, Maureen. "Invisibility/Hypervisibility: The Paradox of Normative Whiteness." In *Privilege: A Reader*, edited by Michael, 155–168. Boulder, CO: Westview Press, 2010.

Reid, Graeme. *How to Be a Real Gay: Gay Identities in Small-Town South Africa*. Scottsville: University of Kwa-Zulu Natal Press, 2013.

Robles, Frances. "Dylann Roof Photos and a Manifesto Are Posted on Website." *New York Times*, June 20, 2015. https://www.nytimes.com/2015/06/21/us/dylann-storm-roof-photos-website-charleston-church-shooting.html.

Rogers, Katie. "Title IX Protections Extend to Transgender Students, Education Dept. Says." *New York Times*, June 16, 2021. https://www.nytimes.com/2021/06/16/us/politics/title-ix-transgender-students.html

Rose, Gillian. "Situating Knowledges: Positionality, Reflexivities and Other Tactics." *Progress in Human Geography* 21, no. 3 (1997): 305–320.

Said, Edward. *Orientalism*. New York: Pantheon Books, 1978.

Sawuck, Stephen. "Beyond 'Don't Say Gay': Other States Seek to Limit LGBT Youth, Teaching." *Education Weekly*, April 6, 2022. https://www.edweek.org/policy-politics/beyond-dont-say-gay-other-states-seek-to-limit-lgbtq-youth-teaching/2022/04.

Schneider, Elena. "The Bathroom Bill That Ate North Carolina. *Politico*, March 23, 2017. https://www.politico.com/magazine/story/2017/03/the-bathroom-bill-that-ate-north-carolina-214944/.

Schwartz, Sarah. "Map: Where Critical Race Theory Is Under Attack." *Education Week*, July 15, 2022. https://www.edweek.org/policy-politics/map-where-critical-race-theory-is-under-attack/2021/06.

Scott, Jessica. "Disruption and Withdrawal: Responses to 21st Century Prides from the South." In *Beyond the Mountain: Queer Life in "Africa's Gay Capital,"* edited by Zethu Matebeni and B Camminga, 171–185. Pretoria: UNISA Press, 2020.

———. "The Distance between Death and Marriage: Citizenship, Violence and Same-Sex Marriage in South Africa." *International Feminist Journal of Politics* 15, no. 4 (2013): 534–552.

———. "Hillbilly Horror and the New Racism: Rural and Racial Politics in *Orange Is the New Black*." *Journal of Appalachian Studies* 23, no. 2 (2017): 221–238.

———. "'Nowhere Does It Say That in the Bible': Tensions between Legal and Symbolic Meanings of Marriage for Lesbian Women in South Africa. *Sexuality and Theology* 20, no. 1 (2014): 56–69.

Scott, Lwando. "The Politics of Pride—Cape Town." *Queer Consciousness* (blog), March 17, 2015. https://queerconsciousness.com/the-politics-of-pride-cape-town/.

Sears, Clare. *Arresting Dress: Cross-Dressing, Law, and Fascination in Nineteenth Century San Francisco.* Durham, NC: Duke University Press, 2014.

Sewell, Summer. "There Were One Million Black Farmers in 1920. What Happened to Them?" *Guardian*, April 29, 2019. https://www.theguardian.com/environment/2019/apr/29/why-have-americas-black-farmers-disappeared.

Socarides, Richard. "Why Bill Clinton Signed the Defense of Marriage Act." *New Yorker*, March 8, 2013. https://www.newyorker.com/news/news-desk/why-bill-clinton-signed-the-defense-of-marriage-act.

Soldaat, Funeka. "Black Lesbian Politics and Organising Spaces." In *Beyond the Mountain: Queer Life in "Africa's Gay Capital,"* edited by Zethu Matebeni and B Camminga, 137–146. Pretoria: UNISA Press, 2020.

———. *uHambo: The Life Journey of Funeka Soldaat.* Cape Town: Free Gender, 2018.

Spade, Dean. *Normal Life: Administrative Violence, Critical Trans Politics, and the Limits of Law.* Brooklyn: South End Press, 2011.

Spurlin, William. *Imperialism within the Margins: Queer Representations and the Politics of Culture in Southern Africa.* New York: Palgrave Macmillan, 2006.

Stafford, Leon. "Despite Progress HIV/AIDS in Georgia Remains Disproportionately Black in Georgia." *Atlanta-Journal Constitution*, February 24, 2022. https://www.ajc.com/life/despite-progress-hiv-remains-disproportionately-black-in-georgia/MOUFBE4GUZFS5GJTOEKAOG2SMU/.

Steyn, Melissa, and Mikki Van Zyl. *The Prize and the Price: Shaping Sexualities in South Africa.* Cape Town: HSRC Press, 2009.

Stoler, Laura. *Duress: Imperial Durabilities in Our Times.* Durham, NC: Duke University Press, 2016.

Swarr, Amanda, and Richa Nagar. *Critical Transnational Feminist Praxis.* Albany: State University of New York Press, 2010.

TallBear, Kim. *Native American DNA: Tribal Belonging and the False Promise of Genetic Science.* Minneapolis: University of Minnesota Press, 2013.

TEDx Talks. "Conversations with Baba | Binyavanga Wainaia." YouTube video. January 16, 2015. https://www.youtube.com/watch?v=z5uAoBu9Epg.

Thomas, Jim. *Doing Critical Ethnography.* Newbury Park, CA: Sage, 1993.

Thomsen, Carly. *Visibility Interrupted: Rural Queer Life and the Politics of Unbecoming.* Minneapolis: University of Minnesota Press, 2021.

Thoreson, Ryan. *Transnational LGBT Activism: Working for Sexual Rights Worldwide.* Minneapolis: University of Minnesota Press, 2014.

Totenberg, Nina. "Supreme Court Delivers Major Victory to LGBTQ Employees." *NPR*, June 15, 2020. https://www.npr.org/2020/06/15/863498848/supreme-court-delivers-major-victory-to-lgbtq-employees.

Trepagnier, J. B. *Attack of the Lesbian Farmers*. Amazon, 2016.

Trotter, Henry. "Trauma and Memory: The Impact of Apartheid-Era Forced Removals on Coloured Identity in Cape Town." In *Burdened by Race: Coloured Identities in Southern Africa*, edited by Mohamed Adhikari, 49–78. Cape Town: University of Cape Town Press, 2009.

Tsing, Anna. *In the Realm of the Diamond Queen: Marginality in an Out-of-the-Way Place*. Princeton, NJ: Princeton University Press, 1993.

———. *The Mushroom at the End of the World: On the Possibility of Life in Capitalist Ruins*. Princeton, NJ: Princeton University Press, 2015.

Tucker, Andrew. *Queer Visibilities: Space, Identity and Interaction in Cape Town*. Malden, MA: Wiley-Blackwell, 2009.

United States Sentencing Commission. "2015 Report to the Congress: Impact of the Fair Sentencing Act." Accessed March 11, 2023. https://www.ussc.gov/research/congressional-reports/2015-report-congress-impact-fair-sentencing-act-2010.

U.S. Census Bureau. "Quick Facts: Buckhannon City, West Virginia." Accessed July 18, 2022. https://www.census.gov/quickfacts/buckhannoncitywestvirginia.

———. "Quick Facts: Elkins City, West Virginia." Accessed July 18, 2022. https://www.census.gov/quickfacts/elkinscitywestvirginia.

———. "Quick Facts: Randolph County, West Virginia." Accessed July 18, 2022. https://www.census.gov/quickfacts/randolphcountywestvirginia.

———. "Quick Facts: West Virginia" Accessed December 19, 2023. https://www.census.gov/quickfacts/fact/table/WV/PST045222.

U.S. Equal Employment Opportunity Commission. "Examples of Court Decisions Supporting Coverage of LGBT-Related Discrimination Under Title VII." Accessed December 16, 2023. https://www.eeoc.gov/wysk/examples-court-decisions-supporting-coverage-lgbt-related-discrimination-under-title-vii.

———. "Title VII of the Civil Rights Act of 1964." Accessed December 16, 2023. https://www.eeoc.gov/statutes/title-vii-civil-rights-act-1964.

Vaid, Urvashi. *Virtual Equality: The Mainstreaming of Gay and Lesbian Liberation*. New York: Anchor Books, 1996.

Wainaina, Binyavanga. "I Am a Homosexual, Mum." *Guardian*, January 21, 2014. https://www.theguardian.com/commentisfree/2014/jan/21/i-am-a-homosexual-mum-binyavanga-wainaina-memoir.

———. "Since Everything Was Suddening into a Hurricane." *Granta*, February 13, 2017. https://granta.com/since-everything-suddening-hurricane/.

Walker, Alice. *In Love & Trouble: Stories of Black Women*. New York: Harcourt Brace Jovanovich, 1973.

We The Brave (@WeTheBraveSA). "Having Made an Appearance in Cape Town, Our Giant Dick Float Will Be at #DurbanPride This Year!" Twitter. July 16, 2016. https://mobile.twitter.com/wethebravesa/status/754329842145832960.

———. "Our #BraveEnough Float is Tweet-Active! Tweet @ Us to Make Our #Cockfloat Blow It's Load with Glitter! #gay #lgbti." Twitter. February 27, 2016. https://twitter.com/WeTheBraveSA/status/703522066381860864.

"We The Brave: The Brave Float." Ads of the World. Accessed March 7, 2023. https://www.adsoftheworld.com/campaigns/the-brave-float.

Wong, Julia Carrie. "LGBT People of Color Alienated by San Francisco Pride's Plan for More Police." *Guardian*, June 22, 2016. https://www.theguardian.com/world/2016/jun/22/san-francisco-pride-police-presence-orlando-shooting-lgbt.

Wray, Matt. *Not Quite White: White Trash and the Boundaries of Whiteness*. Durham, NC: Duke University Press, 2006.

Zouhali-Worrall, Malika, and Katherine Wright. "They Will Say We Are Not Here." *New York Times Op-Docs*, January 26, 2012. https://www.nytimes.com/video/opinion/100000001307281/they-will-say-we-are-not-here.html.

Index

Abbas, Hakima, 11, 14
acceptability, 65, 66–68, 81
accessibility, 34, 91, 94–95, 112
Advocate, The, 48, 77
Ahmed, Sara, 22
Alabama, 123
alienation, 47, 93, 99–100, 133; from home, 4, 89; from land, 16, 37–38, 50–51; from services, 34, 36, 95
Alternative and Inclusive Pride. *See* Pride
Amendment 1, 1, 12, 61, 62, 77, 123–128
apartheid, 40–41, 55–57, 92–93
Appalachia, 37, 71, 129–134
Appalachian Queer Film Festival, 25
Asheville, 3, 61, 62
Atlanta, 18, 33, 98–102
Avashia, Neema, 133

bathrooms, 76
Beam, Myrl, 73
Bennett, Jane, 114, 129–130
Bible Belt, 12, 150
BreakOUT!, 12, 97
Buckhannon, 64, 134, 138
Butler, Judith, 113, 115

Cameron, Edwin, 41, 47
Camminga, B, 5
Campaign for Southern Equality, The, 15, 27
Cape Town, 82–83, 89–93
Cape Town Pride. *See* Pride
Cartwright, Ryan Lee, 12, 33, 50
Center for Transgender Equality, 34
Chasin, Alexandra, 12
cities, 72–74, 76, 83
Civil Union Act, 2, 23, 28, 47, 57, 67, 114
Clare, Eli, 51

colonization, 50, 70–71, 80, 84
coming out, 7, 80, 120–121
Commission for Gender Equality, 54–56, 59
Confederate flag, 145–146, 148–149
constitution: American, 48; South African, 5, 11, 47, 53, 114
constitutional amendment, 1, 2, 61
corrective rape, 5
Currier, Ashley, 13, 22, 85

Defense of Marriage Act, 1, 49, 115
D'Emilio, John, 50–51, 115
displacement, 16, 39, 43, 51, 70–71, 133

Ekine, Sokari, 11, 14, 86
Elkins, 26, 134, 138, 140
eugenics, 70–72

Fairness WV, 13, 25, 136–139
familiarity, 52, 130, 131, 141
family: effects of racism on, 50, 54–59; heirlooms, 31; marriage and, 1; negotiations with, 65, 68, 94, 96, 107–108, 111, 117, 133; queer and trans community as, 125–126, 145; recognition of, 115, 124; shape of, 67
Free Gender, 10, 13, 27–29, 57–59, 91–92, 94, 146
funding: availability of, 101, 119; eligibility for, 10, 70, 86–87, 120; and extractive economies, 78, 126–127; of grassroots organizations, 24, 109, 125, 147; influence of, 116; of LGBT(I) rights work, 14, 69, 113, 116; limitations of, 10, 101, 107–108, 110; opportunities for, 117; questions about, 23

Gay International, 11, 14, 64, 89, 117
Gender Benders, 26–27
Georgia, 98, 100, 102, 104
Georgia Equality, 13
Gevisser, Mark, 4, 9, 41, 47, 63–64, 84
Good, Crystal, 131–134, 142
Gray, Mary, 6, 73, 85, 130, 141
Green Point, 83

Haraway, Donna, 20, 105, 144
hate crimes, 69, 80, 96, 107–108
health: HIV, 101, 103; transgender health, 69
home, 31, 36, 46, 55–56, 67, 106, 125, 150; activism at, 9; alienation from, 4, 37, 51–52, 83–85; attachments to, 16–17, 121; dangers of, 96; displacement from, 41–43; geographical, 18, 122, 129–130, 133, 142–144; meanings of, 98–99, 134–135; political, 123, 125; politics of, 14, 104, 112, 150; rural, 52
Home Affairs, 56–58
Human Rights Campaign, 10, 126
Hunter, Marcus, 6

IGLHRC, 8, 11, 87, 88, 110
isiXhosa, 28–29

Johnson, Colin, 71–72, 87

Kentucky, 6, 52
Khayelitsha, 10, 28, 57–58, 93–94, 146
Khumbulani Pride. *See* Pride
Knysna, 2, 3

language, 10–11, 15–16, 109–112, 120, 146–147, 164–165n6
laws, 115, 128, 130; against cross-dressing, 74; apartheid, 40, 55; bathroom, 76; criminalizing same-sex sexuality, 4, 8, 10, 80, 84, 89, 164n6; nondiscrimination, 66, 69, 78–80, 115, 137, 140; property, 45; restricting mobility, 45, 48, 74, 103; vagrancy, 46, 102; voting, 46
Lorway, Robert, 84–85, 116
Louisiana, 1
Louisiana Queer Conference, 1

Machera, Mumbi, 5
Malawi, 8
Mama, Amina, 20, 21, 22
maps, 7
marriage equality. *See* same-sex marriage
Massad, Joseph, 11, 14, 84, 89, 113, 117
mass same-sex wedding, 2, 3
Matebeni, Zethu, 5, 45, 91–92
methods, 6, 21, 23

metronormativity, and alienation, 19, 34, 83; damage of, 83; logics of, 4, 14; meaning of, 11, 165n12; models of, 85, 91, 98, 105; narratives of, 12, 17, 19, 33–34, 52, 73, 103, 149; perspectives, 93; politics of, 31; proponents of, 36; responses to, 93, 141, 146
modernity, 19, 38, 70–74, 83, 113–114
multi-sited, 21, 23

National Center for Lesbian Rights, 33–34
Ndashe, Sibongile, 112–113
neoliberalism, 22, 113
New Orleans, 97
nondiscrimination, 116–117; in municipal policy, 26, 76, 131, 134–140, 181n24, 181n26; in federal policy, 33, 48–49, 138, 169n3; in South African law, 47
North Carolina, 1, 3, 61, 62, 76, 123–128

Obama, Barack, 9, 33, 35, 63
Out in Africa, 3, 14
out-of-the-way places, 36–37, 86, 90, 108; communities in, 121–122; and extractive economies, 17; in the global south, 113–114; and LGBT(I) rights discourse, 6, 32, 50–52, 86, 128; and metronormativity, 17, 31; and resources, 119–120; spatial politics of, 21–23, 63, 81, 83
OutRight International. *See* IGLHRC
Oyewumi, Oyeronke, 84

pink line, 4, 63, 113, 115, 120, 121
Pink Loerie Festival, 2, 3
policy, 67, 69, 75–76, 108, 135
positionality, 20
Pride, 64, 91; Alternative and Inclusive, 18, 28, 65, 82–83; Cape Town, 18, 28, 65, 82–83, 91–92; Khumbulani, 18, 58, 92, 96; New Orleans, 97; Southern Fried Queer, 98
Puar, Jasbir, 113

Reid, Graeme, 84, 90, 113–114
religion, 110–111; Christianity, 127; Islam, 68
rights, 66, 75–76, 80–81, 84, 123, 149; civil, 48–50, 103; human, 53, 63–67, 70–71, 89; land and, 38–39, 46; language of, 110–112; legal, 55, 60, 67; LGBT, 1, 3–5, 8–18, 29–30, 47, 62, 70–71, 86–87, 91–92, 115–121; property, 74; struggles for, 48, 69
Robinson, Zandria, 6
rural, 3, 26, 33–38, 59–60, 66, 100, 165–166n12; experiences in, 112–114, 119–122, 124–126, 134; fear of, 78; histories of, 102; meanings of, 16, 19, 31, 104; politics of, 12, 51–55,

61–62, 72–74, 83, 148–149; scholarship about, 14, 21, 72, 87, 141; strangeness of, 6, 85

safety: in communities, 13, 58, 68, 73, 95; expectation of, 66, 79; indicators of, 7, 81; for queer people, 4, 6, 17, 51, 69, 97
same-sex marriage, 23, 66–68, 136, 163–164n5; ban on, 1–2, 47–49, 61; campaigns, 12–13; as gay rights, 4, 65, 115–116; mass wedding, 2–3; through the Civil Union Act, 57–58, 114
Sears, Clare, 73–74
Selma, 62–63
Shepard, Matthew, 13
Soldaat, Funeka, 10, 28–29, 57–58, 92
Southerners on New Ground (SONG), 12, 15, 26
Southern Fried Queer Pride. *See* Pride
Spurlin, William, 11

Thomas, Jim, 21, 29
Thomsen, Carly, 13, 14, 21, 85, 86–87
Thoreson, Ryan, 8, 11, 22, 87–89
transition, 64, 65–66
transnational, 21, 22, 87, 113, 114

transportation, 93–95
Trump Country, 37, 133
Tsing, Anna, 20, 21

unAfrican, 6, 11, 60, 86, 97, 146
University of Cape Town, The, 63
urgency, 14, 105–107, 127
USDA, 33–36, 59

violence: against lesbians, 48, 55, 58, 108–109, 118; against women, 95, 116–117; cost of, 84; economic, 122; fear of, 78; of homophobia and transphobia, 47, 59, 65–69, 73, 79–80, 92, 98; by police, 13, 50, 146; proximity to, 93, 95–96, 97, 106–107; of racism, 42, 44–45, 70–72; safety from, 17, 85, 118
visibility, 13, 14, 22, 52, 58, 85–86, 97, 107
Voting Rights Act, 27, 48–49

Wainaina, Binyavanga, 7
West Virginia, 1, 15, 25, 34, 37, 129, 142
whiteness, 17, 18, 30, 90, 93, 124–125, 129, 134, 144–150

Xhosa. *See* isiXhosa

About the Author

Jessica A. Scott is associate professor of gender studies at West Virginia Wesleyan College in Buckhannon. She has published in South Africa and the United States on topics ranging from gender and sexuality to racism in American cultural productions. Her work appears in the *Journal of Appalachian Studies* and the *International Feminist Journal of Politics*, and in the edited volumes *Jacketed Women: Qualitative Research Methodologies on Sexualities and Gender in Africa* and *Beyond the Mountain: Queer Life in "Africa's Gay Capital."*

Printed and bound by CPI Group (UK) Ltd, Croydon, CR0 4YY
02/12/2024

14603672-0001